Black Scholar

Bond in academic regalia, circa 1950
(courtesy of Mrs. Julia W. Bond)

Black Scholar

HORACE MANN BOND

1904–1972

Wayne J. Urban

University of Georgia Press   *Athens and London*

© 1992 by the University of Georgia Press
Athens, Georgia 30602
All rights reserved

Set in Janson Text by Tseng Information Systems, Inc.
The paper in this book meets the guidelines
for permanence and durability of the Committee on
Production Guidelines for Book Longevity
of the Council on Library Resources.

Printed in the United States of America
96 95 94 93 92 C 5 4 3 2 1

Library of Congress Cataloging in Publication Data

Urban, Wayne J.
Black scholar : Horace Mann Bond, 1904–1972 /
Wayne J. Urban.
p. cm.
Includes bibliographical references and index.
ISBN 0-8203-1381-5 (alk. paper)
1. Bond, Horace Mann, 1904–1972.   2. Afro-American
scholars — Biography.   3. Afro-Americans — Education —
History — 20th century.   I. Title.
E185.97.B68U73   1992
370′.8996073 — dc20
[B]   91-13436
                                                              CIP

British Library Cataloging in Publication Data available

In memory of my father,

WALTER JOSEPH URBANSKI

(1908–1953)

Contents

Preface

In 1982, as I was finishing a book on the history of teachers' unions, I had already determined that my next project would be a biography. I was dissatisfied with social-scientific approaches to historical study, and I wanted to try my hand at the more open-ended, humanistic approach afforded by biography. All that then remained was to find my subject.

Because of my work as a historian of education and my interest in the way that historians of education come to pursue their work, I settled on the goal of profiling the life of just such a historian. I knew of Horace Mann Bond's *Education of the Negro in the American Social Order* and *Negro Education in Alabama: A Study in Cotton and Steel*, both published in the 1930s. I also knew that Bond was by profession a historian of education and that, for a number of years before his death, he had lived in Atlanta and taught at Atlanta University. When I discovered the existence of an extensive collection of Bond papers, I settled on Bond as the subject for my biography.

Early in the research of this biography, I learned that Horace Mann Bond's academic career was marked by both great success and great frustration. His youthful educational experiences were uniformly successful, though sometimes accompanied by painful personal relations. His early academic performance, also, was highly regarded. From his college years, he set his sights on the academic life, and his long years of service in several institutions indicate that he found his choice in many respects fulfilling. Yet, in one crucial respect, Bond's academic career was not particularly fruitful. His goal from the time of his graduate education was to be a noted scholar, and his early work showed promise. But he also was extremely ambitious for the kind of recognition and reward that did not usually come to a scholar, particularly a black scholar, in the middle of the twentieth century.

After about a decade of academic work, Bond came to a crossroads. He was confronted with the chance to become a college administrator, a role that often meant the abandonment of such scholarly goals as research and publication. Bond haltingly embraced the role of dean and then college president, but he never completely abandoned his desire to be a scholar. He continued to publish during his twenty years as president of two different colleges, yet, it also must be said, the years spent, with mixed success, as an administrator put him unalterably on a path away from that of an original contributor to scholarship. The conflict between administration and scholarship was one that Bond felt keenly in his mature years. Indeed, a major theme of my biography is that Bond was unable to satisfy these twin priorities: he never would leave scholarship completely and concentrate on his administrative duties, but he never could produce sustained scholarly work after becoming a college president.

As I entered more deeply into the research and writing of Bond's life, I gradually realized that a fully drawn portrait of the man was not to be. Several circumstances hindered me. First, the Bond papers, the major documentary source on which this work was based, are all but silent on his personal and family life. While they are not completely bereft of information on these topics, they do not reveal much about Bond's personal life or his personality. Second, among Bond's family members and close friends, some declined to be interviewed, and others were reticent about revealing the personal side of the man.

Because of this, I have written a biography that concentrates on Bond's successes and failures in his own schooling and in his life's work in educational institutions. Given that Bond spent a good deal of time collecting the material preserved in his papers and, presumably, discarding that which he did not want preserved, it seems that this approach to Bond's life, insofar as it is faithful to what is in the papers, is the one that Bond would have approved. This is not to say, however, that this work is devoid of a personal dimension or attempts at personal interpretation. When it is possible to draw a personal inference or to interpret an event's personal dimension, I do so. In fact, Bond's personality, at least as perceived in his public interactions, is part of the puzzle with which this biography must wrestle.

According to everyone I interviewed, including his wife, Julia Washington Bond, Horace Bond was an extraordinarily formal person. He was always polite and correct in his public interactions with others, and he was seldom, if ever, overtly emotional. Time and again, interviewees commented on the way Bond referred to each of them either by his or her surname or with a formal appellation such as *Mr., Miss,* or *Mrs.* before the surname. I know of no one, outside of his immediate family, with whom Bond interacted on a first-name basis. This does not mean, of course, that Bond was not held in high regard by many of his coworkers and his pupils. He had the respect of many and the warm regard of some, especially those with whom he came into close and frequent contact. Still, Bond's formality, which can only be called excessive, is a problem for one who seeks to tell the story of his life. I will attempt to explain how he came to develop his armor of reserve and how his demeanor sometimes contributed to his difficulties as a university administrator.

A word seems appropriate here about the dynamics of a white author producing a work about a black person. I was aware that I might encounter difficulties, such as individuals declining to be interviewed, that might not have existed for a black American. Yet I also must comment on the unvarying kindness and consideration I received from those individuals, most of whom were black, who agreed to be interviewed.

I have tried my best to portray Bond as I have found him, in his papers and other documents that relate to his life and work and in the accounts of those I interviewed. If my interpretation of his life lacks a sensitivity or awareness that one written by a black person might naturally possess, it is not because I did not endeavor to attain that awareness. I have tried to see the world through Bond's eyes at the same time that I have tried to remain detached enough from him to interpret his actions meaningfully.

Something that helped me to understand Bond was the parallel between his circumstances and those of my father. Members of the same generation, born within four years of each other, they shared the fire to achieve that motivated many Americans, whether they were descended, as was my father, from immigrants, or they were descended, as was Bond, from slaves. Although I was only ten years old when my father died, I have strong memories of his putting in exceedingly long hours in his medical practice in order to achieve his version of the American dream. Bond also worked fervently to achieve his image of that dream. Readers of this book will have to judge if I have adequately portrayed his pursuit of his dream.

I have incurred more than the usual number of debts in writing this book, and it is a distinct pleasure to acknowledge them here. The National Endowment for the Humanities provided a fellowship that freed me from a year's teaching. The Rockefeller Archive Center financed a research trip to their holdings. Linda Seidman, Michael Milewski, and Kenneth Fones-Wolf, archivists at the University of Massachusetts Library, where the Horace Mann Bond Papers are housed, were particularly helpful. I am also indebted to Sophy Cornwell and Emory Wimbish of the Langston Hughes Library of Lincoln University, to Beth Howse of the Fisk University Library, and to Jane Hobson of the Pullen Library at Georgia State University.

I wish to thank numerous other scholars for their help on this work, including Sanford Bederman, Gilbert Belles, Ronald Butchart, Geraldine Clifford, John Hope Franklin, Ralph Luker, Robert McCaul, Michael Sokal, and David Swift. John Matthews, B. Edward McClellan, and Germaine Reed read the entire manuscript and made valuable suggestions for improvement. Of the individuals I interviewed, John A. Davis, J. Alfred Farrell, Martin Kilson, DeForrest Rudd, and St. Clair Drake were especially helpful. Wade Carpenter, Cheon Gie Kim, Deanna Michael, and Ann Ralin, graduate students at Georgia State University, all helped with tasks related to improving the manuscript.

Finally, I would like to thank Julia Washington Bond for her willingness to talk to me many times during the several years in which I worked on this manuscript, for her attendance at a seminar I conducted on her husband and his career, for her permission to quote from the Horace Mann Bond Papers, and for her understanding of the scholarly enterprise. She has been a constant source of guidance during the writing of this biography.

Portions of this manuscript, some in altered form, have appeared elsewhere. Chapter 3 was originally published as "The Graduate Education of a Black Scholar: Horace Mann Bond and the University of Chicago" in the *History of Higher Education Annual* 7 (1987): 29–43. Parts of Chapters 4, 5, and 7 appeared in "Philanthropy and the Black Scholar: The Case of Horace Mann Bond," *Journal of Negro Education* 58 (Fall 1989): 478–93. A part of Chapter 6 appeared as "Horace Mann Bond's *Negro Education in Alabama*," *History of Education Quarterly* 27 (Fall 1987): 363–77. It is a pleasure to acknowledge the permission of these journals to republish this material here.

Black Scholar

Chapter 1

The Prodigy

The name *Horace Mann Bond* seems altogether fitting for a prodigy who excelled in schoolwork at every level and who eventually made his mark in the field of education. The reasons the newborn Bond lad received the name Horace Mann, however, did not relate to the educational career of Horace Mann, the great Massachusetts educational reformer and abolitionist. Rather, young Horace Bond's mother named him in honor of Horace Mann's antislavery activities.

Horace Bond's mother, Jane Browne, met and married her husband while she was a student at Oberlin College, where she had developed a close relationship with Horace Mann's widow, Mary Peabody Mann. Mrs. Mann often told the young black woman stories of her husband's long career in antislavery circles, including his tenure as an abolitionist member of the Massachusetts legislature. Jane Browne was particularly interested in Horace Mann's commitment to desegregation in education at Antioch College, where he served as president in the 1850s. Jane learned that, while at Antioch, Mann threatened to close down the college's dining hall unless two young black women who were students at the college were granted their place at the table. Thus Jane chose the name Horace Mann for her son in honor of Horace Mann's humanitarianism in race relations rather than his considerable reputation as an educator.[1]

Jane Browne had been born in Virginia. Her father, a white man, evinced little interest in his child. Her mother was black, with some Indian forebears. Shortly after Jane's birth, her mother married a black stonecutter who moved the family to Pennsylvania. Jane excelled in school and was reported to have been the first black in her town to finish high school. A wealthy white woman who was impressed by Jane's intellectual promise sponsored her studies at Oberlin, where Jane prepared to become a schoolteacher, her lifelong work. Horace Bond's career in the field of education no doubt pleased his mother.[2]

Despite Jane Browne Bond's ability and interest in the field of education, she was not the major influence in her young son's life. According to his brother Max, Horace was not very close to his mother, and the extant letters between mother and son from a later period reinforce the impression that their relationship was not intimate.[3] This may have been partly because, while the young boy was growing up, Jane Bond was preoccupied with teaching school. Whatever the explanation for their lack of closeness, it is clear that Horace saw his father and his father's family as the major influences in his life. And, for Horace, foremost among the array of Bonds was his father's mother.

Bond's granny, like his mother, was named Jane. She was the second daughter born to Martha, a slave belonging to the Arthur family of Bell County, Kentucky. Jane's father, Henry Crockett, belonged to a family in western Virginia of that famous frontier name. Henry often traveled to Kentucky on business for his master, and Martha was his Kentucky wife; Henry also had a spouse in Virginia. Jane grew up in the Kentucky mountains, where there were few other slaves. Her most frequent companion was one of the Arthur daughters, who was seven years older than Jane. When that daughter married a young farmer and preacher from the Bluegrass region of the state, Preston Bond, Jane was given to the daughter by her parents.[4]

With her new mistress, Jane journeyed from the mountains to the farm of Preston Bond. Relations between the slave girl and her new master were generally pleasant, though marred on occasion by such altercations as when Bond vowed to "whup" Jane and she responded by brandishing a knife in self-defense. When Bond's wife became pregnant, he acted in a not uncommon manner and undertook intimate relations with his slave. Thus, shortly after the birth of Bond's child by his wife, a boy was born to Jane. A few years later, the same circumstances yielded two more children, one born to Bond's wife and a second boy to Jane. James, Jane's first child, was born in 1863. He would become the father of Horace Mann Bond. Henry, Jane's second child, was born two years later. Preston Bond's black and white children and their mothers formed a sort of extended family; all of the children called Bond's wife "Ma" and Jane "Mammy."[5]

Though she had no choice but to acquiesce in the familial arrangement with Preston Bond and his wife, Jane was in no way satisfied with the situation. Shortly after the birth of her two boys, the slaves of Kentucky were freed. Jane promptly left the Bonds and moved back to the mountains to be near the Arthurs, her parents, and her sister. Horace's father often told of the rigors of that journey home, and for Horace this act affirmed the courage and indomitable spirit of his grandmother. Her strength was further illustrated by her actions upon returning to her kin. She worked for the Arthur family and others as a nurse and at a variety of other jobs, and she was able to buy a farm and provide a stable home for her two sons. Although Jane possessed only rudimentary reading skills, she managed to make her way through the whole of the Bible. She concentrated on instilling in her sons a strong moral sense which they in turn would pass on to their own offspring.[6]

According to Horace Bond, the most important inheritances he and his siblings received from their grandmother were her strict moral code and her unconquerable will. Other than the Bible, she read few books; in fact, she thought that reading for pleasure was a waste of time and an indication of moral laxity. An anecdote that Horace frequently recounted shows what happened when these values of the grandmother came in conflict with the literary predilections of the grandson. One day young Horace, who liked to read more than anything else, was hiding from his grandmother, who wanted his help with the morning housecleaning. Hidden with his book in the crawl space underneath the house, the boy heard but ignored his grandmother's calls, thinking himself safely removed from her discovering eye and grasp. When her voice went silent, he settled in for a long session of reading, and, absorbed in his book, he was shocked by a sharp sting on his legs from a long switch wielded by his grandmother. She had found him, and she vigorously flushed him from his hiding place: "Come out from there and help me sweep, you stinking little shit arse." Years later, Horace thought this amusing episode illustrated that his granny was a strong-willed woman who brooked no backsliding.[7]

By her grandson's recollection, Jane Bond's major accomplishment, which she shared with her two sons, was the entire Bond family. When Jane Bond died in 1921, she had fifteen grandchildren, six fathered by James Bond and nine fathered by Henry. In the words of Horace Bond, Jane had "founded an American family, and she deserves her place in history."[8]

Despite her lack of book learning, Jane evidently placed at least an instrumental value on education. Her sons certainly did. At the age of seventeen, Horace's father, James, practically illiterate but hungry for accomplishment, left home for his schooling at Berea College. His brother, Henry, soon followed the same path. Working all the while to earn his own room and board, James took thirteen years to finish high school and earn a bachelor's degree. At Berea, he imbibed the abolitionist spirit and puritan moralism that pervaded the college. They both reinforced much of what he had learned from his mother and became the bases for the ideals he inculcated in his own family.[9]

Berea College, founded in 1855 in Berea, Kentucky, by the abolitionist minister John Fee, was modeled on the emancipationist and puritan principles of its founder; its student body was integrated from the immediate post–Civil War years until the 1900s, when the Kentucky legislature passed a law forbidding mixing the races in the state's schools and colleges. John Fee, who had been born to slaveholding parents in northern Kentucky, became an abolitionist while attending the fervently abolitionist Lane Seminary in Cincinnati. When he preached against slavery from a Presbyterian pulpit in Kentucky, he was dismissed from his synod. He was quickly claimed by the antislavery forces at the American Missionary Association (AMA), and, with the support of that body, he founded Berea College as a bastion of antislavery sentiment in a state that permitted the peculiar institution. Even those Kentuckians who opposed slavery were "caste men"; that is, they did not approve of blacks riding in coaches, taking communion, or attending schools with whites. Thus Berea's stance as both antislavery and anticaste ensured its reputation as a controversial institution. Nevertheless, Fee was able to exercise his ideals at the college. When Fee had the chance to teach black Union soldiers in the waning days of the Civil War, he vowed that blacks would have a secure place at Berea College after the war, a goal that was swiftly accomplished. In the period from 1865 to the mid-1890s, blacks constituted approximately half of the college's enrollment. Most of the blacks who attended Berea left before graduating to teach in Kentucky's black schools. Those who did graduate also generally entered teaching, the occupation followed by James Bond's brother, Henry.[10]

James, however, had other ideas. After graduating from Berea College, he studied for the ministry at Oberlin College, the institution that had produced Berea's first president and the president appointed in 1892, the year of James's graduation. At Oberlin, James found that his racial egalitarianism and moral puritanism were reinforced by the spirit that had made the college a forerunner in racial integration and coeducation of the sexes. Founded in 1833, Oberlin received considerable early support from Arthur Tappan and Louis Tappan, the abolitionist businessmen and philanthropists. From its inception, Oberlin was committed to interracial coeducation, and social equality between the races was encouraged.[11] Oberlin was also affiliated with the Congregational church, the same body that sent the teachers of the AMA to the South to educate the freedmen immediately after the Civil War. In fact, Horace Bond's admiration for abolitionists and for the AMA teachers undoubtedly had their sources in his father's educational experiences.[12]

After finishing his theological studies, James Bond successfully pursued a ministerial career. In 1896 he took a Congregational church in Birmingham, Alabama. Shortly thereafter, he moved to Nashville, where he pastored the Congregational church on the campus of AMA-sponsored Fisk University and served on the theology faculty there. Four of the five Bond boys were born in Nashville, the oldest having come into the world in Birmingham. A sixth child, a daughter, was born after the family left Nashville. Horace, the youngest of the five boys, first saw light in Nashville on November 8, 1904.[13]

James Bond had served as a trustee of Berea College since 1896. In 1907, when the Kentucky segregation law was upheld by the United States Supreme Court, Berea was forced to abandon its policy of integration and maintain, instead, an all-white student body. At this time, James moved back to Kentucky to raise funds for the Lincoln Institute, a school that was to be established at Shelbyville to serve the black students who had previously attended Berea. Horace Bond was two years old when his family came to Kentucky; he would stay in Kentucky until he was eight, when James Bond moved the family to Talladega, Alabama, where James was pastor of a church associated with AMA-affiliated Talladega College. A few years later, the family moved to Atlanta, Georgia, where James served at a Congregational church close to Atlanta University. After the start of World War I, James returned to Kentucky to work among the young Negro soldiers who were being trained at Camp Taylor. Horace stayed in Kentucky this time for only one year, for, in 1919, he left to go to college.

His father and mother, however, would remain in the state for the rest of their lives.[14]

James and Jane Bond became devoted to books and to learning at Oberlin College, and all of their children benefited from their parents' love of education. The two oldest sons did well in school, attending college but failing to graduate after they left to serve in World War I. The three younger sons and the Bonds' one daughter, the baby of the family, all graduated from college and earned graduate degrees. Horace, however, was clearly the intellectual star of the family.[15] A precocious child, Horace developed his passionate love for books at a remarkably early age. In Kentucky, Horace's mother taught at a school headed by her brother-in-law, Henry. Lacking an easy alternative arrangement, Jane was forced to take three-year-old Horace along with her to school. Because his mother needed to concentrate on her students during the school day, Horace was left in the charge of two of his cousins, daughters of his Uncle Henry. They soon found that he had learned to read from observing the lessons taught to the other children. Horace read avidly from his father's small but carefully chosen library and in any other volumes that he could lay his hands on. Though he sometimes accompanied his older brothers in such outdoor activities as hunting and swimming, his small size and meager physical abilities meant that he would not excel in these pursuits and in the sports that his brothers loved. Horace was usually content to remain at home, reading.[16]

Another person who had a significant impact on Horace's early intellectual accomplishments was his mother's sister, his Aunt Mamie. After earning a medical degree from the Nashville institution that later became the Meharry Medical College, Mamie came to Kentucky to practice medicine and to live with the Bonds. Her small practice left her a considerable amount of leisure time, which she devoted to the upbringing of young Horace. Mamie wanted Horace to become a doctor, so she drilled him often in the basics of anatomy and physiology. By the age of seven, Horace could recite the names of all of the bones of the human body. He also had a facility for memorizing numbers of ten or more digits; he could recite long passages from the writings of Julius Caesar; and he was a veritable storehouse of obscure information, such as the number of square miles in the state of Rhode Island. The lad loved the accolades that came from his intellectual performances before family and friends, so he threw himself further into the mental gymnastics of memorization. Mamie also widened

Horace's reading to include history, contemporary novels, and some works of Charles Dickens.[17]

Even though Horace's granny and Aunt Mamie were important female presences in his early life, there is no doubt that the largest influence on the young man was exercised by his father. James Bond was loving and warm to all of his children, particularly to his second oldest son, who was also precocious but who suffered from emotional and physical problems, and to Horace's sister, Lucy, who suffered from a physical impairment. With Horace, James nurtured the young prodigy's intellect, encouraging him to read widely and learn all he could.[18]

James Bond illustrated how much he valued educational accomplishment in a magazine article he published about his own and his brother's children. He began by chronicling the struggles of his brother and himself to earn their way through Berea College and the successes that each had subsequently garnered. Next came an account of the educational accomplishments of the two brothers' wives, both of whom had college degrees. However, the most important chapter in the Bond family's education was just then being written. James described the educational achievements of his own and Henry's children, all of whom had attended college and most of whom had graduated and gone on to graduate school. He also paused to bring his readers up to date on the vocation each of the younger Bonds was then pursuing.[19]

Education and scholarship, however, were not the only priorities for James Bond. He had deep, if somewhat unorthodox, religious convictions. His morals were those of the puritanism that pervaded Congregationalism from colonial times through the early twentieth century. His theology encompassed a liberal streak, however, which undoubtedly flourished during his stay at Oberlin College. The theological seminary at that college had already accommodated itself to nineteenth-century Darwinist doctrines and continued to make its peace with the scientific discoveries that most evangelical Christian sects saw as threatening. James's theological liberalism almost caused his expulsion from the ministerial association in Louisville, Kentucky, because he refused to acknowledge Christ as divine. His religious views continued to evolve to the point that he was on the verge of abandoning orthodox Christianity in the 1920s.[20]

James's puritanical values translated to his children as a strong set of moral convictions and a rigorous set of thou-shalt-nots by which the convictions were reinforced. But Horace also absorbed his father's doctrinal flexibility. This allowed Horace to be comfortable and familiar with the strong religious faith of many blacks without being overcome by the anti-intellectualism and fervid fundamentalism that often accompanied that faith. Horace's ability to weave religious metaphors and conventions into his speeches and interactions would stand him in good stead several times in his career.[21]

However, for James Bond and for his son Horace, more important than religion was the Bond name. Horace remembered that his father had great pride in his family: "He taught us all that the greatest thing there might be in the world would be to have a decent family with children who were not merely ordinary, but exceptional." Horace had fond memories of family outings in which his grandmother, her two sons, and all their children held picnics in places far enough from home to make each event a full-day excursion; the children enjoyed these events as much as or more than their parents did. Also, Horace and his brothers were fiercely loyal to one another: he recounted the brothers' determination to not allow any older boys to pick on their young, small, and bookish sibling. From all of these experiences and others, Horace took away a reverence for and devotion to his family name.[22]

Though he had been brought to the school where his mother taught when he was three years old, Horace was formally enrolled in elementary school for only three months. When he was ready, at the age of eight, to enter school at Lincoln Institute, his reading and memorization skills qualified him for the eighth grade. He was successful at Lincoln and equally successful the next year, when he completed the ninth grade at Talladega College High School. There the teachers lavished much attention on their eager student and widened his reading to include all the novels of the French author Alexandre Dumas, whose ancestry was partly black. One teacher, after making a gift of a book to the young Bond, promised to give him a copy of every children's book that he could read from a new shipment just sent to the school. After Horace earned two large cratefuls of books in just a month's time, the offer had to be, regretfully, withdrawn.[23]

For the next two years, Horace attended the Atlanta University High School. There he excelled in subjects that stressed reading and memory, such as English and history, but he also met his first academic setbacks in subjects for which his background had not prepared him, such as mathematics, Latin, and Greek. Reflecting the immaturity of most ten-year-olds, Horace concentrated on what was easiest and ignored what was most difficult for him. The teachers in Atlanta were more aloof and less nurturing than those Horace had encountered in his other schools. The result was that he accumulated a large number of both superior and failing marks. For Horace's last year of high school, the Bonds returned to Kentucky, and he again attended Lincoln Institute, from which he graduated in 1919. At the tender age of fourteen, he was ready to go off to college.[24]

Like all children, Horace learned much besides what was in books and in the school curriculum of his early years. One important set of experiences that he recalled from his childhood involved relations with the white race. Bond had positive memories of many of the white teachers he encountered at the various schools he attended. He remembered them as inspired with a religious zeal for their charges' education as well as for their social and political amelioration. Particularly vivid in Bond's memory was the time in Talladega when he realized the loneliness that beset the white teachers who worked at the college and its schools. Like the Yankee schoolmarms who were the earliest white teachers of the freed blacks, many of the Talladega teachers held strong emancipationist beliefs and values, and they were ostracized by most of the town's whites. Bond became aware of their isolation and loneliness when he once came upon one of his teachers bird-watching in a field. The enthusiasm she showed at this chance encounter with one of her young black students sensitized Bond to the social and personal loss with which this woman and others like her were struggling. Bond's memories of these and other devoted white teachers of blacks predisposed him to respect many of the whites he encountered later as they labored together in the educational vineyard of the black colleges. The sincere commitment of these teachers to the welfare and success of their black students left a lasting impression on him.[25]

However, some of Bond's other childhood experiences with whites were terribly unpleasant. He was once frightened by a white man who, after Bond's older brothers had harassed him and his girlfriend, shot out the door of the Bond home and terrorized the family for an entire night. Horace also remembered the incident when his brother was hunted down by a mob of white youths out to avenge a young friend whom his brother had beaten in a fist fight. Still another Kentucky memory was of his father taking the family to a Louisville park for a picnic. Acting on a recently passed segregation statute (of which the Bonds were unaware), a policeman roughly evicted the family from the park, angering the father and embarrassing his wife and children.[26]

Bond had especially repellent memories of white policemen. In Talladega, the local white lawman arrested a weekly quota of blacks to fill out chain gangs. In Atlanta, a policeman arrested James Bond after Bond's family moved into a house on the all-white street where the officer lived. Horace wreaked his own form of vengeance on the policeman, his daughter, who had called Horace a "nigger," and her grandfather, whom Bond had imagined to be a Confederate veteran: the young black boy whistled Sherman's song, "Marching through Georgia," every time he walked past the white folks' house.[27]

Bond also remembered Atlanta as the first place in which he was called "nigger." The racial slur was hurled by the son of a Jew who owned a store in the neighborhood, and Horace quickly and almost instinctively responded with a slur of his own: "Christ-killer." Horace was shocked to the point of tears by the venom of his reaction and the response his remark evoked. Horace's other race-tinged Atlanta memories included fearing for his safety if caught alone in a white neighborhood and throwing stones at white boys who ventured into an area frequented by Horace and his black playmates (the boys ran to a safe hiding place before the whites could summon a policeman to punish them).[28]

Bond was exposed to prejudice based on skin color even in his own family circle. The matriarch of the Bond clan, Granny Jane, would have little to do with one of Horace's older brothers, whose skin was noticeably darker than that of the rest of the family. Though James Bond did all he could to care for and reassure his emotionally troubled second son, his efforts proved unsuccessful in overcoming the problems that plagued the young man, who died, prematurely, in the 1930s.[29]

Horace's father held positions that often called for him to be deferential to whites, however they treated him. He was evidently practiced in the arts of appealing to whites, for they looked on him as one of the blacks who were good "leaders" of their people. During his last years in Kentucky, James Bond was active in the interracial work sponsored by the Commission on Interracial Cooperation as well as the YMCA, and the whites he encountered in his work, definitely "liberal" on racial matters compared to other southerners, thought of him as a safe and sane black man.[30] Still, James managed to instill in his children a respect for black achievement and a disdain for white racism. The Bond family library included abolitionist and other antislavery works, pro-Negro volumes from the post–Civil War period, accounts of the exploits of Negro soldiers during that war, the autobiography of Frederick Douglass, and biographies of such friends of the freedman as Charles Sumner. James was also a charter subscriber to W. E. B. Du Bois's *Crisis*, the magazine of the National Association for the Advancement of Colored People (NAACP). In reading the pages of *Crisis*, young Horace learned of the accomplishments of many blacks in several walks of American life. He also learned of the reality of lynchings and other injustices heaped on blacks in the South and in white neighborhoods in northern cities.[31]

One sees clearly in the family background and childhood of Horace Mann Bond the seeds of his academic career and distinction. Recognized as an intellectual prodigy at an early age, Bond himself always attributed his extreme precociousness in childhood to early stimulation rather than some superior genetic inheritance on his part. He believed that most youngsters would have been able to do what he had accomplished in his early life if they had had parents such as his and an Aunt Mamie to encourage them. In addition, the rapid rise of the entire Bond family in terms of its educational accomplishments, from Granny, the functionally illiterate former slave who founded the dynasty, to the third generation, which included Horace and his college-educated kin, was further testimony to Bond's belief in parental will and moral fervor as major catalysts of academic ability.

The social class and educational status of the Bond family are surely relevant in explaining Horace's success, though he seldom discussed such matters. His parents were not well off financially; however, his father's status as a professional and the educational level of both parents clearly meant that the Bonds were part of the "black elite." Both had college degrees and made use of their educational training in their work and in the raising of their children. They provided a rich and stimulating environment for their children. They prized literacy and academic achievement, and they passed on these values to their children. Horace's early accomplishments were recognized and reinforced. He was to be the member of the family who would raise the Bond name to new intellectual heights. This often-spoken desire was shared by both parents and communicated to their son. He bore the burden of these expectations gracefully during the early years of his career, but they must have weighed on him as he attempted to make his way in the world.

Bond would treat his own offspring as he had been treated, encouraging them to achieve all that they could and reminding them of their family

name and traditions. He wrote frequently of the accomplishments of his
own children and his relatives' children. He was proud to be a Bond, and
he nurtured that pride in the next generation.[32] Despite all this, it seems
clear that there was some unhappiness in Bond's childhood. Later in life
he sometimes spoke of a lack of self-confidence engendered by his always
being in school with older people. Perhaps this explains some of his difficulties in relating to those who were not family members. His intellectual
accomplishments and the closeness of his own family circle served as only
a partial antidote to this insecurity.[33]

Bond remained close to his family throughout his life. He corresponded
frequently with his father, mother, and, after their deaths, with his brothers
and sister. Bond's remarkable and supportive family provided him with a
refuge from difficulties when he was a child, and as an adult he would often
look to family members for support in times of crisis.

Chapter 2

Lincoln University

When Horace Bond finished high school at Lincoln Institute, he applied to Fisk University at his father's urging. The Fisk authorities decided that the young Bond was not ready for college-level work; rather than simply refuse him admission, however, they recommended that he take a year of college-preparatory work at Fisk. This decision disappointed James Bond. He arranged for Horace to apply to Lincoln University, where Horace was accepted as a full-fledged freshman.[1]

Horace was only fourteen years old when he entered Lincoln University in the fall of 1919 and eighteen when he graduated in 1923. His youth was accentuated by his relatively small size as well as by Lincoln's older-than-average student body, which comprised many World War I veterans. Despite this disadvantage, he achieved, after a mediocre start in his first two years, an outstanding academic record in his junior and senior years. Socially, Bond was somewhat successful in building relationships with other Lincoln students from the very beginning of his stay there (Lincoln was an all-male institution), the first and perhaps the only time in his life when socializing seemed to be easy for him. On the other hand, the young boy's physical immaturity kept him from enjoying the socializing with young women and dating that preoccupied many of his classmates. All these uncertainties and experiences meant that Bond always looked back on his college years with decidedly mixed emotions.

Lincoln University, which was affiliated with the Presbyterian church, differed significantly from Fisk University and the other colleges that were linked with the American Missionary Association. Lincoln reflected, not the abolitionist traditions of the AMA, but the less-radical colonization tradition associated with its founders and other Presbyterians. Lincoln University was established to prepare clergy and laymen who would evan-

gelize the black man, both in the United States and in Africa. The colonizationist orientation meant, obviously, that Lincoln was less predisposed
than were the AMA-affiliated schools to pursue an agenda of black equality
in America.[2]

Indeed, Lincoln University was a relatively conservative institution devoted to the overtly nonconservative purpose of educating blacks. Located
in the southeastern corner of Pennsylvania, about ten miles north of the
Mason-Dixon line, Lincoln looked south to find many of its students. In
1917, of a student body of 216, the state of Georgia had 26 students enrolled—more students than any other state and 1 more than Lincoln's
home state of Pennsylvania. Virginia, South Carolina, and North Carolina
ranked third, fourth, and fifth in numbers of students enrolled. In conformity with its large number of southern students and its rural Pennsylvania
setting, Lincoln was a nonreformist institution that sought to minimize
militant attitudes and maintain a low profile in the region. Firmly controlled by the white ministers who dominated its faculty and board of
trustees, Lincoln University was one of the last of the black colleges to
hire black faculty; it did not hire a black professor until the 1930s, and it
did not hire a black president until 1945. Thus, when Bond attended Lincoln, he encountered a completely white faculty that, though devoted to
educating its almost all-black student body, was not interested in pursuing
any other part of a black-rights agenda.[3]

Lincoln was a small college; its full-time faculty boasted fewer than
ten teachers at the time that Bond enrolled, and its student body remained small before, during, and after Bond's stay. Lincoln had informal
but real ties to Princeton University: the black college's first president
was a Princeton graduate; many of Lincoln's professors came from the
New Jersey school; and the two institutions shared an affiliation with the
Presbyterian church. Moreover, both Lincoln and Princeton had theology
schools that were tied to the conservative theological currents then dominant in Presbyterianism. In fact, Lincoln was known colloquially through
much of its history as the "black Princeton."[4]

Though Lincoln's tuition and other costs were kept low in the years up
to Bond's enrollment, the students were often unable to pay even those
small fees. The institution simply carried on its books the unpaid bills of
many of its students, often allowing them to graduate with a significant
amount of debt still unpaid. The net results of years of this practice and
a period of rising costs during the time of Bond's stay were a decrease

in endowment and a deteriorating fiscal condition. After Bond graduated, university officials increased tuition and other student fees in an attempt to redress the situation, thereby making Lincoln the most expensive black college in the country. To ease the burden on students, officials provided liberal scholarship aid and continued to refuse to dismiss students for nonpayment. Lincoln saw its mission as the education of deserving, academically prepared black students to make them ready for the professional positions then open to aspiring young blacks: medicine, the ministry, and teaching. This reinforced the ambitions of a largely upwardly mobile student body.[5]

There is considerable evidence that Lincoln University was a successful institution. A 1928 report on black colleges noted that Lincoln had "rendered an excellent service to society" in its "development of leadership in the Negro race," which was accomplished by its training of graduates who excelled as "churchmen, educators, and professional men." The report also praised the Lincoln faculty as academically well prepared for its task and noted that instructors taught a not too onerous number of students and courses. Finally, it commended Lincoln's library as exemplary for a college of its size.[6]

The Lincoln curriculum, which was modeled on that of Princeton and other nineteenth-century colleges, was strong in the classical languages, the humanities, and the natural sciences required for premedical study. Unlike the programs found in many other institutions around the country, the course of study at Lincoln was highly prescribed and allowed for few electives, a curricular pattern that Laurence Veysey has characterized as one designed to inculcate "discipline and piety."[7] Lincoln also refused to adopt the trend toward industrial study that swept black higher education under the leadership of Booker T. Washington. In 1909, after Washington gave a commencement address at Lincoln, an agricultural course of study was announced in the bulletin, but it was never implemented. Lincoln consistently chose an academic path that made it a leading example of an institution devoted to the creation of W. E. B. Du Bois's "talented tenth" of black leaders. Several noted black attorneys, physicians, and teachers and administrators were classmates of Horace Bond's. Alumni from classes of the decade following his graduation included William Fontaine, noted professor; Langston Hughes, influential poet; Thurgood Marshall, lawyer and associate justice of the Supreme Court; and Nnamdi Azikiwe, leader of Nigeria as it emerged from colonialism.[8]

The all-white Lincoln faculty interacted with the student body almost exclusively in class, leaving the students largely in control of their out-of-class activities. Though the school had strict rules which reflected its denominational values, the lack of interaction between students and faculty outside of class meant that the students enjoyed a considerable amount of autonomy in daily life. Only actions that severely breached the rules in ways too obvious to be ignored resulted in a disciplinary response.[9]

Bond's favorable views of the white teachers he encountered in his pre-collegiate education at AMA schools such as the Talladega College High School were not consistently reinforced at Lincoln. Lincoln's teachers were usually concerned for their students, but they were socially aloof and often unconcerned with the black race's quest for justice. One exception to this pattern was Robert M. Labaree. A Presbyterian minister who taught sociology, Labaree was interested in black culture, interacted with students outside of the classroom, and shared the zeal for black rights that fired Bond and his AMA schoolteachers. Bond, like other of Lincoln's noted students, developed a considerable respect and warm regard for Labaree, both of which were reciprocated. As Bond's academic career developed, he frequently wrote to Labaree to tell him of current accomplishments and to solicit advice about future ventures.[10]

However, the warm relations Bond and other students experienced with Robert Labaree were not common. Though students often remembered professors for their dedication in the classroom or gentleness and kindness, sustained personal relationships between students and faculty seemed blocked by racial barriers. Close friendships among students, however, served quite well as a substitute for the lack of guidance from or personal contact with professors.[11]

Because of his youth and small size, Bond was quickly labeled the baby of the freshman class of 1919. One story, not denied by Bond, was that he arrived on campus wearing short pants. His first two years on campus were enlivened by a variety of high jinks. Early in his freshman year, the first-year students had barricaded a room to avoid a bout of hazing from sophomores, the traditional adversaries of the new students. Safely tucked away from their tormentors, the freshmen began a poker game. As Bond remembered it, he was untutored in poker but quickly caught on to the simple game of blackjack. He then proceeded to clean out every other student who entered the game. Bond thus acquired the reputation of an astute gambler, one that he claimed to be unjustified; however, he was not averse to card games.[12]

Surviving evidence about collegiate life for Bond and the other members of the class of 1923 indicates that the youngest member served as a kind of mascot for his class. He was included in most class activities and well accepted by his classmates. He acquired a nickname, "Klops," which was sometimes used in later correspondence between Bond and other students of his era. The nickname seems to have been the result of two events. In Bond's sophomore year, a black eye acquired in a fracas between members of his class and some freshmen led to his being named "Cyclops" for his one-eyed appearance. Shortly after this episode, someone stole chickens from faculty houses; Bond, protesting that he was being unjustly accused, was nevertheless nicknamed "Klops," the Greek word for thief.[13] That Bond was accepted by his classmates, even as they noted his propensity to bedevil them, is illustrated in this description of him, taken from his college's yearbook of 1923, the year of his graduation: " 'Klops' thinks it's nice to be different, and he is. He is opposed to everything including private property, which he proves by taking anything that he wants. The only thing that saves him from murder, is the fact that he is the Class Baby, and we've been hoping that he'd outgrow his shortcomings."[14]

Though he was too young and too small to participate in athletics, Bond became the athletic editor of the student newspaper, thus sharing in the many victories earned by the Lincoln athletic teams, particularly the football team. He also had success in literary activities, served as a member of the debating team, gave one of the speeches at the class commencement, joined one of Lincoln's four social fraternities, and served as an associate editor of *The Paw*, the yearbook of the class of 1923.[15]

Perhaps because of his enthusiastic participation in extracurricular activities, Bond's academic accomplishments in his first two years were mediocre. Lincoln's marking system ranged from 1 to 5, with 1 representing the highest grade, from 90 to 100, and 5 representing a failing grade, below 60. In his freshman year, Bond earned two 1s his first semester, in Bible and in Greek, but none his second semester, a term in which he failed mathematics. In his second year, he made two more 1s, again in Bible and in a poetry class, but made a 4 both semesters in physics. A calculation of his grade average using contemporary designations of A, B, C, D, and F to correspond with 1, 2, 3, 4, and 5, and assigning quality points from one to four for grades ranging from D to A, yields a 2.1 average, or slightly over a C for these two years. By this measure, Bond's first-year grades averaged slightly below C and the second slightly above. In this early period, then, he may be said to have, at best, just gotten by academically.[16]

However, regarding his academic performance, Bond recalled that he underwent a complete change of heart early in his junior year. It was then that a classmate taunted him because of his poor marks. Bond vowed at that moment to become a serious student, and from then on he excelled in almost all of his classes, including his science courses, for which his childhood education had ill prepared him. While there is no way to verify the incident that sparked this academic turnabout, Bond's grades do indicate a decided improvement during his junior and senior years. In these last two years, twenty of his twenty-five grades were 1s, three were 2s, and two were 3s. He also passed practice teaching and earned the highest marks in Bible in three out of four semesters as well as in two philosophy classes, two literature classes, and courses in geography, ethnology, and psychology. In addition, he achieved the highest marks in senior science courses in biology, botany, geology, and bacteriology-embryology. Calculating his average in modern equivalents yields a low A (3.76) average for this period, with the senior-year average higher than the junior average. During Bond's last semester, he earned the highest possible marks in all of his courses.[17]

Because of his sparkling academic record in his last two years and probably also because of his youth, Lincoln officials invited Bond to stay on at the college as a part-time instructor in education for a year after his graduation. Bond could also use this year to study foreign languages and other subjects needed to prepare for graduate school. A common practice at Lincoln throughout the early twentieth century, this was one way that at least a token black presence could be maintained on the faculty without threatening seriously the all-white makeup of the permanent faculty.[18] To prepare Bond for his duties, in the summer of 1923 Lincoln administrators arranged a scholarship for him to study education at Pennsylvania State College. There he was pleased to discover that he could compete successfully with white students, making competitive grades in all three of his courses. In history of education, he earned the grade of 95, in educational measurement a 90, and in introduction to education a 91.[19]

At Penn State, however, a painful experience with a white professor rekindled some of Bond's negative feelings toward whites. In one of his courses, Bond encountered a white teacher's open discrimination against a black student. Ironically, this teacher was somewhat of a celebrity for his "progressivism," since he had transferred to Penn State after coming under fire for his liberal ideas at the University of Tennessee at the time of the Scopes trial; yet this same man forced Bond to sit at the end of a row, away from his alphabetical place, which would have put him next to a white female. Answering Bond's query about the seating, the professor attributed the arrangement to the racial apprehensions of white girls. Bond never forgot this episode.[20] It was a stark reminder that the wounds of segregation inflicted on blacks in the South could be repeated, though in altered form, in nonsouthern settings.

While at Lincoln University, Bond experienced continual frustration in his relationships with young women, an area in which he had never been too successful or comfortable. Lincoln was an all-boys school, and as such it fostered an artificiality that accompanied most contacts with the opposite sex. For Bond, the awkward situation was exacerbated by the fact that he was considerably younger than most of the girls with whom his classmates interacted. He brought this awkwardness along with him from his days in high school, when, again, he had been much younger than all his classmates. In high school, he had often found himself to be the butt of pranks and jokes by older boys and girls who took advantage of his social naïveté. In an autobiographical fragment written in the 1930s, Bond recalled losing his first love at the age of twelve: she deserted him for his older brother, who possessed superior physical attributes and accomplishments. Another time, he recalled that the older girls who were his high-school classmates in Atlanta encouraged him to write florid love letters to a girl who was his own age and who was in the fifth grade. These girls, whom Bond described as "spiteful huzzies [sic]," did not deliver the letters to the object of his affections, as promised; instead, they read them aloud in class to the amusement of all the students except the betrayed and excruciatingly embarrassed young author.[21]

More comfortable with his father than his mother, Horace feared women since early in his life. His apprehensions may have been fueled by dire warnings from his mother about premature contact with girls. This unease was intensified by his experiences with the young black servicemen he encountered at the Kentucky base where his father was working a year or so before his enrollment at Lincoln. Horace was befriended by, and wrote letters home for, several semiliterate soldiers who were married to more than one woman or who tried to keep both a wife and a girlfriend satisfied. He also witnessed the terrors of syphilis through observing the treatment of that disease in the soldiers on the base. He had earlier learned of venereal diseases when, still quite young, he had read widely in his aunt's medical books. All these fears and unhappiness culminated in his bitter loneliness on the night of his college graduation, when he was forced to be alone in his dormitory room while his classmates made merry with their dates in the gymnasium.[22]

In the fall of 1923, when Bond returned to Lincoln University to serve on the faculty, he was also made a prefect of one of the dormitories. By this time he was about the same age as the college freshmen he was supposed to supervise. Bond's dormitory room came to be used by the student residents as a gambling house, where he and an older student took a cut of all the money wagered. When one student's father complained about the money his son had lost playing poker at the college, Bond's complicity in the activity and his own profiting from it became known to the school authorities. Bond was forced to resign from the college, in disgrace, for contributing to rather than preventing the misconduct of his charges. The entire episode proved of great embarrassment to both Horace and his parents.[23] Further, he was shamed by some of the faculty and other members of the Lincoln community. One faculty member, a biology professor named Harold Grim, told Bond that his leaving was a good riddance and that he never would amount to anything. The dean of the college thoroughly chastised the young offender by reminding him that he had betrayed the trust that Lincoln officials had put in him. A noted alumnus also told Bond that he would never be "worth a damn as long as you live." In retrospect, these judgments seem unduly harsh, but Bond did not forget them.[24]

Bond himself attributed this nasty episode and other unpleasant experiences from his early years, including his failures with the opposite sex, to his youthfulness in relation to his high-school and college classmates. On at least two occasions later in his life, he complained of the negative consequences of being a "gifted child," a prodigy. In both instances, Bond argued that the benefits of being advanced because of intellectual precociousness were far outweighed by the costs of being thrown into day-to-day contact with people considerably older than oneself. The result of this was a social adjustment that was at best awkward and at worst harmful to the young person.[25] In one of these recollections, Bond used his own Lincoln experiences to make a case against a proposal to bring gifted high-school students to Northwestern University for collegiate studies. He did not deny that the young students would be capable of meeting the intellectual challenges they would encounter; however, he argued, early and facile academic achievement left them unprepared for the hard work they might encounter in life's other arenas. By and large, prodigies were prone to laziness; they did not know that life was more than the academic games and puzzles at which they excelled. Further, precocious youngsters were subject to the "arrogance" and "intellectual exhibitionism" that often accompanied early accomplishment. But perhaps worst of all, Bond said, the youths' social immaturity, which necessarily accompanied being advanced beyond their age-mates, was quite likely to result in the production of a group of intellectually advanced social cripples.[26]

Upon leaving Lincoln University, Bond was too ashamed of his dismissal to return to his parents' home in Kentucky. Instead, he went to Chicago, where two of his brothers were living. His oldest brother was employed as a postman, and the brother who was his immediate senior, Max, was a student at a Chicago college. Within a few months of his arrival, Horace enrolled as a graduate student at the University of Chicago. He remained at that institution for the next decade, receiving his master's degree in 1926 and his doctorate in 1936, both in the field of education. By the time he received his doctorate, he would also be married and would have risen through the faculty ranks of black colleges to increasingly more responsible positions. The immaturity of his youth would be left behind in the next decade as Bond made his way into the academic world.

Because Horace Bond would spend his career as a professor and administrator in black colleges, the ways in which his Lincoln experience did or did not prepare him for his career deserve consideration. First, as already noted, Lincoln's curriculum stressed the classics and the liberal arts and ignored Booker T. Washington–style vocationalism. This was a quite appropriate preparation for the academic vocation to which Bond aspired. In another important way, however, Lincoln gave its graduates little or no preparation for professional careers. Given its all-white faculty, administration, and board of trustees, Lincoln University sent a negative message to its students and its alumni. Students who desired and alumni who held professional roles in the black community had to face the fact that the institution that claimed to prepare them for these roles refused to allow blacks into the bodies that planned the preparation process and carried it out.

The 1920s, when Horace Bond finished his undergraduate education and embarked on graduate work, were a decade punctuated by protests on black college campuses over curricular and governance issues as well as the paternalistic control exercised by college administrators. This climate of protest and ferment also dominated black cultural life in the decade; the insurgency in black literature was referred to as that of the "New Negro."[27] While Lincoln University heard complaints about the lack of blacks on its board, in its faculty, and in its administration, that protest was entirely mounted by alumni; students played no part in this upheaval.

In the mid-1920s, after the death of the president, the alumni association sought a black president for the college. The trustees demurred, arguing that a white was needed to raise money from the Presbyterian church and nondenominational philanthropies. The alumni could not force the choice of a black administrator, but they did bring enough pressure to bear so that three successive white candidates whom they thought unsympathetic to black concerns were forced to withdraw from consideration. Finally, after three years of dispute, the alumni association celebrated the trustees' choice of a white faculty member whom black graduates felt was not opposed to their aspirations for a role in the college's affairs. Within a year of the new president's accession to office, Lincoln University had its first black trustee, the president of the alumni association. A few years later, the first permanent black faculty member was also chosen.[28]

Lincoln students were totally uninvolved in these disputes. In fact, in the years just after Bond's graduation, student opinion favored an all-white faculty and administration by a two-to-one margin. The reasons students gave for preferring the status quo reveal a remarkable ability to cloak their lack of respect for their own race. Some claimed that, since white philanthropists supported the college, whites should run it. Some argued that there was a shortage of qualified black teachers and administrators. Still others thought that things were fine as they were, with no need for change. Three other sets of comments border on racial self-hatred. Some students said "they just didn't like Negroes"; others claimed that "Negro teachers [would not] have the interest of students at heart"; one student even stated that members of his own race "were not morally capable."[29]

The relation of opinions such as these to Bond's experiences at Lincoln University is not at all clear. First, Bond graduated five years before the students registered these opinions. Inferring that the attitudes of Bond's fellow students and the students quoted above were the same is dangerous. Yet the student body seemed not to have changed much in that brief time, and a similarity between the two groups on this issue can at least be suggested. More significantly, the campus ambience at Lincoln, during and after Bond's student days, seems to have been such that the very students who would later play roles as professors or administrators at black colleges received little help, other than in their academic work, from the faculty at the college. At the very least, they had no black role models whom they might emulate in their own careers.

Thus, though Lincoln University had the kind of curriculum that prepared its students for academic and other professional roles, its campus life lacked the ferment and self-discovery found on other black campuses in the 1920s. While blackness was being valued for its own sake in many black circles in this period, it was not being valued similarly at Lincoln University. When this is added to the other conservative characteristics of Lincoln, it seems that there were many other black campuses in the country where aspiring black academics would have received a more appropriate socialization.

Bond's successful early academic career did not reveal any deficiencies related to his Lincoln experiences. When he returned to Lincoln University as its first black president in 1945, however, the mixed results he achieved there may well have been related to the historically conditioned discomfort that he, the faculty, and some alumni felt.

Chapter 3

Chicago

Horace Bond was not quite twenty years old when he enrolled as a graduate student at the University of Chicago in the spring of 1924. He studied there for the next two quarters and then left to take a full-time faculty position at a black college in Oklahoma. In 1926, Bond returned to Chicago for another year of study, receiving his master's degree in education at the end of the fall quarter and staying for two more quarters to begin work on his doctorate. He then returned to Oklahoma and, later, moved on to other positions at various black colleges in the South. After finally obtaining his doctorate from the University of Chicago in 1936 and embarking on his two college presidencies, Bond maintained contacts with Chicago faculty and some of the students he met there through most of his career.

Bond was initially undecided about his field of specialization. He eventually received both his graduate degrees from the Department of Education, but education was not his first choice. He had an interest in biology that dated back to his childhood regard for Aunt Mamie, an interest intensified by studies in biology and other sciences in his senior year at Lincoln University, but he decided that scientific study was too expensive. He had a strong inclination to study history, but he was turned down by that department because of his lack of undergraduate prerequisites. Lincoln's strictly defined curriculum had allowed Bond room to take only two history courses. The fields in which he chose to concentrate at Chicago, education and sociology, were less costly than biology and less particular about their students' backgrounds than history.[1]

Bond eventually decided to major in education at Chicago. This choice built on his coursework, including practice teaching, at Lincoln, as well as his three graduate courses in education at Penn State in the summer of 1923. It was also a choice to continue in the field in which he had served as instructor at Lincoln in the first semester of the 1923–24 academic year. Bond soon learned that, though the university and the Department of Sociology were particularly hospitable to black students, the Department of Education was not. Black students enrolled in education were not allowed to student-teach at the university's laboratory school but had to arrange to work in black schools in the city.[2]

Like other African Americans, Bond often encountered racist attitudes among faculty members. On one occasion, for example, he felt compelled to write a letter of protest to a professor of education, Frederick Breed, who had lampooned blacks and used the phrases "darky" and "nigger" in a story he told at a convocation. Bond described the story as "quite distasteful to me" and told Breed that the same story had recently been recounted by the Alabama state superintendent of education. Unlike the Chicago professor, the southern white educator did not use offensive words while telling the story and even apologized for relating the anecdote. Bond added that the story and the language Breed used were inconsistent with "academic dignity" and "ordinary considerations of decent respect for the feelings of other people." He concluded, "Not even Amos and Andy are so crude."[3]

Bond faced other difficulties in beginning, and continuing, his graduate studies at Chicago. His adjustment to the city was eased by the companionship of his older brothers. Finances, however, were a constant worry. James Bond considered his sons' educational expenses to be his problem as well as their own. Letters from father to sons in this period typically contained reassurances and encouragement to keep up the good work along with sums of money to pay pressing expenses. The boys were also urged to help each other in times of financial need. Unfortunately, the familial support was not sufficient, and the sons had to find whatever jobs they could to help pay their expenses. Horace, for example, earned much of his way through the University of Chicago by working as a dishwasher in several restaurants.[4]

Because of his difficulties in paying for his education, Bond never studied full-time for more than three consecutive quarters. He would enroll for a period, then drop out to work full-time, return for study, then go back to work, and so on. In spite of this fitful study schedule and continual search for funds, James Bond, at least, never lost sight of the goal. In a letter sent to his son in the same month in which Horace began his graduate studies at Chicago, James began with assurances of forthcoming money and then came to his major message: "Since you are in the fight for your master [*sic*] degree remember that your chief business is to study."⁵ It seems that the young Bond also kept this aim firmly in mind throughout the more than ten years during which he was intermittently enrolled at Chicago. He did well in almost all of his courses and made consistent progress toward the objectives of first a master's and then a doctoral degree.

Bond began his graduate studies by carefully choosing his first quarter's schedule. He took two courses in areas in which he had studied just six months earlier at Penn State: the History of American Education and Mental Tests. For his third class he selected a sociology course on the Negro in Africa, a subject in which he was surely interested and at least moderately well prepared by his and his family's experiences (his aunt had spent time in Africa as a medical missionary), particularly in contrast to the white students who would be enrolled. Bond's careful choices and hard work were rewarded with two A− grades and a B in his first quarter. He was off to a good start at Chicago, and he would continue this success, never making below a B in his master's program and a P (pass) in his doctoral program. The three subjects he initially chose were those to which he would devote most of his major intellectual efforts in his studies at Chicago and in the rest of his career: the history of education, educational testing, and the sociology of blacks in Africa and America.⁶

Charles H. Judd, the chairman of the Department of Education, was the dominant influence in the field of education at Chicago. Chicago's education program had achieved renown at the turn of the twentieth century through its association with such luminaries as John Dewey. Dewey served at Chicago for approximately ten years and was chairman of the Department of Philosophy, Psychology, and Education when he left for Columbia University in 1904. Five years later, Judd came to Chicago and began to dismantle Dewey's edifice. Trained as a psychologist in Germany, where he received his doctorate under Wilhelm Wundt, at Chicago, Judd proceeded to establish education as a "scientific" study, detaching education from its departmental housing with philosophy and psychology and de-emphasizing teacher training and the laboratory school, both of which had been integral to Dewey's approach. Also, in contrast to Dewey's penchant for linking subject and methodology, Judd denied the importance of subject matter in teacher training. He believed that the scientifically trained teacher needed to learn the psychology of teaching the various fields of study, not the subjects themselves.⁷

In place of Dewey's School of Education at Chicago, a primary function of which was to train teachers, Judd started a graduate Department of Education in the Faculty of Social Sciences. Having a graduate department both established the legitimacy of the science of education and offered advanced training to educational leaders. During his thirty years as chair, Judd ruled his department, students and faculty, with an iron hand. All theses and dissertations had to receive the stamp of his approval, and faculty members who did not meet his expectations faced termination or denial of promotion.[8]

Judd stressed an environmentalist concern for learning in education, as opposed to the more genetically oriented emphasis on natural ability that characterized the work of many other notable educational psychologists of the day. This orientation was attractive to Bond and other black graduate students, who were then smarting under hereditarian contentions that blacks' scores on army intelligence tests during World War I "proved" the genetic inferiority of the black race. Yet there is evidence that Judd had no fondness for his black graduate students, a fact that would undoubtedly have been recognized by the young Horace Bond. According to a historian of Chicago's education programs, in order "to discourage nonwhites from matriculating," Judd "tried to deny them financial aid, even where they appeared qualified."[9]

Bond left no detailed account of the three courses or other experiences he had with Judd, but he did acknowledge Judd in the preface to the published version of his dissertation. While completing his dissertation and afterword, Bond wrote frequently to Judd, inquiring about job possibilities or research grants. In unguarded moments, however, Bond revealed a not altogether flattering opinion of Judd: writing to a longtime friend, he recounted that he had finally had his dissertation topic approved "by the demon Judd," and, in another letter from the same period, he described Judd as a stimulating teacher "with whom I disagreed most violently in all the seminar meetings I attended—silently, I must add."[10]

Bond majored in his master's program and minored in his doctoral studies in Judd's field, educational psychology. Bond's favorite professor in this area, however, was Frank N. Freeman, who specialized in intelligence testing. Both Judd and Freeman were trained in psychology, not in education, and Judd had been on the faculty and Freeman a doctoral student at Yale University before they came to Chicago. This emphasis on pure psychology may have had some impact on Bond, since he reported

to W. E. B. Du Bois in 1926 that his field of study for the doctorate would
be psychology, not education.[11]

At Yale, Freeman had specialized in intelligence testing. Brought to Chicago by Judd, he taught in the Department of Education for the next three
decades. Bond took two courses from Freeman at the master's level, including Mental Tests in his first quarter of graduate study in 1924, and two
more courses at the doctoral level.[12] Frank Freeman's balanced views on
intelligence test scores were one reason that Bond sought him out. Freeman's outlook was compatible with the strongly environmentalist position
taken by black intellectuals who sought to explain the low scores of black
soldiers on World War I tests. Freeman's criticism of genetic explanations
of score differences was a persistent theme in his work. In a 1937 study
that he coauthored, Freeman and his colleagues concluded that, while they
could reach no general solution to the problems raised in the nature-
nurture (heredity-environment) debate, they believed that "what heredity
can do environment can do also." Freeman studied the environmental
aspect in intelligence in his own work and directed several dissertations
in this area. In one such thesis, the student concluded that environment
modifies both intelligence and the Intelligence Quotient (IQ) that measures it and that, while IQs are valid measures of intelligence, environment
must be considered if IQs are to be used for purposes of prediction over
long periods of time.[13]

Bond frequently acknowledged the importance of Freeman's teaching
as well as his kindness. Freeman was not initially responsible for Bond's
strong interest in mental tests, however; rather, the Chicago psychologist allowed the young black scholar to build on an interest he already
had when he came to Chicago. "Scientific" arguments about the genetic
inferiority of blacks had been promulgated in America at least since the
turn of the century. The army's intelligence test scores reflected only the
latest version of this scientific racism. Black intellectuals had become practiced at refuting allegations of genetic inferiority, though largely in forums
known only to black audiences, as black scholars' access to mainstream
scientific and popular journals was severely restricted. Bond's interest in
the topic had been piqued in a sociology course taught by Robert Labaree
at Lincoln University. And at Pennsylvania State College in the summer of
1923, he became personally and intellectually aroused when he overheard
a white student argue that IQ tests proved the inferiority of blacks.[14]

Bond published two articles on black intelligence scores in the summer of 1924, so he was clearly at work on this topic before enrolling at Chicago in March of that year. In the first, published in W. E. B. Du Bois's *Crisis*, he tried to show the errors in fact and interpretation that whites used in employing test scores in a racial war against blacks. He castigated white psychologists for misusing the data from the army tests, stating that the source of any deficit in black scores in relation to whites was environmental. In support of this position, he described the results of a series of intelligence tests he had given at Lincoln in which northern black students scored considerably higher than their southern counterparts, an imbalance also reflected in the high-school records of the two groups. In contrast to many white psychologists' studies, which explained regional differences in test scores by claiming that intelligent blacks had migrated to the North, Bond's studies showed that regional differences in scores diminished significantly during the years the students were at Lincoln. The university environment, then, had an equalizing influence on the students' performance. Bond went on to claim that circumstances similar to those he found at Lincoln would likely occur wherever "an intelligent effort has been made to make allowance for the environmental factor."[15]

One month after the publication of his first article, Bond published an article on testing in *Opportunity*, the journal, edited by Charles S. Johnson, of the National Urban League. Here Bond discussed an aspect of the army intelligence scores that was ignored by psychologists who claimed that whites' higher scores proved them to be innately superior to blacks. Bond showed that blacks from some northern states—namely, Illinois, New York, Ohio, and Pennsylvania—scored higher than whites from the southern states of Mississippi, Kentucky, Arkansas, and Georgia. Bond also attacked testers who attributed whites' superiority on the tests to their Nordic blood. He showed that whites from northern states, where there were considerable numbers of immigrants from southern and eastern Europe, scored significantly higher than whites from southern states, who more closely resembled the ideal of Nordic racial purity. In this article, as in the first publication, Bond stressed the environmental factors that explained regional differences among white scores and racial differences between black and white scores. He concluded that the army's and other intelligence test results had to be interpreted with the following fact in mind: "All tests so far devised and given have shown differences in social degrees of rating; and all so-called racial differences can be resolved into social differences."[16]

However, Bond refused to condemn intelligence tests per se. At the end of his article in *Opportunity*, he noted, "It is not with intelligence tests that we have any quarrel: in many ways they do represent a fundamental advance." He added that tests were useful for diagnostic purposes and standardizing American education, a necessary step if environment were to be truly equalized for students. In fact, if properly used, intelligence tests could even be "a remedy of the classic faults of teachers' judgment." [17]

Frank Freeman's encouragement of Bond's interest in tests and test · scores was unusual in the climate that prevailed in American universities of that time. Bond later noted that only at Chicago under Freeman and at Columbia under William C. Bagley were students encouraged to combat racist determinism. Bond retained his ties with Freeman and his interest in the use and abuse of intelligence testing throughout his years at Chicago. Throughout his long career, Bond maintained his environmentalist stance and his opposition to hereditarian explanations of black scores on intelligence tests. [18]

In addition to his two courses with Freeman at the master's level, Bond took another testing course from the psychology department. His master's thesis, "An Investigation of the Nonintellectual Traits of a Group of Negro Normal-School Students," did not involve intelligence test scores, but it did use personality tests in an effort to highlight nonintellectual traits that might explain the performance of black teachers. [19]

Bond never hid his contempt for the ideas of a third Chicago educational psychologist, Guy Buswell. Though he took no courses from Buswell at the master's level, he enrolled in one Buswell course and another cotaught by Buswell at the doctoral level. Shortly after completing the master's degree, Bond was called in by Buswell to discuss Bond's score on an intelligence test, a required screening device for doctoral study. The professor told the young black that he had done quite well on the test, though he did not reveal his score. Buswell asked Bond to explain his high marks, since blacks did not usually do well on the test. Bond answered that his score reflected his prodigious amount of reading; Buswell, evidently dissatisfied with that explanation, remarked, "It probably is your white blood," and dismissed Bond with congratulations on his performance. This encounter soured Bond on Buswell and undoubtedly had something to do with his contrasting "the agony of a lecture by Dr. Buswell" with the stimulating lectures he encountered in other courses. [20] In later years, when Bond remarked, "I must acknowledge a bias against educational psychologists,

at least those of my generation," he was undoubtedly thinking of his experiences with Buswell and probably those with Judd. Frank Freeman,
however, was the one psychologist from whom Bond learned a great deal
and for whom he expressed great respect.[21]

From the first quarter of his graduate studies, Bond took work in the
sociology department. His interest in sociology emerged under Labaree
at Lincoln, where he developed a strong desire to understand the plight
and improve the conditions of his race. As a graduate student, he enrolled for ten sociology courses, five each at the master's and doctoral
levels. Robert E. Park taught three of them. According to Bond, Park was
one of two "great teachers" he encountered at Chicago, the other being
Edward Sapir, an anthropologist who also taught in the sociology department. Park held a German doctorate and had worked for seven years with
Booker T. Washington, the noted black educator, spokesman, and president of Tuskegee Institute. Park was greatly interested in the culture of
black Americans, in both its African and its American origins. The sociology department at Chicago, and particularly Park's classes, became a
haven for black students. Charles S. Johnson, editor of *Opportunity*, future
head of social sciences at Fisk University, and, later, the president of that
institution, studied with Park. E. Franklin Frazier, perhaps the most noted
black sociologist of this century, also received his doctorate at Chicago.
Park was a giant in the development of the field of sociology and a prime
mover in establishing the University of Chicago as perhaps *the* place to be
in the development of that discipline. Also, it was under Park's influence
that the department developed race relations as one of its specialties.[22]

Largely because of Park, the department's eminence, and its favorable
orientation to studies of blacks and their experiences, it seemed for a time
that Bond might switch to sociology. He corresponded frequently with
Park in the late 1920s, after he had received his master's degree and had
begun his doctoral work. Park responded positively to Bond's plans to
engage in more environmentally oriented studies of black intelligence and
discussed the possibility of Bond writing a dissertation on the topic of
blacks as "marginal men." The concept of marginality, fairly new in sociological literature, was largely associated with and developed by Robert
Park and the Chicago department.[23]

Park also arranged for Bond to publish an article in the 1928 *Annals of
the American Academy of Political and Social Science*. In his brief essay, Bond
noted the progress of blacks since Reconstruction and related it to their

ability to maintain their self-respect in the face of racial slights. He showed how Booker T. Washington, by the very success of his career at Tuskegee Institute, was instrumental in helping blacks retain their dignity. Bond concluded that a recent humorous article in which a black author noted the whimsical ways of "our white folks" was a healthy indication that black self-respect was increasing. Bond's essentially optimistic analysis of the condition of blacks coincided with Park's own views of the present and future of the race. Park posited a process of racial accommodation and saw assimilation as the natural and favorable outcome of that accommodation. This view was easy for a white academic to maintain, as he could selectively interpret events in terms of his framework. It was also a convenient view for an aspiring black academic to use in interpreting current events. It overlooked, however, the horrid conditions under which most blacks struggled and the turbulence then sweeping through the black intellectual circles influenced by the New Negro movement in arts and letters and the black masses who were following Marcus Garvey, the black nationalist.[24]

Although Bond always praised Park lavishly in public and profited from his sponsorship, he also indicated that he was aware of the unrealistic optimism and the fatalism implicit in Park's theory of race relations. Bond's privately expressed views of Park also revealed a complex interaction between the two men. In an autobiographical fragment, Bond recounted an occasion when Park chastised him for his "intense dislike for practically all white people." Park correctly read Bond's suspicious attitude toward some whites, particularly those whom he did not know, but Park delivered his assessment with a gruffness that the young black student would never forget, although Park's cantankerousness was well known throughout the department. Professors often had to persuade graduate students to continue working with him, even after he had offended or insulted them (he once called a student a "damn fool"). In a letter to a close friend in 1935, Bond complained about Park, writing that "that old sob" Park had become convinced, erroneously, that Bond was having personal problems. In his characteristically insensitive style, Park ignored Bond's protestations that there were no problems and thrust his nose into his student's private affairs.[25]

It was in Bond's professional interest, however, to maintain cordial relations with Park. The two kept up a steady correspondence as Bond's career developed in the 1930s. By that time the sociologist had retired from Chicago and gone to teach at Fisk University in Nashville, where Charles

Johnson was head of the Department of Social Science and where Bond was a sometime faculty member. When Bond left Fisk to go to Dillard University in New Orleans in the mid-1930s, he reinforced the tie by inviting Park to study conditions among rural blacks in Louisiana.[26]

Of course, Park was not the only sociology faculty member at Chicago who aided Bond. In a course taught by Park's colleague Elsworth Faris, Bond was assigned to review a treatise on the genetic basis of IQ, and Faris arranged for the review to be published in a 1927 issue of the Chicago-sponsored *American Journal of Sociology*.[27]

Bond also reported that it was in a sociology course that he learned how to do research. After being instructed in a method of gathering data on index cards, he was paired with another student to research a particular topic. When he compared his work with that of his colleague, a more advanced student in the department, he was embarrassed to find that he had accomplished a fraction of what she had. She then took him to the library and showed him how to research a topic thoroughly. Bond always remembered this lesson, and this method and thoroughness in doing research would stay with him throughout his career. While president of Lincoln University in the 1950s, he instructed students in the art of research by index card, taking them to the library and showing them how to make a comprehensive study of a topic.[28]

Bond flirted with the idea of switching to sociology for his doctoral dissertation before deciding to stay with education as his field of record. At one point, he considered staying in the Department of Education but having Park supervise his thesis. Transit of faculty and students between the two areas was not difficult since both were departments in the Faculty of Social Sciences at Chicago.[29] Bond's decision to remain in education thus may not have been as significant as it seems to modern academics, who are accustomed to the walls erected by ever more specialized departments and the tension between education and other subjects. His ability to work in both sociology and education in his early academic jobs testifies further to the relative permeability of the boundaries. The numerous opportunities for blacks in education, provided by the existence of segregated black schools in the South and the emphasis on teacher training in most black colleges, may well have been the deciding factors in Bond's choice.

Bond selected a dissertation topic in the history of education, not in educational psychology, the subject of his master's thesis. In 1929, he wrote to the Department of Education, inquiring as to how much remained in his work on the Ph.D. requirements and outlining his plans for completing his residency. In addition, he discussed three possible dissertation topics, two of which were historical: "As a thesis, I should like to take either of the following subjects: 'The Constitutional and Legal Basis of Negro Education in the United States since 1865'; 'The Financing of Negro Education in Southern States since 1865'; 'The Achievement of Negro Grammar School Students in Certain Typical Southern Counties.'" [30]

As already noted, when he arrived at Chicago, Bond was not allowed to follow his interest in history because of his deficiencies in undergraduate coursework. What the Chicago history department's rule about prerequisites ignored, however, was the wide reading that the young man had cultivated since his childhood, much of which had been in historical works. [31] In contrast, the Department of Education allowed Bond to explore the history of education and did not worry about the presumed shortcomings of his background. His mentor in this area was Newton Edwards, from whom he took four courses, three at the master's level and one at the doctoral level, and who advised Bond in his doctoral studies and directed Bond's dissertation. The young black scholar obviously learned his lessons well: Bond's doctoral thesis on Alabama Negro education received a prize as the best dissertation in the department, was published soon after its completion, and was reprinted in a paperback edition in the 1960s. [32]

Newton Edwards, a South Carolinian, had received an A.B. from Trinity College (now Duke University) and a Ph.D. in history at the University of North Carolina. He had a reputation for working closely with all of his students, and Bond often testified to the importance of his influence. In the preface to the published edition of his dissertation, Bond acknowledged the "painstaking counsel" of Newton Edwards, "who has given much time to the manuscript while it was being prepared." Over a decade later, in a talk given to a group of educational historians, Bond recalled that it was "through that great teacher Newton Edwards, whose student I take pride in being, that I came long ago to regard the history of education as the veritable Queen of all disciplines." Bond described how he had learned from Edwards that the history of education, properly conceived, was a part of the history of a social order. To understand educational institutions and their development, one must look at "all of the social institutions, . . . the Family; the Church; political and economic institutions, and the economy on which they rest; all these become the necessary content and object of the student of the history of education." [33]

Edwards's published ideas on the history of education clearly reflect this focus. A textbook he coauthored with Herman Richey, a Chicago graduate and faculty colleague, sees the changing array of social forces as the determiner of the essential tenets of the school. For Edwards, educational history thus becomes a part of social history. Edwards's text divides American history into different periods animated by different social orders: "In each social order studied, attention is directed first to the essential features of the social order itself, to the dominant ideology, to the social structure, to the clash of economic interests, to the sources of political power and the form of political institutions, to the workings of the prevailing economic, political, and social arrangements." [34]

This heavily socioeconomic orientation was not uncommon in academic work since the early 1930s. History, as well as other disciplines, experimented with a variety of approaches in analyzing the crises caused by the Great Depression. Yet, in historical study, the socioeconomic emphasis predated the depression; it descended from the work of the progressive historians of the early twentieth century—Frederick Jackson Turner, Vernon L. Parrington, and Charles A. Beard—all of whom stressed the importance of economic factors in American history. This orientation was attractive to black scholars who wished to explore the history of their current troubles and indicate the ways in which those troubles were not simply inevitable, but rather part of a historical process that might be subject to change. Horace Bond's dissertation on black education in Alabama illustrated these lessons well. [35]

Thus far in this chapter, I have focused largely on Bond's formal education, but no account of the graduate education of any scholar should be devoted completely to coursework and to professors. Much of what is learned in graduate school takes place out of the classroom, in other forums where students interact and debate intellectual issues.

However, the social aspect of Bond's own education was diminished by several factors. We recall his difficulties in relating easily to individuals outside of his own family. Race was another factor limiting his personal contacts. Black students clearly did not have the easy relationships with fellow students that whites did. While black students found friends among their black peers, their numbers were not large and the places for comfortable intellectual and personal contacts among blacks were not plentiful on and around the campus. While a few white students might befriend blacks, the contexts in which this type of interaction might take place were distinctly limited. In addition, the constant financial pressure experienced by Bond and most other black students hampered the continuity of their on- and off-campus life. Working part-time while going to school and intermittent attendance at the university, with time taken out frequently to pursue full-time work to finance further study, were not conducive to a vigorous extracurricular experience.

Despite these limiting conditions, however, Bond made links with the Chicago black community and participated in debates on such topics as the New Negro literary and political movement of the 1920s. He also attended a Communist party meeting to speak on the topic of mental tests and the Negro. At this meeting he signed his own name to a roster of attendees, instead of using a "party name," as did the rest of those in attendance. Bond's later recollection of this event was that he had merely accepted an invitation to speak and had participated as a "perfect innocent," one untutored in the realities of American politics, mainstream or radical. He also reported that, though he sympathized with Communist ideas, they would not bear fruit in the American situations with which he was familiar. Whatever political positions Bond held during his early graduate-school days, his top priority at that point in his life was not politics but to get his education and not to alienate those who might be in a position to help him in his career.[36]

These few instances of off-campus activities were the exception to the rule, however. Bond spent most of his limited spare time with his siblings who lived in Chicago. The rest of his time was spent working, going to class, or studying. It was a stark, spare existence for the young man, but one that he did not dislike.

Perhaps the most important way that the University of Chicago affected Horace Bond's life was by aiding his incorporation into the network of black academics being developed by the Julius Rosenwald Fund and the General Education Board (GEB). The Rosenwald Fund, headquartered in Chicago, had enjoyed a long-standing relationship with the university through its founder, Julius Rosenwald, who lived but a short distance from the campus. Several Chicago faculty members, including Charles Judd, served on its board of trustees. John D. Rockefeller provided initial funding to both the GEB and the University of Chicago, and both retained close ties to the Rockefeller family and its interests.[37] The relationships between Bond and these philanthropies, however, are best described in the context of his early career as a black academic in a number of black colleges.

Chapter 4

Young Scholar and Academic

While Horace Bond was completing his first two quarters of graduate study in the summer of 1924, finances forced him to seek a full-time position for the fall of that year. Given that Horace was not yet twenty years old and that his father was well connected with many black professionals, it is not surprising that James Bond took the lead in finding a suitable position for Horace. On behalf of his son, James wrote numerous letters to black high-school and college administrators in several southern states. One of James's contacts paid off, and Horace was offered a position as director of the Department of Education at the Colored Agricultural and Normal University of Oklahoma, in Langston. After Horace had accepted the position, his father advised him on how to negotiate for a better salary. The strategy was for Horace to use an offer from another institution as a bargaining chip, but to be very careful not to alienate either college's president with behavior that could be interpreted as unseemly or overly aggressive.[1]

Horace Bond would remain at Langston for the next two academic years and be on leave for a third year while he returned to Chicago to continue his graduate studies. Throughout his Langston tenure, Bond continued to receive advice and encouragement from his father. He shared his dreams and his concerns with his father, seeking advice, for example, on whether or not to study for the ministry in order to further his academic career. The elder Bond replied that a ministerial qualification might help his son obtain a post as president of a prestigious college, such as Fisk University. In other letters, James told Horace that a year's study in Europe would be good for an aspiring academic, that Horace might well become the first black faculty member at Oberlin, and that Horace would be a college president by the age of thirty.[2]

Horace's affairs were not the only topic discussed by father and son. For example, after consultation with his father, Horace arranged to have his older brother Thomas come to study at Langston. After Thomas's graduation from Langston, James and Horace also managed to get him admitted to Lincoln University after Horace wrote Thomas's letter of application.[3]

In the summer of 1926, as Horace prepared to go back to Chicago and graduate school, his father wrote approvingly of his plans. He encouraged his son to finish his master's degree and get started on the doctorate, pointing out that financial help could come this time from James, Tom, and another of Horace's brothers, Max. (During his two years in Oklahoma, Horace had sent part of his salary to his brothers.) The elder Bond reminded his youngest son of the importance of his educational career. Even while granting that the future of his brothers was important, James told Horace, "I am going to see you through because my hopes are 'set' on you."[4]

It would be a mistake, however, to attribute Horace's early academic accomplishments completely to his father. The young scholar quickly moved to ensure that he could use his time at Langston to establish himself in academe. Less than three months after his arrival in Langston, Bond published an account of the teacher-education curriculum then in place there. Writing in James McKeen Cattell's *School and Society*, Bond referred to the innovative curriculum as the Langston Plan and was careful to credit Langston's president for its support. Bond described the Langston Plan as a course of study that stressed the problems and the unique circumstances found in black schools. In tests and measurements, for example, the norms established were appropriate to black students, an approach strongly preferred over the use of the inappropriately high, general norms, which demeaned black students' achievements. Similarly, in the history of education, the problems of black education received considerable attention alongside more general concerns: the "ideals of Booker T. Washington," for instance, "[were] studied and discussed, and compared with the opposed school of Du Bois and others."[5]

Bond engaged in substantial research in mental testing while at Langston, giving an intelligence test to several black youth who were children of Langston faculty and pointing out, in an article he published in W. E. B. Du Bois's *Crisis*, the exceptionally high scores they achieved. He attributed the high scores to the youngsters' unusual environmental advantages: their parents were very well educated, and they were raised in a collegiate community. Bond continued to cultivate his relationship with Du Bois, writing to the *Crisis* editor for advice on gaining admission to the graduate school at Harvard. Bond also participated in a larger study of common schooling for blacks throughout the nation, a study that Du Bois published in a two-part article in *Crisis*. In his contribution, "The Negro Common School in Oklahoma," Bond copiously documented the stunted educational arrangements that blacks were forced to endure because of penurious white politicians' reluctance to authorize any but the most rudimentary of educations for blacks.[6]

Of course, Bond did more than publish articles in his two years at Langston. He taught several courses in education, and he was active in extension work with black teachers in several Oklahoma locales, where he learned a great deal about the political realities for blacks in the state as well as the substandard conditions under which black teachers worked. Despite his youth, Bond was not naive about Langston and its place in Oklahoma politics. Shortly afterward, he wrote an unpublished account, "Politics in Negro Education," in which he exposed Langston's president, I. W. Young, as an unqualified political hack who had been given his job because he delivered the black vote to the Democratic candidate for governor in the election of 1922. One can see that, while Bond followed his father's admonition to support his president during his years at Langston, he did not refrain later from criticizing the situation at the college and the qualifications of its president.[7]

Langston had been founded in a town where, when Oklahoma was still a territory, radical blacks had migrated in hopes of founding a separatist settlement that would eventually become a completely black territory. Langston was established as the college that would help realize that goal. Its curriculum was based on the liberal arts, in repudiation of Booker T. Washington's focus on industrial education as the appropriate curriculum for blacks. Statehood for Oklahoma blunted separatism, however, as whites moved to establish political control in Oklahoma and blacks had to deal with the emerging power structure. The result was the kind of machinations that politicized the Langston presidency. In the curriculum, whites forced Langston to adopt a plan for industrial education at the same time that blacks fought a rearguard action to preserve the academic courses they had established.[8]

Though Bond exhibited a political understanding unusual for someone so young, his youth managed to show itself in other aspects of his life at

Langston. Still finding it difficult to socialize comfortably with women, he tried to overcome his inadequacies with the fairer sex by fortifying himself with alcohol before social engagements. Bond claimed that this was his first contact with alcohol, made available to him by his landlord, who was acquainted with numerous bootleggers. Whether or not alcohol was the vehicle he used to conquer his fear of women, he did learn to dance at Langston and even fell in love with a woman ten years his senior.[9]

While he may have improved his social life at Langston, Bond clearly perceived that to enhance his professional career, he should stay there no longer than absolutely necessary. Thus, when he left Langston to return to Chicago for graduate study in the academic year of 1926–27, his status of being officially on leave did not prevent him from seeking a more advantageous position. The first job that Bond landed was as director of extension work at the Alabama State Normal School for blacks in Montgomery. This institution was not much more prestigious than Langston. Nevertheless, Bond again took advantage of his situation to improve his professional qualifications. His responsibilities included organizing and conducting classes in thirty-five centers throughout the state. Over twelve hundred teachers were enrolled in these classes, and Bond got to know many of them and other educators as well as other black Alabamians who lived and worked around the various centers. He used this wide-ranging contact with the black citizens of Alabama to develop his public-speaking abilities as well as his understanding of black farmers and workers. Following a pattern of publishing he had established at Langston, Bond translated his experience of accompanying a black convict to the electric chair into an article that was later published in the journal *Phylon*. [10]

While in Chicago and before going to Montgomery, Bond began a campaign to secure his future as an academic. He wrote to President Thomas Elsa Jones of Fisk University in an attempt to secure a teaching position for the summer of 1927. Though a position did not materialize at once, Bond continued to petition Jones for employment in Nashville, as did Bond's father. In April of 1928, while Bond was finishing up his second semester at Montgomery, Jones offered the young scholar a position. Bond was to work with Charles S. Johnson in social research, to supervise dormitory students, and to teach in the areas of history and education.[11]

Fisk had recently endured a student rebellion against the completely white administration's paternalistic regulation of their lives. Jones, a white Quaker, was chosen president in February 1926 and given a mandate to modernize the school, and he moved to consolidate support from students and alumni by appointing a black faculty member as dean of the university and bringing black scholars to the campus to help raise student morale and Fisk's standing among black institutions. One of these scholars was Charles S. Johnson, who held the title of research professor in the Department of Social Science.[12]

Bond had had previous contact with Johnson through Robert Park and the Chicago sociology department and had published in *Opportunity*, the journal that Johnson edited for the National Urban League. Johnson would author and edit numerous volumes during his years as head of social science at Fisk, giving that department a solid reputation as an academic leader in its field. Bond seized the opportunity to come to Nashville and to capitalize on his ties to Johnson, a leading black intellectual. Within a few months of Bond's arrival in Nashville, Johnson was writing to James Bond, reporting the good work his son had done on the education section of a study scheduled for presentation at a national conference.[13]

Bond's father was proud of his son's latest appointment. He cautioned him to remember that everyone in Nashville (presumably all of the Bonds' former friends and acquaintances from the family's days at the Congregational church adjacent to Fisk's campus) was watching him and that "you must therefore watch your step." James added, however, that he had "every confidence" in his son's ability to do the job. While Horace's father worried about his son's engaging in behavior that might embarrass the family, James himself sought employment at Fisk for other family members, an act that might well have caused the family a loss of face if it had become known. Shortly before Horace was to begin teaching at Fisk, his father wrote to President Jones seeking a position at the university for his wife. James Bond also urged Horace to get the president to hire Horace's brother, Max. Horace evidently did nothing in response to this letter, perhaps aware that such efforts on behalf of his mother or brother might be misinterpreted. A few months later, James Bond died, leaving his son and other family members to make their own way in the world.[14]

After his father's death, Horace continued on the course of success the two had mapped out jointly. He sought to preserve the memory of his father by editing and attempting to publish an autobiography that his father had compiled.[15] Though he did not succeed in this venture then or later, he never failed to honor his father or to acknowledge his father's significance in his own life.

While it was a coup for the young Bond to be hired at Fisk, he also helped the institution. A young black scholar who had earned his master's degree and had begun work on his doctorate at a prestigious graduate center, he had also proven himself in successful stints at two other colleges before he quite successfully filled a variety of roles in Nashville. But, despite the numerous attractions of the position at Fisk, Bond left after just one year, making sure, however, that he left on good terms with the president and that he would be welcomed back (as he was twice more during the next decade). In the fall of 1929, Bond left Fisk to embark on still another phase of his career: a fifteen-year relationship with the philanthropic organizations then transforming black education in America.

Bond's contacts with the philanthropies and their agents owed much to his father. In July of 1924, while Horace was in his second quarter of graduate school and looking for his first academic position, James wrote a letter to Julius Rosenwald, head of the Sears, Roebuck empire in Chicago. Rosenwald, who had spent considerable sums of money on constructing schoolhouses for rural blacks in the South, was beginning to finance fellowships for black graduate students. James reminded the retail magnate of their contacts in the years when the elder Bond served as the financial agent for the Lincoln Institute in Kentucky. He also told Rosenwald of the promise of his son, who "is dedicating his life to the profession of teaching and is anxious to continue his studies with the Ph.D. degree as his objective." James's efforts did not bear fruit this time; there is no record in the Bond papers of a reply from Rosenwald, and Horace worked full-time for the next two years.[16]

Undeterred, James Bond turned to the General Education Board, funded by John D. Rockefeller, for financial aid for Horace. He wrote to Leo Favrot of the GEB and urged Horace to write also to Favrot and to another GEB official. Favrot replied that, while Horace was certainly "a very brilliant young man," he lacked experience, a deficiency he could remedy by working for three or four more years before finishing his doctorate.[17]

In 1928, Bond's prospects of obtaining support from the Rosenwald interests improved dramatically. In that year Julius Rosenwald systematized and institutionalized his philanthropic efforts. Following the model of the Rockefeller Foundation, on whose board he had served, he created the Julius Rosenwald Fund. Edwin Embree was hired away from the

Rockefeller interests to become the first president of the fund. James Bond apprised Horace of these events and urged him to write immediately to Embree, whom James had met at Berea College when James was a student and Embree was a young lad living with his parents at Berea, the college that his grandfather, John Fee, had founded. Through the years, James had maintained contact with Embree, and now, with Embree serving as president of the Rosenwald Fund, he thought that this relationship could pay off for his son. James told his son to "cultivate" both Embree and S. L. Smith, the field agent for the fund.[18]

Horace evidently followed his father's advice. In the fall of 1929, he joined the Rosenwald Fund full-time, working as a research assistant on a project that examined schools for blacks in sixteen counties in three southern states—Alabama, North Carolina, and Louisiana. Bond traveled through all three states, visiting over seven hundred schools and testing almost ten thousand children during the two-year study. He also made valuable contacts with white state officials responsible for black schools as well as with board members, administrators, and teachers in the numerous city and county systems he visited. In Alabama, he became reacquainted with persons met in his extension work at the State Normal School in Montgomery and during a summer of teaching at Tuskegee Institute in 1929. In fact, he taught again at Tuskegee in the summer of 1930.[19]

Bond's supervisor in the Rosenwald work was Clark Foreman, who used the results of the survey in his doctoral dissertation at Columbia University. Foreman came from a prominent Atlanta family; his uncle was Clark Howell, who edited the *Atlanta Constitution* in the early twentieth century. According to Bond, Foreman became a "radical" white on the issue of race after a lynching he witnessed in Athens, Georgia, when he was a youth. Foreman would stay with the Rosenwald Fund until shortly after the completion of his study, when he left to take a job in the Department of the Interior under the Roosevelt administration. He would later work for other government agencies and then for civil liberties groups. Relations between the young black and the young white were amicable and close. Bond cultivated Foreman's friendship, carefully considering the white man's schedule before arranging mutual visits to schools.[20]

Bond also enlisted Foreman's help in his plan to study at the London School of Economics (LSE). He asked Foreman, who had spent two years at the LSE in the mid-1920s, to help him obtain a fellowship. Studying in England would involve some maneuvering for Bond, since President Jones of Fisk, where Bond still maintained an affiliation while working for Rosen-wald, wanted his young staff member to proceed with his doctoral studies at Chicago rather than detour from his path for a year of foreign study. Bond dallied with the London plan for almost a year before ultimately deciding to go back to Chicago and finish his doctoral coursework.[21]

Foreman argued that environmental factors held down the achievement of black students in the South. To prove the point, Stanford Achievement Tests in reading and mathematics were administered to black students in rural and urban counties that supported their schools either relatively gen-erously or penuriously. Generous support and other environmental advan-tages were seen as explanations for success in student achievement. This line of argument was congenial to Bond, who had used it since his earli-est days in graduate school. Thus he threw himself energetically into the work with Foreman, hoping to cement his standing with his supervisor and the Rosenwald Fund and convinced that the work he was doing was both intellectually valuable and of benefit to his race.[22]

Bond used his experiences in researching Alabama schools as the basis for two articles, one published in the Chicago-based *American Journal of Sociology* and the other in *Harper's*. In the first, he described two mixed-race communities in counties in the Mobile, Alabama, area. Though both communities were biracial, their other characteristics were substantially different. The residents of one group lived in well-tended homes and sent their children to a school where achievement was high. Residents of the other lived in shacks, gave but the slightest attention to education, and had schoolchildren who achieved at extremely low levels. After describ-ing these groups, Bond concluded that the extreme differences between them certainly contradicted any hereditarian explanations. Even if white blood was hypothesized to account for the success of the first group, which would have been the hereditarian explanation, it would also have to account for the failure of the second. Bond's own explanation for the difference was tentative; he suggested that the strong religious orientation (Roman Catholic) of the prosperous group contrasted severely with the irreligious-ness of the other. He concluded, "Whatever the explanation, certainly one needs some other explanation than that of hereditary racial superiority or inferiority to account for the vast social distance that separates these two racial islands."[23]

In the *Harper's* article, Bond indulged his penchant for popular jour-nalism. (He had written several journalistic pieces in the late 1920s and early 1930s and for a time even considered journalism as a career.) He established his credentials and those of other southern blacks as "real" southerners: they had lived in the South for generations and loved it every bit as much as any white man did. He interpreted black obsequiousness to southern whites, behavior demanded by these whites, as instinctive exercising of the gentlemanliness that characterized southern black behavior in the nineteenth and twentieth centuries. The manners of whites, however, had deteriorated. Unlike the plantation owners and other gentlemen of the Old South, modern white southerners were crude, loud, and offensive. Their politicians, the Vardamans and Bilboes, also reflected this crudeness. What whites needed was a good dose of the manners of their ancestors. Perhaps the money taken away from blacks to educate whites would provide some benefit to blacks if it were to reinfuse white southerners with some of the manners that they had lost.[24]

One cannot be sure that Bond believed everything he said in this article. His frequent use of irony and subtle sarcasm casts doubt on his allegiance to the piece's substantive points. His documentation of the severe diminution of financial support for black schools was probably what he really wanted to get across to his readers. If a call for the rebirth of white manners was the vehicle he had to use to call attention to this unequal educational expenditure, the end may have justified the means. However that may have been, the publication of this article in a national literary and current affairs periodical was surely a feather in the young man's cap.

While working for the Rosenwald Fund, Bond maintained his relationship with President Jones of Fisk and his affiliation with that institution, and he relied on Jones's assurances of a place for him at Fisk when he took the president's advice and turned down a college presidency in Kentucky. Jones was especially solicitous of Fisk's young black faculty member. He allowed Bond to delay his return to Fisk to work another year on the Rosenwald project and to delay still another year in order to finish his doctoral coursework at Chicago, with a scholarship from the Rosenwald Fund. Of course, Jones had numerous reasons to be considerate. Bond was obviously an up-and-coming black scholar who could enhance Fisk's academic reputation. Further, Jones was dependent on the Rosenwald Fund and other philanthropies for funds for Fisk's development; he certainly would not wish to alienate the philanthropies by thwarting the plans of one of their prime black beneficiaries.[25]

As Horace Bond was astutely using the opportunities provided by the

Rosenwald Fund and Fisk University to progress in his professional life, he also was making major changes in his personal life. While at Fisk, the young man met the woman who would become his wife. Julia Agnes Washington was the daughter of a prominent family in Nashville's black society. Her father had been a mathematics teacher and then principal of Pearl High School, the public high school for blacks that was adjacent to the Fisk campus. Her mother had graduated from Fisk's normal school, and the Washington family attended the Congregational church that Horace Bond's father had pastored. In fact, Julia's parents were married by James Bond.[26]

Julia Washington's maternal grandfather, Joe Browne, had become quite wealthy through his flourishing floral business, which he had taken over from a German for whom he had worked. After Browne's death, his wife, Callie, became something of a social mavin for Nashville's black elite. At her home, she held frequent parties and receptions where the social set could meet newcomers, particularly those who joined the Fisk faculty. Mrs. Browne's granddaughter, Julia, was a history major at Fisk until her teacher took a leave of absence, whereupon Julia changed her major to English literature rather than be taught by a young substitute about whom she knew nothing. That young substitute would eventually ask her to marry him, and she would accept. In December 1929, Julia Washington and Horace Bond were married in Chicago, where the bride was in graduate school and where the Rosenwald Fund, for whom the groom was working, was headquartered. They would have to have a second wedding in Nashville, a year later, so that Julia's grandmother could see her granddaughter married in the proper fashion.[27]

Julia Bond was tied closely to her Nashville roots and to Fisk University. She was influenced by the Fisk faculty "from childhood," and it seemed only natural for her to earn her bachelor's degree there. She went on to study English literature as a graduate student at the University of Chicago and to teach for a brief period at the Kentucky State College in Frankfort, Kentucky. Eventually, she received a master's degree in library services from Atlanta University in the 1960s and worked in the library at Atlanta University. Her interests were in the areas of history and sociology, particularly the latter, and she once remarked that she had been profoundly influenced by Charles S. Johnson and E. Franklin Frazier, both of whom taught sociology at Fisk when she was a student there. She was an avid believer in the AMA philosophy of education for all men and women, regardless of color, the philosophy on which Fisk was founded and by which it was nurtured.[28]

During the first two years of their marriage, Horace and Julia were frequently apart. While his wife was in graduate school in Chicago, Bond was traversing the back roads of the South studying black-school achievement for Clark Foreman. Both Bonds were unusually reserved; surviving correspondence yields few of their letters to one another, and these few letters usually contain scant information on personal matters. None of this is to say, however, that they were unloving or unhappy in their relationship. Coming from families that paid attention to the proprieties of the world in which they lived, both Horace and Julia seemed unusually mature in their attitudes about marriage and in their sense of planning for the future as well as living in the present. At the beginning of their marriage as well as later, they were able to take periods of separation in stride, without weakening the cement that would bind them together for the next four decades.

Horace Bond's marriage stood him in good stead as he developed his academic career. Because Julia Washington Bond had been raised in a city with a black community proud of its private black college, she knew the ins and outs of social life in a collegiate setting. Her family was prestigious and reasonably well-to-do, and she was a cultivated young woman who would become a devoted wife and mother to her three children. It is not surprising, then, when, a few years after the Bonds' marriage, an old friend asked about his personal life, Horace responded that he was quite pleased to have married Julia Washington. That pleasure was rooted in both the personal regard he and his wife had for each other and the realization that he was well prepared through marriage to continue an academic career.[29]

Given that Horace Bond received a steady income while working for the Rosenwald Fund and also maintained his affiliation with Fisk, a relationship that included the opportunity to teach part-time, it seems fair to say that the Bonds did not feel the full impact of the economic crisis devastating Americans, both black and white, in the early 1930s. At the behest of Clark Foreman, who was delighted to have his young associate continue working on the school survey for a second year, Bond received a 10-percent raise in pay in the fall of 1930. For the 1931–32 academic year, Bond received a Rosenwald fellowship to return to Chicago to work full-time on his degree; his wife also continued her studies in that year. Bond's request for slightly over two thousand dollars was cut by over a fourth by the fund, to the level of support other fellows were receiving.

Upon completion of this year of study, Bond returned to Fisk to a full-time faculty position as an associate professor. During this and subsequent stays in Nashville, the Bonds lived rent-free in an apartment built for them as an addition to Julia's grandmother's home.[30]

Even with their good fortune, however, Horace and Julia Bond were not completely immune from the consequences of the depression. Because of the decreases in philanthropic foundations' income and disbursements, and the problems students had in paying their expenses, Fisk University markedly declined in the first four years of the depression. In 1932, faculty were forced to return a portion of their salary to help the college pay its bills. Fisk faculty also feared worse effects from the depression, including a loss of position. In addition, Horace's travels through the South made him keenly aware of the hardships that both blacks and whites were facing in the region, including the budget cuts that were being inflicted on black schools in the South and elsewhere. Still, a position in an educational institution, as long as it was not lost, helped its occupant to weather the economic storm more successfully than most Americans, black or white. Indeed, Bond's reported salary from Fisk—slightly more than three thousand dollars for the 1933 calendar year—indicates that he was surviving the depression reasonably well.[31]

As Bond was making his way in the world—adjusting to a new marriage, finishing his Ph.D. coursework, and settling into a comfortable place on the Fisk faculty—he was also engaged in defining his intellectual stance. His point of view did not at some point emerge full-fledged; rather, it developed in fits and starts, as Bond explored first one position in the black ideological spectrum and then another. For most black intellectuals of the 1920s and 1930s, the poles of the spectrum were still the positions explicated by Booker T. Washington and W. E. B. Du Bois in the earlier part of the twentieth century.

Bond's views of both Washington and Du Bois were complex and nuanced. For one thing, the young academic understood the realities his predecessors had faced. Bond did not resort to simplistic affirmation of either leader's views; he was not an uncritical devotee of either the Tuskegeean's industrial education or Du Bois's "talented tenth." His own place as a fledgling member of the liberally educated black elite might have inclined him toward Du Bois; but his father's southern background and personal dispute with Du Bois, as well as his own experience in the homes of rural black southerners, left him somewhat suspicious of the black spokesman from Massachusetts and more understanding of the respect that rural black southerners had for the man from Tuskegee.

Bond developed his own position on the Washington–Du Bois controversy in a series of scholarly and popular articles published in the 1920s and 1930s. In 1925, while still in Oklahoma, Bond published in the *South Atlantic Quarterly*, a leading periodical of social and literary criticism, an article on black leaders in the years since Washington's death in 1915. Bond began with a look at the ideas of Washington and Du Bois in the early twentieth century, and here he paid homage to the Tuskegeean's popularity in the homes of ordinary blacks, particularly southern blacks, and noted the lack of rank-and-file support for Du Bois's ideas. After Washington's death, however, the situation had changed in several particulars. Du Bois, through his editorship of the *Crisis* and involvement in the NAACP, had managed to attract a group of admirers in the literary, journalistic, and political arenas. Bond mentioned James Weldon Johnson as typical of the new breed of NAACP leader as well as a mainstay of the black literary movement of the 1920s. Other writers who were cited as evidence of the influence of Du Bois's ideas included Countee Cullen and Jean Toomer. The black weekly journals that were springing up in many cities reflected Du Bois's assertiveness and activism far more than the cautiousness of Washington and the Tuskegee Institute. Politically, the concentrations of blacks in several northern cities, such as New York and Chicago, meant that, for the first time in decades, blacks could wield influence over their own affairs by following a bipartisan line which looked to both political parties for a favorable response. This was a significant improvement over blacks' half century of blind allegiance to the Republican party, an allegiance, now taken for granted, that had been fostered by Washington and that had not stopped the economic and political debilitation that had plagued blacks in the South at least since the 1890s. Bond went on to praise Du Bois's pan-Africanist philosophy as a solid attempt to get blacks to work together throughout the world. He contrasted the hard work and serious commitment of Du Bois's pan-Africanism with the opportunism and transience of Marcus Garvey's African romance.[32]

Turning to the situation in the South, Bond noted that none of Booker T. Washington's successors at Tuskegee Institute could claim accomplishments approaching those of the founder. Bond characterized Robert Moton, principal of Tuskegee since Washington's death, as distinctly in-

ferior to his predecessor. Others associated with Tuskegee had equally
undistinguished records of accomplishment, with the exception of George
Washington Carver, the indefatigable agricultural chemist. About the
South's interracial movement, which was made up of organizations
through which blacks could communicate with whites who were "moder-
ate," if not liberal, on racial issues, Bond was favorable. Du Bois had criticized this movement as being a continuation of obsequiousness of southern
blacks toward whites, an attitude he claimed was encouraged by Washington. The prominence of Bond's father in this movement was a source of
suspicion between Du Bois and the Bond family, and Bond's treatment of
the interracial movement tried to acknowledge and deflect simultaneously
Du Bois's criticism. He pointed out that, while the interracial movement
may have reflected a continuation of black passivity in social and political
affairs, it represented an honest attempt at amelioration in those arenas as
well as an affirmation of Du Bois's educational philosophy and a repudiation of southern blacks' blind faith in Washington's industrial education.[33]

   In his concluding paragraphs, Bond stated, "Du Bois . . . is the most vital
and . . . compelling figure in the Negro world of today," but then he went
on to mitigate that praise. For Bond, if blacks had not migrated from the
South to the North, the message of Du Bois would have fallen on deaf ears.
It was the difference in situations between southern and northern blacks,
as much as anything, that had led to the climate in which Du Bois's ideas
could flourish. Moreover, Du Bois's success owed something to the economic philosophy espoused by Washington, for only through the creation
of a strong economic base for blacks could the intellectual and political
aspirations of Du Bois and his followers be realized. As for the South, it
was the interracial movement, which built on Washington's insight that
cooperation between the races was necessary if progress were to be made,
that was the best hope for the region's blacks—if hope or progress were to
be had.[34]

   Although late in his life Bond came close to repudiating this article,
calling it the work of "an opinionated young fool," it does not fit that description. Rather, it is a careful weighing of the situation and an attempt
to contextualize the problems and issues. Perhaps Bond was referring to
his criticism of Moton—the least subtle, and possibly the most insightful,
judgment in the article—as foolish opinion. Leaving that aside, however,
the article represents the work of a careful young man trying to sort out
the intellectual and political currents in which he would be swimming

for the rest of his life. His affirmation of Du Bois is clear, though less than complete, and not in any sense adulation. His defense of his father and other workers for the interracial cause is also clear, poignant, and prophetic of the situation in which he would find himself and the values that would guide his work for at least the next two decades of his career.

Intellectually, Bond followed Du Bois's educational, political, and social philosophy, but his followership was tempered by the realities of dealing with southerners, black and white, as well as by a healthy historical understanding of the situations in which he found himself. Bond's allegiance to Du Bois can be attributed initially to his early and continuous reading of Du Bois's *Crisis*, which also published several of Bond's articles, and Bond's participation in a research project headed by Du Bois.[35]

Bond's ties with Du Bois loosened considerably, however, in the early 1930s. In 1931, he sent Du Bois an article to be considered for publication in the *Crisis*. Prepared with the students in one of his Fisk classes, the article documented the relative stature of leading black colleges by counting how many of those listed in *Who's Who in Colored America* graduated from each college. Bond's interest in the information may have been related to the fact that Lincoln University, his alma mater, was the leading institution in terms of its production of *Who's Who* listees. Whatever his personal motivation, he undoubtedly thought that the topic and treatment would appeal to Du Bois's interest in the origins and output of the "talented tenth" of black people.[36]

Du Bois did not publish the article, however. Instead, he printed, with only a brief comment, a small chart from the larger work, and did so without notifying Bond of his plans. When Bond saw only the chart in the pages of the *Crisis*, he sent to Du Bois a letter of protest, claiming that he had been treated "very shabbily" by the decision to reduce his article "to a skeletonized, almost meaningless table." Du Bois apologized, stating that he had wanted to publish the article in full but that it had to be cut considerably to fit into that issue of the *Crisis*. He added that he had failed to notify Bond of the abstract's publication because he was editing the magazine from a distance (Du Bois was then on the faculty at Atlanta University, and the *Crisis* was published in New York) and was also currently writing a book.[37]

In the midst of this contretemps, Bond wrote a scathingly critical essay on Du Bois as leader of the black race. Bond described the "insolence" and "impudence" that had characterized Du Bois's writings in the student newspaper in his days at Fisk and that still permeated his writing. After acknowledging the contributions Du Bois made in his doctoral dissertation and other early scholarly writings, Bond returned to the theme of impudence as he assessed Du Bois's tenure as editor of the *Crisis*, noting that "the old bitterness of phrase, the easy fluency of diatribe . . . of his younger days were now reasserted with an intensity almost savage." While granting that Du Bois and other blacks had legitimate cause to be bitter, Bond questioned whether Du Bois really sought the welfare of all black people; indeed, Du Bois's protests against race snobbery might be "less vehement . . . if America practiced some sort of system of selective segregation, by which the members of the black intelligentsia received a special consideration and were freed from the proscription that now includes the Negro generally."[38]

Bond went on to contrast Du Bois's elitism with Booker T. Washington's devotion to the ordinary members of the black race and Du Bois's recklessness and rashness with Washington's caution and accommodation, which were "not . . . [the result] of cowardice but rather . . . prompted by the demands of strategy." Using military metaphors to evaluate the positions of the two leaders, Bond defended Washington and attacked Du Bois: "Shall we thrust with the biting point of a keen rapier, hilt to hilt, to the bloody death, or shall we study cannily the disposition of the opposing forces, understand the psychology of the opponent, take advantage of his prejudices, seize upon them for our own devices?" He then attacked Du Bois's criticism of the patronage granted to black politicians and clergymen as typical of what whites would say about the same phenomenon. Finally, he exposed an instance of obvious intellectual inconsistency, contrasting Du Bois's active support of World War I with his later condemnation of that war for the hardships it brought upon blacks.[39]

Certainly some of Bond's criticism of Du Bois may have been due to his resentment of the way his article was treated, yet this should not be taken as a full explanation of Bond's position. Rather, his paper reflected views Bond held deeply and on the basis of which he would often act. Horace Bond was a southern black, a man raised and educated in the South, and his experience made him suspicious of activists from the North who did not understand southern blacks' burdens and who seemed as intent on feathering the nest of the black elite as on improving the lives of ordinary folk. The enormous gulf between northern and southern students that Bond remembered from his days at Lincoln University also made him wary of northerners' solutions to southerners' problems. Moreover, Du Bois's criticism of workers in the interracial movement, including Bond's own father, also must have rankled.[40] Whatever the complete explanation, it seems clear that Bond's attitude toward Du Bois was ambivalent, and his paper reflected his reservations. He respected the accomplishments of this leading black intellectual, but he also felt that Du Bois's elitism made him insensitive to the tribulations of ordinary blacks, particularly those who struggled daily with the manifestations of deep-seated racism in the South.[41]

In any case, Bond's assessment of Du Bois remained private, for he did not publish his paper. Charles S. Johnson, Bond's mentor at Fisk, read the paper, and, on Johnson's advice, Bond decided against its publication.[42] As mentioned earlier, Johnson became the leading black social scientist in the South in the 1930s; his work was equaled in later decades only by E. Franklin Frazier, who taught under Johnson at Fisk before moving to Howard and establishing his own reputation. Johnson conducted several studies of the conditions of rural black southerners and earned the praise of white southern sociologists, such as Howard Odum of the University of North Carolina. Johnson was also part of the ruling council of the Rosenwald Fund, helping to decide which black academics the fund would support. In some respects, Johnson can be seen as Booker T. Washington's successor as the black leader in the South with whom whites were most comfortable. His advice to his protégé was to not publish an article that could inflame relations between Johnson and Du Bois, and Bond complied. Bond's compliance was partly explained by his respect for Johnson, but it also seems that Bond shared his mentor's desire to avoid, rather than to create, controversy.[43]

None of this is to say that Bond was an accommodationist and a willing accomplice in the continued enslavement of his people. Rather, he was a young academic working his way up "in the system," which consisted of the black colleges in the South. As an insider, he knew the rules, which often included ingratiating oneself with certain whites by telling them what they wanted to hear. For example, Bond wrote to his Rosenwald supervisor, Clark Foreman, that the blacks in rural Louisiana were "dumb as cattle, shiftless, improvident," and added that Mr. Rosenwald might make a profit on a scheme for "farm-sharing" among these people. Bond also knew how to cultivate his Fisk president, Thomas Elsa Jones. In late 1932, Bond visited the Atlanta University campus to see how the graduate programs recently started there might serve as a model for Fisk's future efforts. On the issue of whether white or black staff were doing, or could do, a better job teaching black students, Bond told Jones what a white administrator in a black college would want to hear, not, necessarily, what black faculty believed: that black students often preferred whites to blacks as administrators or teachers in their colleges, for reasons that were quite defensible and understandable.[44]

As one who was on his way up in the world of southern black colleges, Bond could be highly critical of those who attacked this system, even to the point of ignoring its weaknesses. While discretion was involved in his decision not to publish the critique of W. E. B. Du Bois, discretion yielded to defense of self and system in Bond's review of a book openly critical of black colleges, Carter G. Woodson's *Miseducation of the Negro*, published in 1933. Woodson, an independent black historian, was then on the outside of the black intellectual establishment; he was fighting philanthropic foundations that sought to have him affiliate with a black college before they would fund his research, and he was also battling most black intellectuals over control of a proposed encyclopedia of black history.[45] Recipient of a Ph.D. in history from Harvard and founder of the Association for the Study of Negro Life and History, Woodson was a prolific researcher and writer in black history, particularly in the 1910s and 1920s. He was also a cantankerous individual who, by the 1930s, was at odds with other black scholars and most black colleges, particularly the private colleges. Thus, his blanket attacks on these colleges, on black professionals in medicine, law, and the ministry, and on blacks with doctorates, whom he regarded as inferior teachers, were salvos in the war he was then waging with his scholarly enemies.[46]

Bond's review focused mainly on the excesses of Woodson's attacks and the weaknesses in his argument. Bond exposed such contradictions as Woodson's criticizing black religion as a pale imitation of white religion and then indicting black religion for focusing exclusively on hellfire and damnation while white religion was progressing to humanitarianism. Bond also noted other inconsistencies, such as Woodson's damning northern teachers of the freedmen and then criticizing anyone who would utter a derogatory word about the teachers. Bond concluded by claiming that the considerable accomplishments of Carter G. Woodson, the noted black scholar, contradicted the book's very premise.[47]

Bond was for the most part correct, yet it is also true that he ignored the book's core argument and focused exclusively on the points where Woodson was vulnerable. Woodson's theme was that the curriculum in black colleges, particularly in black liberal arts colleges, neglected the black experience as a focus of study; instead, they aped the essentials of the white liberal arts curriculum. The consequences were disastrous; by concentrating on Shakespeare and other European writers, for example, black students were taught to ignore the contributions of black writers, many of whom had flourished since the New Negro movement of the 1920s. According to Woodson, unless black colleges' curricula paid attention to black history, black literature, black music, and other black contributions, the institutions would continue to be estranged from the experience of black citizens. This could do nothing but widen the gap between the black elite and the rest of the black world.

Bond's failure even to mention Woodson's theme is strange, particularly when one considers Bond's orientation to black issues. We have already seen his publicity of the black emphasis in the Langston teacher-education curriculum. Later, as a teacher and administrator in black colleges, he would emphasize black studies as appropriate in liberal arts colleges and studying and improving black rural life in land-grant colleges, actions that indicate that he was not unsympathetic to Woodson's main point. His negative review thus can be seen as reflecting his own ties to the black intellectual establishment. It may also have reflected his resentment at Woodson's criticisms of the education he had received and the intellectual values he (as well as his minister father) embraced. Clearly, the publication of his negative review of a book by an author who was then at odds with almost everyone in the black intellectual world would not harm Bond's career, as an attack on Du Bois might have done.

Horace Bond was becoming increasingly well known among the black intelligentsia. In his second stint at Fisk, he taught social sciences, this time as an associate professor. After a year of teaching, he worked for two months in public relations and promotional activities for Fisk. He thus became increasingly visible to Fiskites off-campus as well as on-campus. Next, under Charles Johnson's oversight and the Tennessee Valley Authority's sponsorship, he supervised a survey and statistical analysis of the socioeconomic and educational conditions of blacks in 115 counties in Virginia, North Carolina, Georgia, Alabama, Mississippi, Tennessee, and Kentucky.[48] Bond was becoming increasingly familiar with conditions for blacks in several southern states and increasingly visible to the leadership, black and white, in the region.

Bond's affiliation with the Rosenwald Fund also enhanced his prominence and influence. He was able, for example, to recommend others for positions with the fund, such as Roy Davenport, a Fisk graduate, who worked with Bond and Foreman as analyst of their survey data. Bond later helped Davenport to find a job teaching at Langston, where Bond had obtained his first faculty position. After a few months on the job, Davenport wrote Bond that the Langston president was fearful of a Rosenwald Fund–hatched plot to take some on-campus dissent, blow it up into a major issue, oust the chief executive, and replace him with Horace Bond. There is no evidence that this scenario had any basis in reality, but the invocation of Bond and the Rosenwald Fund as villains in the story testifies to Bond's visibility as a favored son of the fund and the power of an individual well connected with the fund.[49]

Bond's prominence was, indeed, increasing. In 1932, he signed a contract with Prentice Hall Press for a book on black education, and his book, *The Education of the Negro in the American Social Order*, was published in 1934. Also, Bond was often asked to consider other job possibilities, such as positions at a public college in Georgia or at Lincoln University. However, the prestige of Fisk and the Rosenwald connection made him reluctant to move.[50]

This picture of Bond as a black academic on the way up should not be taken as a complete portrait of him and his ideas during this period. There was a more activist, a more radical side of Bond that influenced his activities at times in these years. The two books he published in the 1930s both contained trenchant analyses of the educational inequities that whites foisted on southern blacks.[51] It seems fair to say that, throughout Bond's career, scholarship was the arena in which he would most often exhibit his more radical leanings on race relations as well as on other issues.

It was not just in scholarship, however, that Bond would evince his more activist commitments. In an episode at Fisk in the early 1930s, he showed his radical side to Fisk colleagues who disappointed him with their inability to stand up to injustice. Ishmael Flory, a Fisk student, proposed a strike and picketing in downtown Nashville to protest the lynching of a black who was abducted from his home, just a block from the Fisk campus, by a white mob. When the Fisk administration forbade Flory's response to this atrocity, the students countered by picketing the campus itself. Bond served on a faculty discipline committee (elected to represent faculty radicals, he claimed), which would decide Flory's fate. According to Bond's recollection of the event, he cast the lone vote against Flory's expulsion, but he was overruled by five votes, including that of his fellow faculty radical, E. Franklin Frazier. When Bond asked Frazier why he voted for such a harsh penalty for the student, Frazier replied that Bond had defended the student because he, Bond, had never been fired from a job. Frazier was awaiting his appointment to the Howard University faculty and did not wish to risk an unfavorable recommendation from the Fisk administration.[52] Though we have only Bond's recollection of this event, it does not seem to be an act out of character with his values and orientation.

Indeed, in 1934, Bond wrote a letter to the editor of a black newspaper in Cincinnati in response to an article on the compromises forced on young blacks who wished to make their way in the world. After discussing the virtues of butting one's head against a wall to protest racial injustice or befriending those who built the wall, Bond concluded that neither of these was a satisfactory response. He added a perceptive account of his own ambivalent actions and thoughts: "I am in one of those frightful muddles characteristic of my generation. I can never quite decide just how far to carry protest, or accomodation [*sic*]. I am opinionated enough to believe that by a determined effort, by assiduous practice of the art of fooling the white folks, I can become a great Race Man or a big Niggra as they would have it. However, I cannot bring myself to smile the little smiles and say the little things that pave the way for grandeur." He added that, on the other hand, he could not abandon his academic career for the militance of a radical religious prophet, such as Elijah, or a committed political activist, such as Lenin.[53]

While much of this chapter seems to recount Bond's artistry at conciliating or fooling the white folks, it also seems fair to say that he knew what he was doing and that he acted at least partially in the hope that he could achieve a position where he could act for the genuine benefit of his people. He did not intend to "desert his people," the sin that Allison Davis had urged black scholars to avoid. And it should also be remembered that many of the whites with whom Bond was dealing were committed, in their own minds and in his mind, to the betterment of the black race. Yet he seldom could be completely sure of the depth of any white man's commitment to blacks, and he had to maintain a wariness in his relations with his white friends, lest he be unexpectedly and bitterly disappointed by them.

Chapter 5

Dillard University and the Rosenwald Fund

In their tone and in their deference to the white benefactors of the black race, Horace Bond's interactions with the Rosenwald interests through-out the 1930s and early 1940s echoed those of his father. When Julius Rosenwald died in 1932, for example, Horace wrote for the Associated Negro Press news service a panegyrical obituary in which he linked Rosen-wald with the Great Emancipator of the black race, Abraham Lincoln. Bond also mentioned that Rosenwald was a Jew and lauded the affinity between the two long-suffering races of Negroes and Jews. Finally, he in-voked Booker T. Washington as the one who had first induced Rosenwald to contribute to black schooling in the South, stating, "Washington and Rosenwald are not less emancipators than Abraham Lincoln. Both saw the truth of the age-old way by which races must go forward." [1]

Bond also carefully cultivated his relationship with Edwin Embree. He frequently corresponded with Embree while studying at Chicago during the 1931–32 academic year, and they continued their correspondence after-ward. In August 1931, he wrote to congratulate Embree on the publication of an article about Embree's grandfather, John Fee, and Berea College. A year later, back at Fisk, Bond kept Embree apprised of the status of his own historical research and proposed coauthorship with Embree of an article he was preparing on Booker T. Washington. He invited Embree to visit "our humble home" whenever the Rosenwald official came to Nashville. On the occasion of such a visit, Bond promised to show Embree his library, which, in its number of volumes on the Negro, he was building up to the point where it might approach the noted private collections of others. [2]

Edwin Embree was not the civil rights radical that his grandfather had been. A Yale graduate who, after a few years working as a fund-raiser for Yale, spent most of his adult life working as an administrator in philanthropic foundations, Embree is best described as an archetypal early-twentieth-century southern liberal, a perhaps naive optimist about the present and future conditions of the darker race.[3] Embree's agenda was to benefit individual black scholars and institutions, mainly in the South, as a way to pave the road for the forthcoming black advance. He and the Rosenwald Fund supported black southern universities as places where black leaders could "learn the civilization" that would help their own and their people's progress. If Embree had harbored any more radical ideas than these doctrines of racial uplift, he would have had considerable difficulty getting them past the white southerners who made up a significant part of the board of the Rosenwald Fund.[4] This is not to say that Embree or the Julius Rosenwald Fund was not genuinely interested in helping southern blacks. It is to say, however, that the philanthropy's notion of black interests was not the same as that of their black clients. Blacks who sought help from Embree and the Rosenwald Fund, including Horace Bond, were surely aware of this gap.

Early in 1934, while Bond was teaching at Fisk, Embree asked him to come to the Rosenwald Fund's headquarters in Chicago for the summer to do some editorial work. Bond quickly agreed. Before leaving for Chicago, however, he received an offer to become academic dean at Dillard University in New Orleans, a new university that had been created with the support of the Rosenwald Fund and the General Education Board. Dillard's part-time white president, Will Alexander, who was also affiliated with the Rosenwald Fund, extended the offer to Bond.[5]

This was not the first time Bond had been approached to do administrative work. In 1931, he told Edwin Embree that Leo Favrot of the GEB had asked him if he would be interested in an administrative job at one of the universities the GEB was then developing. Bond told Embree that he had been "non-committal" to Favrot and solicited Embree's opinion on the matter. Bond added that his major priority was to continue his dissertation research in educational history, whatever position he finally accepted.[6]

Bond's own attitude toward administration was cautious. Though his father's fond dream was for Horace to become a college president by age thirty, Horace was not overly enthusiastic about the prospect of administrative work. Now, at the age of twenty-nine, he was being asked to become a dean. Julia had married him with the admonition that she did

not want to become the wife of a college president. Her feelings about a
deanship were not completely positive, particularly since the post was in
far-off New Orleans, a long distance from home and family in Nashville.[7]

When Embree and Alexander first discussed prospects for the new Dillard faculty, in 1932, Bond's name was mentioned for a position in history.
Two years later, with the university set to open in another year, Alexander offered Bond the dean's job. Dillard's president stressed the "creative
opportunity" that a new institution provided for an academician. Bond's
letter of acceptance to Alexander referred to his appointment to "the faculty" at Dillard, perhaps an indication that he thought that an academic
dean was still first and foremost a faculty member. While working for the
Rosenwald Fund in Chicago during the summer of 1934, Bond studied the
curriculum for undergraduates at the University of Chicago to discover
whether it would be suitable for Dillard's students.[8]

In fact, Dean Bond did use the undergraduate curriculum at Chicago as
a model for the Dillard course of studies. In 1929, under Robert Maynard
Hutchins, Chicago had reorganized its undergraduate program to break
the hold of specialization that the graduate departments had exercised over
undergraduate studies. Hutchins detached the college from the graduate
faculties and redesigned the undergraduate curriculum. The first two years
were now called the junior college and consisted almost completely of required work in the humanities, social sciences, and sciences. Completion
of the junior college, however, was to be based not on passing courses but
on passing a series of examinations in various subject areas. After passing the exams, a student would then go on to the senior college, pursue a
major, and prepare for graduate or professional study.[9]

Following the Chicago model, which was also being used at Fisk University, Bond divided the Dillard undergraduate curriculum into a junior
(first two years) and senior (second two years) division. He maintained
the examinations that Hutchins had instituted at Chicago, but, unlike his
model, Bond made the passing of courses a prerequisite for taking the
tests. The reasons for requiring the passing of courses at Dillard were several: students at a new institution were interested in the transferability of
their course credits, a circumstance that did not obtain at the established
and prestigious University of Chicago; a new school such as Dillard had
to adopt a course format in order to give accreditation agencies a basis
on which to approve its program; and the experiment in deemphasizing
courses at Chicago had meant a decline in students' tuition payments,

a situation that could not be tolerated at the fledgling Louisiana school, which needed every dollar it could earn.[10] However, Bond did more than borrow the Chicago curriculum for Dillard. He added an emphasis on the special contributions of blacks to Dillard's courses, an obvious, though not necessarily common, feature of studies in black colleges. He also stressed the social sciences, since these areas of study both provided the means for analyzing the problems blacks faced and pointed the way to their possible amelioration.[11]

Bond's pleasure in designing a curriculum was echoed in some other activities he pursued as an academic administrator. He had a hand in recommending candidates for faculty appointments to Alexander, a task he embraced with enthusiasm. No doubt with Bond's approval, the early Dillard faculty included such noted young black scholars as Allison Davis in anthropology, J. G. St. Clair Drake in sociology, and Laurence Reddick in history. All of these men became longtime colleagues. The dean also made it his business to stand for high academic standards at Dillard, a position he seemed to advocate with special conviction. Further, he had an opportunity to solicit help in building Dillard's library, a task he first undertook to discharge by requesting aid from Louisiana's governor, Huey Long. Bond's priorities of high academic standards and enriching the library were not always shared by the president; however, the dean did not seem to mind being occasionally the only administrative voice standing for intellectual excellence and enrichment on his campus.[12]

Other duties connected with the deanship, however, intensified Bond's ambivalence about administrative work. Since Alexander was a part-time president who was almost always away from the campus, Bond was forced to take on additional administrative duties, ceremonial and clerical, that he ordinarily might have avoided. He was also plagued by a rivalry with Dillard's chief fiscal officer; their dispute over their areas of purview and the decisions for which each was responsible was not adjudicated by the president but, rather, left to fester unresolved.[13] In addition, Bond faced alone the large number of complaints and conflicts that always seem to arise from a faculty working in a new institution, where new rules were being made rather than old ones followed. For example, two young, activist faculty members were pictured in a New Orleans newspaper and described as leading a group of black picketers in the downtown business district. Bond, though sympathetic to the cause of the picketers, had to explain their activities to Dillard's board president, a pillar of the New Orleans establishment who did not look kindly on the image of Dillard as a den of demonstrators. It is not surprising, then, to find Bond, less than one year after Dillard's opening, writing to President Jones at Fisk University to ask about returning to Nashville or perhaps teaching at Lincoln University. In a letter to one of his professors at Lincoln, Bond contrasted the relative peace and satisfaction of a recent two-month stint at scholarly work with the rough-and-tumble of personnel and student problems he encountered on his return to Dillard.[14]

Bond's dissatisfaction with administration was not unknown to Edwin Embree. When Will Alexander revealed his intention of relinquishing the Dillard presidency, Embree compiled a list of possible successors that included the name of Horace Bond. After naming Bond, however, Embree commented, "He does not like administrative work, is not particularly good at it, and I think he would make a serious mistake from his own standpoint to turn from his chief interests in research and teaching to an administrative post." Bond's own evaluation of his work at Dillard was not far from Embree's, and he made no effort to pursue the presidency at a time and place where he might well have made a strong bid. Writing to his old teacher, Robert Park, Bond recounted the difficulties he had had as a dean and added that, in contrast, he gained great satisfaction from such activities as writing a successful grant proposal for Dillard to the General Education Board. In a perhaps overstated but revealing insight into his own views after one year of Dillard's operations, Bond told Park: "My first year at Dillard is leaving me with many changes of personality and character. I am becoming more patient—more of a liar—scheming and contriving—disgustingly dishonest—and a new experience, widely and enthusiastically hated."[15]

Bond threw himself into grant writing, an obvious relief from the day-to-day personality clashes and political intrigues of his job. He simultaneously pursued a return to Fisk or Lincoln as an alternative to staying at Dillard. He ultimately turned down an offer of a faculty position from Lincoln, but not because he did not want to leave the Dillard deanship; as he confided to Robert Park, he could not leave Dillard after such a short time because it would be an admission of failure, and he thought his wife had a point when she argued that he should stay until the end of the next academic year, June 1937, which his contract as dean specified as the end of his tenure. Salary had to be another concern: while Bond was making $3,600 at Dillard, Lincoln offered him $2,700, a pay cut amounting to one-fourth of his salary. Another and perhaps the most important reason to stay at Dillard was the fact that Bond did not want to bite the hands of the foundations that were feeding him, and feeding him well. In a telegram to the president of Lincoln, Bond rejected the offer and summarized the situation: "Conversation with Favrot geb this morning stop he suggested that I should stay here next year stop Embree of Rosenwald fund of same opinion stop believe it well to follow these suggestions stop will probably enhance possible usefulness Lincoln or elsewhere in future to retain this good will stop therefore seems advisable to stay stop regret greatly inability to come."[16]

Going back to Fisk did not present the same difficulties Bond faced in considering Lincoln's offer, since the Rosenwald Fund was intimately involved in Fisk's activities and would not see a return there as an instance of disloyalty. Here, however, Bond ran up against a different barrier: presidential prerogative. Fisk's President Jones was ready to bring Bond back until informed by the new president of Dillard that Bond was needed in New Orleans for at least one more year.[17]

So Bond stayed on at Dillard through the first year of the new administration. Throughout that year, however, he sought various kinds of grants and fellowships for the next year, using the recent completion of his dissertation at Chicago as well as his experiences with the GEB and the Rosenwald Fund as evidence of his qualifications in research. He sought, unsuccessfully, to obtain a Guggenheim Fellowship through the sponsorship of Charles Judd of Chicago's Department of Education, who also was a member of the board of the Rosenwald Fund. Getting a grant or a research position with the help of his Rosenwald or GEB contacts would not alienate Bond from these groups, and neither would going back to Fisk. He would soon accomplish both of these objectives, but in stages. He began by, with the help of Embree, arranging a leave of absence from Dillard and accepting a Nashville-based position with the Rosenwald Fund to study the training of rural black teachers. Not long after arriving in Nashville, he was released from his duties at Dillard, and he rejoined the Fisk faculty as chairman of the education department, assigned to the Rosenwald project until its completion.[18]

In assessing Bond's experience as an academic administrator at Dillard University, one needs to emphasize his personal dissatisfaction with the job. It does not seem that the Dillard experience alone, however, turned Bond against administration; he also had a generally negative attitude toward administrators at black colleges. He once reported being on a train with a group of black deans on the way to a conference and feeling quite out of place. His fellow deans were "puritans" who neither smoked nor drank, since they had to maintain their image. Further, they seemed incapable of casual exchanges with other faculty members.[19]

Bond was reluctant, however, to close the door on administrative work and unreservedly pursue a life of teaching and research, and the research position in Nashville provided an immediate and honorable release from the pressures at Dillard. Bond thus used the Rosenwald Fund to extricate himself from an unpleasant situation that was unlikely to improve. That he managed to use the fund to remove himself from a position to which it had appointed him is testimony to his effectiveness in employing the fund for his own career purposes without alienating its officers.

Bond would stay with the rural teacher-training study for the next two academic years, until the summer of 1939. Though more urban than rural in his upbringing, he had become familiar with rural black educational problems since embarking on his academic career. His experience in the Rosenwald study of rural black schools in three southern states in 1929 and 1930 had been supplemented with a stint as a Rosenwald "Explorer" in 1934, when he was on the Dillard staff but before the institution opened its doors.

While the venture into the liberal arts at Dillard University marked something of a new direction for the Rosenwald Fund, the work in rural schools was a continuation of the Washingtonian emphasis on practical and basic endeavors. According to the fund's officers, the Explorer experiment marked the beginning of an expansion of Rosenwald's earlier work in building rural school buildings: the fund now sought to investigate what was going on inside of the schoolhouses built with its money. Reflecting an affinity for the anthropological approach favored at the University of Chicago, the Explorers were to live in rural communities and to observe all aspects of residents' experience, with particular attention paid to the relationship of the rural school to their lives. The Explorers wrote up their findings as case studies and met with each other to discuss their results and to make recommendations. At an initial meeting, the researchers described the orientation of their work: "Rural schools should prepare for rural life." Thus, the major finding of the Explorers' study—that the rural schools were utterly unrelated to the realities of rural life—seems unsurprising, if not preordained.[20]

As their assignment for the Explorer project, Bond and his wife lived in and studied the Star Creek district of Washington Parish, Louisiana. Their report decried the teachers' poor backgrounds, the low quality of instruction they offered, and the students' sporadic attendance. It also laid out the tortured relations between blacks and whites in the area, where conduct other than obsequiousness by blacks resulted in resentment and recriminations from whites.[21]

While the Bonds were away from Star Creek in January 1935, a young black man, who had been involved in an altercation in which a white man was killed, was taken from the jail in the town of Franklinton, beaten, and lynched by a white mob. Horace hesitated to return to Franklinton, fearing for his life, and that of any black, in the circumstances then prevailing. He reported his concern for his own safety in Franklinton to the Rosenwald officials, who inquired into the episode and then advised him to make his own decision on further participation in the project. After some thought, he decided to return to Franklinton. While there, he interviewed the father of the youth who had been lynched and used the interview as the basis of an article he submitted to *Harper's*. He also wished to combine the interview with his historical and observational studies of blacks in Louisiana and the South into a book-length manuscript entitled "Forty Acres and a Mule." These publication plans, however, bore no fruit.[22]

Bond's anger at the lynching and its aftermath erupted in two letters he wrote to a black journalist. He noted that whites were chagrined mainly at black reaction to the lynching, since the black maids, fearing for their own safety, refused to cross the railroad tracks and enter the homes of their white employers. Bond also recounted that white residents forced the family of the slain youth to leave town, whereupon Bond sought to find a farm elsewhere in the South for the family, as an alternative to the sure dissolution and despair they would face if they were to emigrate to a strange urban environment in a northern city. At the end of his stay in Franklinton, Bond spoke at a commencement exercise at the black school. Contending that both blacks and whites in Louisiana suffered under the legacy of slavery, he came dangerously close to open criticism of the white power structure. Three white ministers also spoke on that occasion, one trying to contradict him and the others mouthing platitudes of spiritual uplift intended to show blacks that whites were still their friends. The principal of the black school, whom Bond had criticized in his report on the district for being completely beholden to the white powers, had started a campaign for a new schoolhouse for blacks. This campaign, in Bond's words, was supported by whites who wanted to "show the Negroes and the world that, although they did lynch Jerome, it was all in good clean fun and no hard feelings exist[ed]." [23]

The anguish that Bond experienced over the situation in Franklinton was of little significance to the white officers of the Rosenwald Fund. They simply filed the Bonds' report with the reports of other Explorers, compiled in a nine-volume mimeographed document.[24] Based on these reports, the fund decided that the key to remedying the problems in rural schools, both black and white, was to concentrate on the training of the teachers. This decision ultimately led to Bond's employment in the fall of 1937 to study the training of rural teachers. In offering this position to Bond, Edwin Embree indicated he would take care of any difficulty the new Dillard president had regarding Bond's participation in the project. The plan was for Bond to be on leave officially for the first semester of the 1937–38 academic year; the fund would later request leave for the second semester. He would be headquartered at Fisk University in Nashville, since the study itself was to be administered from the George Peabody College for Teachers in that city. Embree pictured the proposed work as "the ideal preparation for the man who expects to make his career in the professional field of education" and for a man who "might influence greatly the direction of teacher education and rural education throughout the South." In a final paragraph, Embree assured Bond that the move, though on the surface somewhat doubtful from the viewpoint of an academically oriented career, was in his own best interests: "As you know, I am not anxious to interrupt your regular career. I would not make this proposal to you (however much we wanted you) unless I felt it was a natural step in the orderly progress of your teaching and research under university auspices." Given Embree's reassurances, Bond's uneasiness with the situation at Dillard, and the fact that the fund increased his salary, it is no wonder that he accepted the offer to return to Nashville with enthusiasm. It is also testimony to his ability to calm the ruffled feathers of his superiors that he was ultimately succeeded as dean at Dillard by his brother, J. Max Bond.[25]

Within six months of going to work on the study of rural teacher training, Bond was appointed chairman of the Department of Education at Fisk. While holding this position, he continued to work on the Rosenwald grant. Though Bond had considered several other positions, his choice of the Rosenwald project freed him from the day-to-day drudgery of administrative work but allowed him to keep the title and prerogatives of head of department and developer of programs.[26]

The agenda of the Julius Rosenwald Fund for its work in rural teacher training was compatible with, but not identical to, the personal objectives of Horace Mann Bond for his work in the field of education. The fund wished to continue its focus of observing rural schools and testing their students, as Bond and Clark Foreman had done eight years earlier. The fund sought to develop a picture of a good rural school, to come up with a profile of what constituted a good teacher in that school, and then redesign teacher-training curricula to meet that profile.[27] In true Washingtonian style, the curriculum of formal educational institutions would be changed to reflect the realities of black rural life.

An internal document of the Rosenwald Fund indicated some specific directions that the revision of teacher education for rural schools might take. Teachers were to be educated to meet the actual conditions they would encounter in rural settings; this was to be accomplished by "setting up practice schools out in the country as well as on the campus" and by instituting courses in rural life that would acquaint the prospective teacher with "farming, handcrafts, homemaking, and health" — in short, rural conditions, rural children, rural experiences, and "the special needs of the southern region," not the "blind application of a fixed curriculum." The education of rural children would be based "on their own heritage," "a variation from a standard." All of these statements indicate a change from the normal pattern of collegiate teacher-education curricula.[28]

Bond's own educational priorities for black southerners were not opposed to the rural emphasis of the fund. However, he had a broader program than just the work at rural schools. His prescriptions for the training of rural teachers were not so slavishly tied to rural life. Bond believed that a focus on urban schools and teachers was as important as that on rural schools if all the educational needs of black southerners were to be met. In July of 1937, he told Embree that the fund's withdrawal from urban education was a "great loss," pointing out that one-third of the black population of the South lived in cities. While at Dillard, he had started, with Rosenwald help, a summer school for city children in New Orleans, and he was proud of what the children had accomplished there. He believed that experimental urban schools should be supported as models of excellence in settings where black youngsters had typically been shortchanged. Model urban schools for blacks would benefit middle-class black young-

sters, many of whom had extremely high IQs, and black students would
be encouraged to strive and achieve at the highest levels. Here Bond was
echoing the theme of black excellence, which he had developed a decade
earlier in an article on black children of high ability. He would repeat
his New Orleans proposal when he moved to Nashville and proposed to
provide a model school for black children at Fisk.[29]

Bond showed a knack for gaining Rosenwald Fund support for traditional academic answers to rural school problems, answers that did not
rank high in the philanthropy's own list of solutions. For instance, he
touted to Embree the idea of publishing a newsletter on problems in rural
schools as well as a scheme to beef up students' personal libraries at black
teacher-training schools, for he believed that teachers needed to become
aware of the fact that "books are a part of their natural environment" and
that funds should be set up "to encourage book buying and library building
by students in Negro colleges and normal schools." Embree's response to
both of these ideas was positive, but he added that he wished Bond to think
of a third point, the stirring up of interest in "the inside of a rural school."
We have here not a clash of views, but a definite difference in emphasis.
In all of these arguments, Bond was seeking to incorporate in the Rosenwald effort traditional notions of academic excellence; Embree, however,
stressed the fund's commitment to redesigning the school to conform to
the realities of rural life.[30]

In February 1938, after becoming chairman of the Department of Education at Fisk, Bond proposed three projects to be supported by the Rosenwald Fund and other philanthropies. Of these three, two were related
to the rural-education efforts of the fund, but the third, an experimental school to be held on the Fisk campus, reflected his long-standing and
deep interest in the cultivation of educational excellence among blacks.
Bond also stressed excellence in his recruiting of students for Fisk, under
the sponsorship of the Rosenwald Fund or with funds from the National
Youth Administration. He told an official at Florida A & M College that
he was particularly interested in "especially good students."[31]

To conduct his teacher-training study, Bond visited rural schools and
black colleges that claimed to train teachers for rural schools. In one report on four black teacher-training schools, he decried the divorce between
federally funded work in agriculture and home economics and the regular work in education. He then noted that prospective teachers had little
"theoretical understanding of the background—social and economic—of

their students, and of the communities to which they are to go." Further, he was critical of the practical teaching experience at every school except one, the Alabama State Teachers College, where he had served as director of extension work in 1927–28. Even there, he observed, the absence of courses in sociology or rural sociology prevented "widening the appreciation of the student-teachers for their problems."[32] In criticizing this lack, Bond was advocating the traditional academic means of coursework to bridge the gap between teachers in training and the rural schools where they would be working. Thus, in many ways, he saw reform as a process of providing the proper academic experiences for students as well as a process of binding theory with practical work.

The notion that Bond had an educational agenda distinct from that of the Rosenwald Fund can be developed further by considering his recommendations to black audiences in settings not dependent on philanthropic support. In late 1938, he responded to a request from the president of West Virginia State College for an enumeration of the most important problems in "Negro education." Bond noted three specifics: first, the lack of a climate of self-respect in the black community, which meant that its members did not have faith in their own futures; second, the failure to select and stimulate the intellectually gifted young blacks so that they might be encouraged to excel; and, finally, the failure to develop "a rigid and severe discipline" in black schools. This last lapse began with teachers not insisting on careful and accurate work; it resulted in students who did not develop habits of thoroughness.[33] Bond's list of problems had little to say about any lack of relevance between the school and its teachers, on the one hand, and the communities and black students and parents, on the other. Rather, he indicated that, in his mind, the fundamental problem was a lack of commitment to the traditional goals of excellence and achievement. It is clear that his specifics did not reflect the same priorities that the reform-oriented members of the Julius Rosenwald Fund would endorse.

There were times when Bond's personal correspondence with close friends revealed an opportunistic, sometimes even cynical, way of dealing with the philanthropies. For instance, a 1939 letter from an old academic friend characterized quite graphically Bond's successes with the General Education Board and the Rosenwald Fund: "So you are sopping up some GEB gravy too. Good for you. A little beef mixed with the Rosenwald pork should prove a nice combination." A year later, a classmate from Lincoln days sought Bond's advice on how to solicit philanthropic support for graduate study: "I know you are a big shot with the Rosenwald people et al. Tell me how to get a big fat grant, and help me to do so." In his reply, Bond mentioned several persons who should be contacted but cautioned against being too specific in outlining research ideas, since these same individuals might very well appropriate them for themselves. This response was in marked contrast to his reply, earlier that same year, to an applicant whom he did not know: "There is little I could tell you that would help in obtaining a Rosenwald Fellowship as I am not a member of the Committee . . . which grants these Fellowships." These examples illustrate the general point Bond made in a letter to his good friend and colleague, Allison Davis: "Do as good for yourself as you can, whether through [Charles] Johnson [of Fisk], [W. Lloyd] Warner [of the University of Chicago], [Will] Alexander [of Rosenwald], or the devil himself." These and other exchanges reveal that Bond and his friends knew that there was a game being played with the philanthropies, and they were intent on being successful in playing that game.[34]

All of this is to say that, although he was a favored son of the Rosenwald Fund, Bond was more than an extension of the fund and those who presided over it. He knew that he was beholden to the fund for much of his advancement, but he attempted to maintain his own identity in his scholarly work and in his advice to other black educators. How much of that identity he might have to sacrifice, or at least to downplay, would become apparent in a decision Bond made in 1939, when he was offered the presidency at the Fort Valley Normal and Industrial School.

In 1939, Bond experienced two great milestones in his life: his mother died, and his first child was born. Jane Bond died in April 1939. Although her relationship with her son was not as deep or intense as that which had existed between her husband and her son—Jane's infrequent letters to Horace usually contained family news, requests for money, and exhortations to her son to stay on the path of righteousness—the loss of a mother for most children is profound, and there is no reason to believe that this was not the case for Horace Bond.[35]

Horace and Julia Bond were childless in the first eight years of their marriage. They were not initially worried about their inability to produce offspring, but as the years went by, they became concerned about whether or not they would be able to have children, and they contemplated adoption. The birth of their daughter, Jane Marguerite, in the summer of their ninth year of marriage, alleviated this concern and brought great delight to the Bond household.[36]

Jane's arrival also brought a new urgency into her father's educational work. In the Baltimore newspaper, the *Afro-American*, he had a somewhat bitter exchange with another black over the deadening handicaps that faced all black children in public schools in the South. He asked his opponent not to take offense at what he had said and hoped that it would not be taken as a personal attack; he added, however, that he now had a personal, as well as a professional and intellectual, stake in improving black educational opportunities. "I now have a little daughter, six months of age, and when I contemplate the unequal educational chance she is bound to have right here in the city of Nashville, when she comes of school age, it both terrifies and angers me."[37]

In 1939, the year in which these two landmark events occurred, Horace Bond faced the Rubicon of his professional life: the offer of the presidency of the Fort Valley Normal and Industrial School in rural middle Georgia. The school at Fort Valley was not unknown to Bond: in November of 1937 he had visited there as part of his work for the teacher-training study. Fort Valley had enjoyed a long-standing relationship with various philanthropic agencies, particularly with the Rosenwald Fund and the General Education Board. In 1937, a proposal was made to shift the school's major source of financial support from the Episcopal church–affiliated American Church Institute to the state of Georgia, with the financial cooperation of the Rosenwald Fund. The president of Fort Valley died early in 1939, just as the plan for state affiliation was coming to fruition.[38] Bond's work with several rural teacher-training institutions, as well as his affiliation with the Rosenwald Fund, made him a prime candidate for the Fort Valley presidency. At first, he was even more reluctant to accept this post than he had been to go to Dillard as academic dean. However, Embree seemed set on getting Bond to accept the presidency and pushed hard for that outcome. Bond agonized. First, he suggested that his brother Max was more suited to the post. Next, he flatly refused the position, citing a wavering in the state's financial commitment as his reason. Then, he accepted the job but reneged after a careful study of the institution's financial situation.[39]

Bond's reluctance to become a college president mainly stemmed from his desire to continue his scholarly work. Publication of his dissertation, which would be his second book, was imminent. He told Embree that, given five to ten graduate students to work with at Fisk, he could make himself a scholar. He noted the publication of a recent book by E. E. Just, a black biologist with a Ph.D. from Chicago who was on the Howard University faculty, and reminded Embree that Just was about the only black scholar who had devoted a twenty-five-year career to scholarship. Bond concluded this discussion, no doubt thinking of himself, with the remark that it might be "more worthwhile for one or two persons to do that sort of thing for a like period of years." [40]

Embree persisted, and Bond eventually accepted the Fort Valley presidency, though only on an acting basis; again he took leave from Fisk. This time, however, a rift soon developed with Fisk's President Jones, after Jones hired a full professor to replace Bond, an action that Bond took as an indication that Jones was not counting on him to return. Bond felt that he had no choice but to resign and to throw himself fully into his Fort Valley duties. [41]

Several serious misgivings dogged Bond's decision to become president of Fort Valley Normal and Industrial School. In addition to his scholarly pursuits, which he feared would suffer, the political minefield of the presidency of a black college in the Deep South concerned him greatly. Given the racial and political climate in Georgia, he worried that the state's commitment to Fort Valley could easily falter. Moreover, Fort Valley would have to compete for state funds with two already existing state-supported black colleges, one each at Albany and at Savannah. Still another factor weighed on his mind—his family. The Bonds had an infant daughter, and Julia was now pregnant with another child. Rural Georgia was not as stimulating an environment as urban Nashville for raising children. [42]

Despite all of these concerns, Embree persisted and eventually did see Bond accept the presidency at Fort Valley. Embree did not force the office on Bond; he did, however, put a considerable amount of pressure on the young black academic to accept it. Bond's eventual acquiescence was surely due, at least in part, to his reluctance to offend his philanthropic benefactor at this stage of his professional career. Of course, the high status of a college presidency, which was one of the few avenues available for upwardly mobile blacks in the segregated world of higher education, was no doubt part of the attraction. Another incentive was the salary of $4,800, a distinct increase in remuneration for Bond and an even greater lure when considered in relation to the low cost of living in rural Georgia. For Bond to have remained a faculty member at a black college meant facing a life with high teaching loads, poor pay, little research support, and consignment to an existence in the shadow of his administrators. Horace Bond did not wish to live in that shadow.[43] The only way in which he could possibly have succeeded as a scholar would have been to have support from philanthropies. As it was, the Rosenwald Fund preferred for him to go into administration, and he accepted. From the perspective of what he had already achieved and experienced—the establishment of his reputation as a scholar and his distaste for administrative work at Dillard—his decision was questionable, but understandable. From the perspective of what he would encounter—success at Fort Valley followed by a cataclysmic end to his twelve years as Lincoln University president—his decision was a tragedy.

Chapter 6

Scholar of Black Education

Before I recount the particulars of Horace Bond's eighteen years as a college president, I need to examine his achievements as a scholar, for it is as a scholar that Bond made his most important contributions to black education and intellectual life, and he made the greatest portion of these contributions during the 1930s, before he moved into college administration for good. The two books and several articles that Bond published in the 1930s began a long career of writing and publishing on the history and social analysis of black education; he would produce four other books and a large number of articles in the rest of his working years.[1] The two books he published in the 1930s, however, represent his most serious and sustained scholarly treatments of the educational and social experience of black Americans, and his reputation as a scholar rests mainly on these two works.

Bond first proposed publication of a textbook on the subject of Negro education in a letter to Prentice Hall Press in July 1932. Accepted within a month, the projected work was to be part of a series edited by George Payne, the dean of George Peabody College for Teachers, whom Bond had most likely met during his work in Nashville at Fisk University. Bond's publisher envisioned his book as a text that black colleges would use in their education courses. Because this was the first textbook written specifically for courses in black colleges, a market in which sales could not be accurately predicted, a contract calling for slightly less than the usual royalties was agreed upon. Within two years of the initial contact with Prentice Hall, Bond's work was published under the title *The Education of the Negro in the American Social Order*.[2]

Bond's conceptual strategy of locating black education in its "social order" owed much to his mentor in the historical study of education, Newton Edwards of the University of Chicago. Bond had taken several of Edwards's courses, and, in the fall of 1931, less than a year before proposing publication of his book, Bond had completed another of Edwards's courses, "The School in the Social Order."[3] Edwards's point of view was heavily socioeconomic, a novelty in educational history and other educational studies in that period but a common approach in many fields of study during the Great Depression. At its best, the socioeconomic focus properly located educational events in their social and economic context and prevented glib analyses and facile solutions to educational problems. At its worst, it resulted in doctrinaire, usually Marxist analyses that identified injustices in society but spoke little, if at all, to educational problems. Bond's effort was decidedly on the more scholarly and less doctrinaire end of this ideological spectrum. Though he devoted the bulk of his pages to educational issues and problems, he noted that the social order was the proper context in which to study schooling, and he cautioned against regarding the school as a "panacea" by which to solve social problems.[4]

The Education of the Negro was divided into three parts: the first dealt with the history of black education since Reconstruction, the second with the issues of economics and finance in education, and the third with current problems. In the historical section of the work, Bond covered the pre-Reconstruction era, Reconstruction, and the post-Reconstruction politics of black education, highlighting the positions of various groups of whites in terms of their members' social and economic backgrounds. He showed how poor whites had little in common with wealthy plantation owners and their families; instead, poor whites' economic interests were with freed slaves in such government programs as those that provided liberal amounts of public schooling. Both poor whites and blacks were overly devoted to education, particularly in the period immediately following the Civil War.[5]

Bond then turned to the radical nature of congressional Reconstruction and the generous educational proposals of the Reconstruction legislatures of the southern states, heavily influenced by blacks, poor whites, and northerners who came south. He also discussed the white "Redeemer" reaction to this situation, identifying it as a diminution of educational privileges for black children and a concomitant maintenance of some of these privileges for poor whites. The wealthy whites were able to break the coalition of mutual economic interest between poor whites and blacks by short-changing the latter group, for benefits for poor whites were made to appear dependent on the disadvantages of blacks. Bond then noted the brief resurrection of a biracial coalition between whites and blacks in his discussion of the Southern populist movement of the 1880s and 1890s in the South. The ultimate failure of this coalition was due, again, to the rejection of blacks by white farmers, who were manipulated by wealthy whites and white politicians. Seeing educational provisions as part of the larger struggle for political and economic power in the region, Bond graphically depicted the victory of the powerful whites who opposed spending money on schools for blacks and, instead, financed schools for white children with public money provided ostensibly for all the states' youth.[6]

The picture that Bond painted was not unreservedly gloomy. He was careful to highlight the contributions of the Freedmen's Bureau, the American Missionary Association, the Yankee schoolmarms who came down and taught the freed slaves, and the northern philanthropists who aided the cause of black education in the South. In none of these descriptions was Bond uncritical, however. He noted the limits in the commitments of all of the white benefactors at the same time that he chronicled the progress made with their help. He also highlighted the contributions of blacks to the financing and conduct of their own schooling, contributions that seem truly heroic given the depressed economic state in which they found themselves in the postwar world. Booker T. Washington was discussed extensively as the leading black educator and spokesman for southern blacks in this period.[7]

The three chapters in the section on economics and finance were the shortest of the three sections; however, they provide readers with at least two insights. The first, developed in the initial chapter of the section, was that black children and their families migrated in great numbers from rural to urban areas in the immediate post–World War I years. Responding to the horrible conditions for rural southerners in general, as well as to the vicious racial discrimination that accompanied these conditions, southern blacks began to migrate to cities, mainly in the North but also in the South. Bond's insight—that the educational problems of blacks should, in the future, be conceived as part of the urban problem—was not stressed by most other scholars in the 1930s.[8]

In the last chapter of his section on financial issues, Bond described the discrimination that stifled the economic opportunities available to southern blacks. He noted the South's depressed economy in relation to the rest of the nation, which meant that Mississippians or Alabamians would have to tax themselves at rates five or six times as great as the rates in a wealthy state, such as California, in order to produce a similar investment in education. Thus, southern educational expenditure was doomed to remain at the low levels that the relative poverty of the entire section mandated.[9]

When considering the plight of black children and schools, however, this situation became even worse. The commitment of southern states to separate-but-equal systems of schools, as sanctioned in *Plessy* v. *Ferguson* (1896), meant, in reality, that these separate systems would be maintained in ways that allowed whites to benefit from the low amounts expended on black schools. Quoting from an article he had published in a 1933 issue of *School and Society*, Bond calculated that separate schools for blacks in the region meant that each white child had available for his or her education $1,922 more than the sum available for a black youngster.[10]

In a discussion of the county system of school finance prevalent in the South, Bond showed how the substantial numbers of black children in a county enabled the white citizens of that county to finance education for their children solely on the state appropriations to the county on a per-capita student basis. Whites simply skimmed off the state funds available because of large black enrollments and used them for white pupils; black children received only the droppings, after the whites were taken care of. This system also induced the powerful white politicians in the rural areas, where most of the black-majority counties were located, to fight off attempts by the white-majority counties to finance schooling through local taxation.[11]

Even when southern states instituted "equalization" measures in school finance in the post–World War I years, they merely equalized whites' opportunities to rob black schools for the benefit of their own children rather than achieved any genuine equalization of educational expenditures. Bond concluded from his analysis that, until there could be genuine equality in the financing of black schools, there could be no realistic hope that black students would realize any equality in educational opportunity.[12]

In the third and final section of Bond's textbook, "Current Problems," he discussed a variety of topics, many of which he had studied and written about in the decade since he began academic work in 1924. A chapter on teachers, undoubtedly informed by Bond's teacher-education experiences in Oklahoma, Alabama, and Tennessee, described the low level of ability among black teachers, which he attributed mainly to low salaries. As a solution, he advocated both higher salaries and better supervision of teachers and also indicated that teacher-training institutions should take care to admit and turn out better-qualified teachers. A chapter on black students, entitled "The Forgotten Child," detailed the extreme poverty and other deprivations that plagued most black children, and Bond showed how these conditions were related to the poor attendance records of black youth in schools.[13]

In a discussion of the capacity of black children, Bond used much of the work he had done on IQ testing early in his career, reprising his critique of the army IQ tests from his earliest articles, as well as his studies of black children of high ability and of the nonintellectual traits of blacks. He concluded by stating his strongly held beliefs that the IQ test and other measures of the abilities of black children were largely dependent on these children's environment. He cited approvingly an article by Frank Freeman, who argued that racial differences in intelligence were quantitative, that is, of a kind that can be lessened by environmental intervention, rather than qualitative, which would indicate that interventionist strategies are not likely to improve the situation. Bond praised the views of one expert who estimated that environmental deprivation might depress an IQ score by twenty points, and he conjectured that a slump of twenty points was probably too low of a figure for some of the most deprived black children from rural poverty or urban slums.[14]

Bond next devoted a chapter to the achievement of black children. He summarized the data from the study he completed with Clark Foreman and discussed several other studies. In all cases, he advanced analyses related to the environmental conditions of the children. He singled out the black schools run by the Tennessee Coal and Iron Company in Birmingham, Alabama, for special mention. In these schools, the achievement of black children, which was almost identical to national norms, was far superior to that of black youth in the county schools for blacks. Bond attributed this difference to the fact that the schools run by Tennessee Coal and Iron had substantial financial support and were "excellently managed, equipped, and supervised." He concluded that, "altogether, this is probably the best system for Negro children in the entire South."[15] In conformity with his emphasis on the significance of social forces, however, Bond cautioned that Tennessee Coal and Iron's schools were not totally responsible for the situation: "Rather, it is the entire complex which is involved, for the industrial company managing these plants has not restricted its program of social betterment to schooling alone." Similarly, in his conclusion to the chapter, Bond reminded his readers that educational improvements, though desirable and necessary, could not substitute for the very real changes necessary in the out-of-school environment of black Americans if they were to compete on a level field with their white counterparts. "So long as the efforts of educators are restricted to an improvement of the method and means of instruction, we must resign ourselves to several centuries of continued struggle before the ultimate will be even in sight." So that his readers did not interpret his conclusion as an invitation to stop their work, he added that this did not mean that black teachers should slacken their efforts to improve their charges' educational opportunities.[16]

Bond then briefly treated the topic of higher education for blacks. He described industrial and liberal education as competing goals for black colleges but then deemphasized the significance of the difference in the approaches. Moving to a discussion of the schooling of blacks in the North, he compared segregated schools carefully, but generally unfavorably, to racially mixed schools (though he did not support the latter as explicitly as he did in an earlier article in a black newspaper). He stressed the administrative problems peculiar to black schools, noting the ways in which genuine vocational education might be appropriately employed in black schools, as opposed to the existing and inappropriate policy of blanket consignment of black children to menial tasks and occupational tracks.[17]

After these discussions, Bond returned to his theme of the relation of education to the rest of the social order. In evaluating the social setting in which black schooling occurred, Bond dealt with socioeconomic problems that confronted African Americans, particularly southern African Americans. On the question of farm tenancy as the characteristic form of black rural life, he noted that there was little that the school could do. Land reform, to use a modern term, was what the black farmer needed. During Reconstruction, when the phrase "forty acres and a mule" served as shorthand for the redistribution of land to the freed slaves, the typical black farmer came as close as he would ever come to becoming a landowner. Since this redistribution did not happen, however, the black tenant faced insurmountable odds in making his farming pay off, at even a subsistence level. Without land reform, blacks would, and should, continue to abandon rural areas for greater opportunities in the cities.[18]

In detailing the incidence of crime, Bond again argued that schools could have little influence over the phenomenon. Crime was a result of deprivation and social disorganization, two areas in which schools were severely limited in what they could accomplish. In the area of health, however, schools could do more. After discussing mortality rates, the incidence of tuberculosis, and the rate of syphilis in the black population of the South, Bond noted that teaching health practices and standards in school would go a long way toward combatting these problems as well as dealing with other health concerns.[19]

In arguing that the school was ill equipped to deal with land reform and crime but was quite well equipped to help raise health standards, Bond saw the school neither as the great panacea for reform nor as completely ineffective. Rather, as he had done earlier in his book, he tried to indicate realistic goals for the schools and teachers.

In his concluding chapter, Bond addressed the future prospects of black education, arguing that the financial inequities suffered by black children and black schools were the problems that needed to be addressed most urgently. The racial prejudice responsible for school segregation was so deeply entrenched that it was beyond the reach of educational policy. However, equalizing expenditures—ideally effected by federal aid—was a more tangible and perhaps reachable objective. Unfortunately, the political climate, which featured both racial prejudice and fear of federal control over schooling, militated against achieving this relatively simple solution. Equalization at the state level seemed a goal just as illusory. Southern whites were simply not interested in equipping black children with tools equal to those given to whites.[20]

More practical improvements might be accomplished, however. In the rural areas, more efficiency in counties' administering of black schools, as was taking place in one Arkansas county, could lead to better opportunities. In urban areas, a minimal increase in expenditures over a lengthy period of years could gradually lead to equalization. Bond used Nashville, Tennessee, as an example, suggesting that, for the relatively small sum of fifty cents for every one thousand dollars of assessed property valuation, teacher salaries and other expenditures for black schools could be equalized in only twenty years.[21]

Unfortunately, neither his rural nor his urban solutions really spoke to the massive problems plaguing black schools. To argue that more efficient administration in rural counties would erase problems of expenditure differences that were as large as twenty or thirty to one in favor of white children over black was like trying to kill an elephant with a flyswatter. To project a tax increase, no matter how small, for a twenty-year period, as Bond did for Nashville, was to ignore the psychology and social structure that made southerners reluctant to pay for schools at all, let alone for black schools. As he ended his book, Bond was not facing reality. Black teachers and black children confronted huge obstacles every day, and, realistically speaking, nothing short of a social revolution could ameliorate their conditions. And Bond was not about to advocate that social revolution—not because he did not want it, but because he did not think that it could happen. His closing sentences exhorted black educators to work in their vineyard, not with the expectation that they would see tangible improvements, but with the conviction that they were on the side of righteousness. Improving black educational opportunity was, then, a good fight that needed to be fought for the sake of principle and whatever small gains could be made. It was not necessarily, or even probably, a battle that could be won.[22]

In many ways, *The Education of the Negro* was a tour de force. It brought together into coherent form an immense variety of information and successfully utilized several disciplinary approaches. Sympathetic readers of the book could marvel at its author's synthetic ability and find much in it with which they agreed. This was precisely the reaction of Bond's old professor, Robert Labaree: while congratulating Bond on his book's publication, he noted its effective integration of varied material and indicated his agreement with Bond's criticism of segregated schools in the North.[23]

Because *The Education of the Negro* was a textbook pitched to black colleges, Bond's work was not widely reviewed. Three of the four reviews I located were positive. E. Franklin Frazier noted in the *American Journal of Sociology* that Bond attacked "the problems of Negro life in as fundamental and comprehensive a manner" as any other book had done. Frazier praised the "objectivity" of the study as well as its "thorough research and understanding of the fundamental factors involved." He concluded, "Every teacher and school administrator in this country should read this book, for no one can have a realistic picture of the educational problems of the Negro without a knowledge of its contents."[24] Charles Thompson reviewed the book favorably in the *Journal of Negro Education*, a periodical he had recently started at Howard University. In *Survey*, Ambrose Caliver, another leading black educator, also praised Bond's work and noted its rare combination of scholarship and practicality, calling it a "scientific production that is at once accurate, dramatic, and emotionally appealing." He went on to list it with Carter G. Woodson's *Education of the Negro prior to 1861* as necessary reading for black educators and intellectuals.[25]

Woodson's own review, however, published in the *Journal of Negro History*, which he edited, was not so favorable. Woodson thought the work "unscientific," episodic, and superficial. Its main deficiency, however, was its assumption that black education was similar to white education. Woodson also objected to Bond's contention that reducing financial disparities between black and white schools would go a long way toward solving the problems, for Woodson thought that black education ought to be seen, not in terms of its support relative to that given to white education, but in terms of the social problems of black people. Woodson here was repaying Bond for the negative review that the young scholar had accorded to Woodson's *Miseducation of the Negro* a few years earlier. Rather than analyze Bond's points, Woodson restated the position he had developed in his own book. For Woodson, black education, like the rest of black culture, suffered most from the black educators who transmitted it, because they insisted on aping white education and culture instead of attending to their own concerns in their own way.[26] Woodson ignored the major points of Bond's work, just as Bond had ignored his. The scholarly score, in Woodson's eyes, was now even.

Bond wrote his book in order to graphically describe the educational, social, and economic realities of black Americans. In a painful illustration of some of those realities, he responded to pressure from Edwin Embree and revised some particulars about the Rosenwald Fund in his book. The changes were minor but significant in that they revealed the power that philanthropic agencies and officers could exert over the work of their black beneficiaries. In the original manuscript of the book, Bond mentioned "large defalcations" of funds by the white administrator of Rosenwald programs in Mississippi. At Embree's prompting, the word "large" was omitted from the published version of the book. Also, Bond's reference to diversion of Rosenwald dollars from black schools to white schools in "several" southern states was changed to read as follows: "The writer knows of three instances in two other states" where such diversion occurred. Forcing Bond to depict the financial abuse as dependent on his own knowledge relativized that phenomenon and watered down any inferred criticism of the Rosenwald Fund in particular or philanthropic agencies in general.[27]

Sales of Bond's book were not overwhelming. In 1938, he reported total sales of approximately eight hundred books, adding that it was then selling about one hundred copies per year. The steady sales over a four-year period indicate that there was a small market for the work, and the fact that it was reprinted in 1965 and again in 1970 is testimony to the notion that the ideas it propounds were important.[28] As a first effort by a young scholar, yet to receive his Ph.D., it is an impressive piece of work. While some of its sections report the results of original research, its textlike approach and treatment of many topics meant that it could not be recognized as an original work of scholarship in a specialized field of study. Bond's second book, however, established his reputation as a scholar in the field of educational history.

Bond's greatest contribution to scholarship was his doctoral dissertation, "Social and Economic Influences on the Public Education of Negroes in Alabama, 1865–1930." Completed in 1936, the work was published in 1939 under the title *Negro Education in Alabama: A Study in Cotton and Steel.* In the preface, Bond acknowledged his debt to his doctoral adviser, Newton Edwards, and mentioned that Edwards had first called to his attention "the importance of social and economic analysis of educational institutions," the kind of analysis that made Bond's book distinctive.[29]

Bond had considerable difficulty finding a publisher for his dissertation. He first approached Charles Thompson and suggested that the work be the first of a series of monographs published by the *Journal of Negro Education.* Thompson, who was still struggling to place his journal, which was less than five years old, on a firm footing, could not accommodate his friend. Bond next tried the presses of the University of North Carolina and the University of Chicago. The southern press was initially positive, but ultimately demurred. The press at Bond's alma mater was interested, but only if the manuscript were shortened, a revision that Bond felt would severely damage his work. Soon, however, he received the good news that the dissertation had received a prize and a small cash award from the University of Chicago and a grant of $500 toward publication from the Rosenwald Fund. Combining the prize money and some of his own funds, Bond was able to offer a subsidy of seven hundred dollars to Carter G. Woodson's Associated Publishers, which published the book in 1939. Bond was initially reluctant to approach Woodson because of the negative reviews the two had recently exchanged. Woodson, however, was evidently willing to overlook the past, for he recognized in Bond's work a study of great substantive value as well as usefulness in combating the racist accounts of Reconstruction written by southern historians.[30]

One should not pick up a copy of *Negro Education in Alabama* expecting to find a literary masterpiece. As Bond's contemporaries and reviewers pointed out, the book had stylistic flaws. It smacked of the dissertation from which it had emerged, most notably in its habit of repeating introductory statements almost verbatim and in its use of excessively formal, jargonistic language. Because of his heavy workload as dean at Dillard and subsequently as department chair and faculty member at Fisk and also as researcher for the Rosenwald teacher-training study, Bond was not able to revise the dissertation before its publication.[31]

Despite the negative consequences of Bond's failure to revise his dissertation, the book was well received almost immediately upon its publication and for years afterward. W. E. B. Du Bois praised Bond's book in a review published in the *American Historical Review*, and it was also treated favorably in the *Journal of Negro Education*, the *Journal of Southern History*, and the *Mississippi Valley Historical Review*. One year after its publication, the noted historian Howard K. Beale relied on Bond's work for part of his landmark article on Reconstruction history, published in the *American Historical Review*.[32] The continuing importance of Bond's book is demonstrated by the fact that numerous recent works in history, educational history, and black history cite it as a source and that a paperback edition published in the 1960s remained in print into the 1980s. To trace the scholarly significance of Bond's ideas, one should first look at its historical and historiographical contributions to Reconstruction studies.[33]

In a 1936 letter to a noted student of black history and culture, Arthur Schomburg, Bond indicated the historians whom his book targeted: "I am all set to demolish Fleming, McMaster, Rhodes, Dunning, and Du Bois." It seems odd to see Du Bois, the black radical, linked with William Archibald Dunning and other historical apologists for the South. Indeed, Du Bois had written *Black Reconstruction* (1935) to correct the bigoted views of the Dunning school of Reconstruction historians; in Du Bois's highly ideological interpretation, the freedman and his participation in Reconstruction politics are seen as a dictatorship of the proletariat. Some years later, in a letter to a former student, Bond explained why he had placed Du Bois in the company of white racist historians: "All of his stuff is from secondary sources, and what he did was to take the 'facts' reported by the Dunning-segregationists, and read into them his own interpretation—which was highly creative, but—since the first guys didn't have the 'facts,' Du Bois therefore missed the *real* stuff. Note that I am not objecting to the Marxist approach; what I deeply regret is to see so damned many pages of rehashing of superficial stuff, while the facts, that would have been enormously more convincing, were apparently quite unknown to Du Bois."[34]

Bond's main target was not Du Bois, however, but Walter L. Fleming, author of a then-standard work, *Civil War and Reconstruction in Alabama*. Fleming had been a student of William A. Dunning at Columbia University, and his dissertation served as the core of his published work on Reconstruction in Alabama. He had risen to a deanship at Vanderbilt University and was acknowledged as one of the leading lights of the contemporary South. Some years later, in a letter to John Hope Franklin, Bond claimed that Fleming's footnotes revealed him to be an unreliable scholar, one who twisted quotations to fit his preconceptions and who labeled the ideas of diehard southerners as those of northerners. Indeed, Bond told Franklin, this kind of work was "downright skulduggery."[35]

Bond's own discussion of Reconstruction omitted the beloved figures of what he later called "the vaudeville of what has been Southern History": the "vicious carpetbagger" and the "equally vicious Scalawag"; the stereotypical "ignorant, misled Negro voter and politician"; and the equally stereotypical "noble southern White Man" striving "desperately to preserve 'the Southern Way of Life.'" In place of these caricatures Bond offered an interpretation based on underlying economic patterns: "I saw Alabama Reconstruction History as the struggle between great aggregations of capital, seeking in this, and other States, to weld together economic empires. These I typified by studying the railroads, that were the basic skeletal framework on which empires were then built. I saw the Democratic Party as the party of the Louisville and Nashville Railroad; . . . I saw the Republican party . . . as the party of the Alabama and Chattanooga Railroad (now the Southern)."[36] Bond attacked Fleming's view that the Reconstruction government of Alabama, heavily influenced, if not controlled, by blacks, saddled the state with an onerous debt of thirty million dollars; instead, the debt was a result of political commitments made to the various railroad interests, and the amount of genuine debt incurred under the Reconstruction government was comparable to that incurred by pre–Civil War and post-Reconstruction regimes.[37]

By the 1950s, Bond's work, along with the work of such historians as Roger Shugg, Vernon L. Wharton, Francis Simkins, and Robert H. Woody, had become known as the revisionist school of Reconstruction history. Selections from Bond's and other revisionists' works, along with selections from traditional historians of Reconstruction, were anthologized in a 1952 volume that highlighted the conflicting interpretations of the period. By the 1960s, revisionist interpretations such as Bond's had gained the ascendancy.[38]

Since the 1960s, however, students of the Reconstruction have sought to move beyond the debate between the traditionalists and the revisionists. In the 1970s, several historians stressed that radical northerners in Congress and in the Freedmen's Bureau lacked real commitment to the freedman; these scholars bypassed both the traditionalist attack and revisionist defense of Congress and the bureau. Though Bond was a vigorous defender of Thaddeus Stevens, O. O. Howard, and other northern "humanitarians," he discussed Reconstruction-era education in Alabama as exemplifying both humanitarianism and the political opportunism of northern capitalists. Thus he was not completely unaware of the forces that later historians viewed as critical to a proper understanding of Reconstruction.[39]

The failure to provide "forty acres and a mule" to the freedman is another important point for contemporary historians of Reconstruction, and it is one that Bond did not overlook. Speaking of the freed slaves, he remarked: "These masses . . . knew exactly what they needed. . . . They asked for a subsistence farmstead—for forty acres and a mule." Taking land reform as a beginning point, some recent historians have used comparative studies of emancipation in several slave countries to show that the formation of classes was perhaps the key event of Reconstruction. A particularly influential recent work, Jonathan Wiener's *Social Origins of the New South*, uses the categories suggested by Bond in his work to chronicle the battle for economic hegemony among planters, merchants, and industrialists in Reconstruction and post-Reconstruction Alabama. Like Bond, whose work is cited in the notes but not discussed, Wiener highlights the freedman as central to this economic conflict.[40] Thus Bond's contribution to Reconstruction history is of contemporary as well as historical significance.

In the last three chapters of his treatment of Reconstruction as well as in the bulk of the remaining chapters in his book, Bond turned to the topic of education. Following the ideas of Newton Edwards and his own work in *The Education of the Negro*, Bond maintained the economic focus that characterized his chapters on Reconstruction. His emphasis on social and economic forces as influences on educational events was unusual in educational histories, whether written in the 1930s or afterward. Merle Curti's *Social Ideas of American Educators*, published in 1935, was one history of education that resembled Bond's work in its use of an economic perspective as well as in its critical stance toward the actors and institutions it studied. Bond's dissertation, completed one year after the publication of Curti's book, contains no reference to Curti, although Bond knew of Curti's work, since the two men had corresponded shortly after its publication. Curti dealt with the South in only two chapters, though there his treatment shared much with Bond's.[41]

Bond's major foil in the history of education was Edgar W. Knight, who had studied history with William A. Dunning as part of a doctoral program at Teachers College, Columbia University. In his treatment of Reconstruction, Knight followed the Dunning school and thus downplayed the educational accomplishments of the Reconstruction-era governments; instead, he emphasized the educational achievements of antebellum southern whites and the post-Reconstruction redeemer regimes. In contrast, Bond properly credited Alabama's Reconstruction government for establishing common schools in Alabama; but he also noted that it failed to provide for racially mixed schools, an idea that surely would have made Knight apoplectic.[42]

In discussing late-nineteenth-century Alabama education, Bond located its main development in the gradual fiscal strangulation of the black public schools. In 1887 white planters arranged for passage of a law that made the apportionment of state funds for schools a matter of local discretion, thereby allowing whites in counties with black majorities to divert the per capita funds to white schools. A constitutional convention in 1901 disfranchised Alabama's black population and adopted limited local taxation for white schools, a concession to white-majority counties that did not have enough black students to sufficiently finance the white schools. Bond argued that this local tax was much more significant in improving educational opportunities for whites in Alabama than the "southern educational revival" so cherished by Edgar Knight and other southern historians, for these two tax measures allowed whites to discriminate in varied ways to ensure that the public schools' funds could be manipulated to their advantage. Disfranchisement robbed blacks of any opportunity to contest the situation politically. Here Bond documented in detail his views on school finance, as set forth in *The Education of the Negro*, and, in its treatment, tone, and illustration of the tragic outcomes, his discussion of the racial consequences of public school financing in Alabama anticipated Louis Harlan's 1958 study of race and school finance in five southern seaboard states at the turn of the century.[43]

The final section of Bond's book was composed of four chapters on black schools in Alabama from 1900 to 1930, when educational opportunities for black children in rural areas were dismal. Philanthropic foundations provided the one bright spot on the educational horizon for destitute rural blacks in the early twentieth century, and Bond devotes a chapter to the Peabody Fund, the Slater Fund, the Jeanes Fund, the Rosenwald Fund, and the General Education Board. Anticipating late-twentieth-century scholarship, Bond was critical of philanthropies' activities. Like Merle Curti in *Social Ideas*, Bond noted philanthropies' acquiescence in the racial status quo in Alabama. Their tendency to favor vocational rather than academic courses of study for blacks and to cultivate local white elites was a sure sign that any opportunity provided to blacks would have distinct limits.[44]

One thing that rural blacks could do to alleviate their plight was to move to the industrial cities of Alabama and the North. In Alabama, industrial development centered in Birmingham, where, as in *The Education of the Negro*, Bond found that genuine improvements in living and educational conditions were achieved by black workers, who benefited from company housing, schooling, and other welfare measures. However, that corporate assistance was at least partly industry's hedge against labor unrest. Here, again, Bond anticipated the views of contemporary historians of education.[45]

Bond's contribution to the historiography of education involved more than anticipating recent scholarship, however. The subtlety and complexity of his interpretations exemplified an admirable historical sophistication. A prime example of this interpretive virtuosity was in his chapter on Booker T. Washington. Bond began by warning his readers against simply adopting a great-man approach; rather than falling into the "common error of attributing momentous changes to the impress of a great personality" such as Washington, Bond contended that the lives of even admittedly great men "merely illumine the slow and sub-surface movements of human events." The bulk of the chapter illustrated the subsurface movements and factors that help to account for the accomplishments of the eminent Tuskegeean. Bond noted, as did Merle Curti, that Washington's personal influence in Alabama could not be considered apart from that of the white agent of the Peabody Fund, J. L. M. Curry. Bond carefully outlined Curry's conservative, privileged background and showed that Curry's commitment to philanthropic support of black education was never allowed to become a repudiation of his conservative political principles.[46]

Bond then showed that Washington's advocacy of industrial education for blacks was not a principled devotion to an innovative educational
philosophy; it was, instead, a means to accommodate black educational
development to the suspicions of Curry and other whites who felt that
blacks might one day seek opportunities equal to whites'. Bond argued
that what Washington learned at Hampton Institute was not industrial
education, but the fundamental moral lessons that Samuel Chapman Arm-
strong, Hampton's headmaster, sought to instill in his students. The industrial training Washington implemented at Tuskegee was, then, a matter of
moral discipline, an emphasis that was also the animating force behind the
classical curriculum at such institutions as Fisk and Atlanta universities.
This was a point that he also had made in his discussion of Washington in
The Education of the Negro. [47]

For Bond, the main difference between Tuskegee Institute and the traditional baccalaureate schools such as Fisk lay, not in their educational
schemes, but in their "fundamental attitude toward racial equalitarian-
ism." He contrasted Washington's circumspection in addressing this issue
with the actions of colleagues at Fisk and Atlanta, individuals described by
J. L. M. Curry as "misguided fanatics" who refused to compromise with
their environment.[48] Thus Bond characterized Washington's major failure as political rather than educational and as related to Washington's
dependence on whites such as Curry.

Bond's critique of Washington was not punctuated by any personal rancor. Anticipating modern-day apologists for the "wizard" of Tuskegee,
he acknowledged that, in terms of Washington's educational and political strategy of appealing to the dominant class of whites, "it is entirely
possible, of course, that no other strategy was feasible." Moreover, Bond
concluded his chapter on Washington by attempting to balance his largely
negative evaluation: he mentioned, on the positive side, the success of
Tuskegee Institute itself, the services provided by its many graduates, and
Washington's profound effect on public opinion. In fact, for Bond, Washington's claim to greatness rested more in the area of "thought, and feeling,
and opinion," than in any tangible accomplishments: "In his own time
Booker T. Washington was a vivid, towering personality; even in our time
he has become a legend. And who shall deny the importance of legends, as
social forces, in affecting the course of human history?"[49]

These sentences seem to make clear that Bond located Washington's
historical significance in his reputation rather than his accomplishments.
In his earlier treatment of Washington in *The Education of the Negro*, Bond

was still fair but more favorable than in *Negro Education*. In the earlier work, Bond stressed the educational accomplishments of Tuskegee Institute, which trained numerous teachers for black schools in the South, as providing testimony of the value of Washington's career. That approach was no doubt appropriate in a textbook that would be read by aspiring black teachers. In his scholarly historical study, however, Bond was free to provide the most critical evaluation of Washington that he would ever produce.[50]

Bond suggested that the final assessment of Washington would have to be made by a later generation of historians with access to tools sophisticated enough to deal with the areas of personality, thought, feeling, and opinion. And, indeed, the current generation has the benefit of Louis R. Harlan's magisterial works in forming its own judgments of Washington. Harlan examines the voluminous Washington papers to construct a sophisticated analysis that, while it makes use of much source material, that was unknown to Bond, on Washington's secret life, does not contradict the thrust of Bond's interpretation.[51]

It is thus quite clear that Bond made a respectable scholarly contribution to the study of Reconstruction history and the history of education. Yet Bond also made a major contribution to what has since become an important specialization: black history.

In black history, Horace Bond's work stands out as one of the premier studies in the early development of this specialty. By 1940, according to August Meier and Elliot Rudwick, eighteen doctoral degrees had been granted to black scholars in history or the history of education. Bond was one of the eighteen, and the publication of his dissertation, along with the publication of *The Education of the Negro in the American Social Order*, marked him as a scholar of great promise. Bond was among the few black historians who developed independently of the network created by Carter Woodson, founder of the Association for the Study of Negro Life and History. Though Woodson's publication of his dissertation brought Bond closer to the Woodson orbit, he never became part of the group and subject to the personal domination that Woodson could and did exercise over others' scholarship.[52]

When one considers Bond's contribution to black history, it is important to note that, despite his socioeconomic orientation, he never became a complete economic determinist. It would be extremely hard for a black scholar who faced the viciousness of racism in a variety of ways in his academic and personal life to adopt a mode of historical analysis that relegated discrimination to a minor role. What was creative in Bond's book was his combination of economic emphasis with racial sensitivity. This resulted in a work that rang truer to the complicated reality of the American experience than had the mechanistic economic analyses of slavery, the Civil War, and Reconstruction produced by scholars such as Charles A. Beard. Beard's emphasis on economics, to the exclusion of all other factors, could be, and was, easily twisted by southern apologists into an argument that the South's treatment of its black population was not an important issue. In contrast, Bond noted the failure of black and white farmers to join in a coalition based on their common economic interest during Reconstruction and, again, later in the nineteenth century, when agrarian movements were on the rise. In this instance, economic interest did not overcome racial antagonism.[53]

In writing about blacks and whites during Reconstruction and afterward, Bond encountered one issue that arises in all subspecialties of history but that is particularly thorny in black history: the problem of advocacy in scholarship. Black scholars have taken a number of approaches in dealing with what John Hope Franklin called one of the great dilemmas of the black American scholar. Most, as Franklin noted, engage in polemics to protest the humiliations they have endured in the white-dominated academic world.[54] Bond's position on the issue deserves the careful attention of those who wish to be both scholars and advocates. In an article published in the 1950s, he remarked: "I have long had the conviction, and now declare, that every scholar has the primary obligation, to whatever public his word may command, of announcing, by way of preface, where he stands ideologically." Of course, such forthrightness does not absolve the scholar of his commitment to fairness and the facts, but it does give the reader or listener a sense of his position and an orientation to what is to follow, and, as such, seems a useful practice for those who write about potentially controversial topics.[55]

As a doctoral student whose degree was dependent on the approval of a doctoral committee composed of white scholars, however, Bond decided that he could not take his own advice and state his own ideological predispositions in his dissertation. The preface to *Negro Education* is made up of acknowledgments to the various academics and librarians who helped him in his research. A careful reader will note, however, that Bond did indicate his orientation, though only subtly:

As a matter of pure sentiment, I should like to conclude these acknowledgments by referring to a Negro trusty known to me only as
Amos, who was in 1930–1932 attached to the Alabama State Department of Archives at Montgomery. By now I understand that Amos has
paid his debt to society, and presumably is working out his destiny as
a free member of the social order. By his thorough knowledge of the
materials in the Alabama Archives, and his unvarying solicitude for
the comfort of my wife and of myself, Amos remains as more than a
pleasant memory. He has been a constant source of inspiration in the
pursuit of this study.[56]

Bond's appreciation for and invocation of this black convict suggests that
his study of Alabama education for blacks involved more than a dispas-
sionate, scholarly rendering of the subject.

A careful reading of Bond's book will show that his commitments to the
cause of black freedom and progress were there, though not passionately
paraded. Like other works published in this era, such as J. Hugo Johnston's study of race relations in Virginia, Bond's work does not showcase
its ideological orientation. Instead, these works drove home their commitment through the force of their scholarship. Winthrop Jordan testified to
the attractiveness of this approach in his preface to the 1970 published edition of Johnston's 1925 thesis. In words that could easily apply to Horace
Mann Bond's *Negro Education in Alabama*, Jordan noted: "Some readers
today will find his discussion . . . too gentle, and lacking in appropriate
moral outrage. . . . It is precisely the attention to and respect for the 'facts'
which give this study its special value."[57]

After *Negro Education in Alabama* was published in 1939, Bond did not
produce another historical work until his history of Lincoln University
was published, posthumously, in 1976. He devoted the rest of his productive years to administration, serving as president at Fort Valley until
1945, as president of Lincoln University from 1945 to 1957, and as dean
of education at Atlanta University from 1957 until shortly before his retirement. Bond's withdrawal from research and publication was common
among black historians. Those who did not go into administration were
overwhelmed with heavy teaching and service duties at the black colleges
where they worked. In the middle decades of the twentieth century, with
the exception of the work of John Hope Franklin, Rayford Logan, and a

few others, black history was a field in which much of the work was done by white scholars.[58]

Bond did not abandon historical study completely, however. During his Lincoln years he developed and taught a course in African history and one in African-American history as part of his attempt to make African studies important in the Lincoln curriculum. In 1953, he responded to a call from the NAACP to participate in preparing a brief for the celebrated legal case *Brown* v. *Board of Education.* Working with John Hope Franklin, C. Vann Woodward, and other historians, Bond wrote a paper on Reconstruction-era educational legislation, and his work was used in the NAACP's answer to several questions posed by the Supreme Court. He also worked long and hard on his Lincoln history, almost from the time he became president of that institution in 1945.[59]

It must be marked as a tragedy in Horace Bond's career that, in the years after his dissertation was published, he was never free to follow his inclinations and talent for historical scholarship. As already suggested, the misfortune belonged not only to Bond but also to most of those inclined to scholarship in his generation. In the years of Bond's two college presidencies and his deanship, he never lost his desire to be involved in scholarship. That desire, however, would be fulfilled, at best, only partially and fitfully.

Chapter 7

Fort Valley President

Horace Bond overcame his initial reluctance and committed himself fully to the presidency at Fort Valley State College.[1] After six years there, he had taken the school from the status of a junior college to that of a comprehensive, baccalaureate-granting institution. In this process, he had become a respected spokesman for his college and the rural black constituency it served. He also had made his peace with the diverse nonscholarly tasks a president is expected to perform, and he mastered some of the arts of political manipulation, public relations, and bureaucratic maneuvering that were crucial to the success of a black college president in the Jim Crow South of the mid-twentieth century. At the same time he maintained his ties to the academic world beyond Fort Valley through contacts with more prestigious institutions such as Atlanta and Fisk universities. He also continued to publish in books and journals, though his efforts were distinctly less scholarly than they had been before; his publications were now devoted mainly to analyzing and promoting the activities and image of his college. As Fort Valley president, he also tried to respond to the crisis of World War II and its aftermath with a combination of mostly unsuccessful scholarly and programmatic initiatives.

By the time Bond left Fort Valley for the presidency of Lincoln University in the fall of 1945, he was a much more polished individual than he had been six years earlier. He was also drifting, though not without some regret, away from the scholarly accomplishments that he had achieved in the 1930s. In short, he had become a committed professional administrator who was also gaining a powerful voice within the segregated world of black higher education.

Acceding to the presidency of a public college in the Deep South was a step not to be taken lightly by any black academic. Although Bond had the support of a major philanthropic agency, the Julius Rosenwald Fund, which provided substantial funds to his college, much of his initial hesitancy in embracing the presidential role stemmed from his suspicion of the motives of white Georgians who would also have to support and contribute to his college. Of course, white Georgians were not all of the same mind regarding higher education for blacks; in fact, Fort Valley owed its existence to the fact that they were divided. A white supporter of black higher education, Walter D. Cocking, had been hired as dean of the College of Education at the University of Georgia in 1937. A year later, Cocking decried the woeful lack of opportunities provided in Georgia's two separate public black colleges. Partly because of Cocking's ideas, the Georgia Board of Regents decided to add the college at Fort Valley as a third black unit in the university system. Cocking had known of Bond and had worked with him in Tennessee, factors that may have persuaded the regents that Bond should be the president of the new black college.[2]

Bond knew, however, that support from a political body such as the board of regents in a Deep South state, where race could become an inflammatory issue at any time, might swiftly disappear in the heat of whatever new racial crisis or "incident" could be concocted by politicians. In addition, the reluctance of the board of regents to provide the funding that they had promised when they took Fort Valley into the university system increased his suspicion that their support was lukewarm at best. Perhaps because of his unease, Bond seemed to devote an inordinate amount of his time and attention to the pursuit of increased state funding, a task at which he was unsuccessful in the first few years of his tenure. At times he became so depressed about the lack of state support that he urged Rosenwald officials to consider reducing their own financial commitment to the college, a withdrawal designed to call the financial bluff of the regents and the chancellor of the university system.[3] In contrast, in the later years of his presidency, Bond would successfully engineer significant increases in state funding for his school and adopt a more sanguine view of its future.

Before that change in the financial fortunes of the college could take place, however, it and the other black units in the university system had to navigate through an extremely dangerous political situation. The major protagonist in this drama was Eugene Talmadge, then governor of Georgia. Known as "the Wild Man from Sugar Creek," Talmadge was the self-proclaimed spokesman for the wool-hat boys, the rural poor whites of the state, and he was certainly not above race baiting as a way to retain his popularity with his white constituents.[4]

In early 1941, Talmadge was invited to speak at Fort Valley in honor of a recently retired black educator and sometime Talmadge supporter. Much to Bond's surprise, the governor accepted; surprise, however, quickly turned to trepidation. Two events led Bond to expect trouble on the occasion of Talmadge's visit, scheduled for May 9, 1941. The black honoree whom the governor was to recognize in his speech died, removing what Bond thought was a moderating influence on what the white politician might say to his black audience. Also, just before his visit, Governor Talmadge had vetoed an appropriation for nearby Macon's training school for black girls, an action that removed any hospitality that the black students and citizens of Fort Valley might have been willing to extend to Talmadge. Bond became increasingly concerned about what kind of message this politician would send to his listeners and, just as importantly, about the response he would receive. The visit came off without incident, however; the fabled "populist" came, made a short, relatively innocuous talk, was given a reserved but polite response, and left the campus.[5]

One month later, an editorial in the *Atlanta Constitution* mentioned the governor's visit to Fort Valley in a criticism of his use of the race issue in his reelection campaign. Bond was afraid that, by publicizing Talmadge's visit to Fort Valley, the newspaper might provoke some type of reprisal against him or his school from the governor. Fortunately, nothing of the sort materialized, although Talmadge did go on to support punishment for those who advocated race mixing in his state's colleges.[6]

In November 1941, Talmadge moved to dismiss Walter Cocking from his deanship at the University of Georgia. In a full-page advertisement in the *Constitution*, the governor reported that the education dean had recently endorsed establishing a black school close to Athens, a school that whites could also attend. The ad quoted at length from a black-education conference that had been conducted by Cocking in 1938. Bond, who in that year was working on rural education in Tennessee, was cited by name in the advertisement and identified as an employee of the Rosenwald Fund. In many of his speeches Talmadge had pilloried the fund as a tool of the Jewish interests that financed it and that were behind its alleged program for race mixing in Georgia. Bond prepared for trouble. In his own mind, however, an occurrence during Talmadge's visit to Fort Valley saved the college from direct damage. It seems that the governor had been photographed, along with Bond and other black educators, on the steps of a building constructed with Rosenwald funds, and one of Talmadge's supporters in Fort Valley who was also a longtime supporter of the college told the governor of the existence of this photograph. Bond believed that Talmadge's fear of being shown in a biracial situation caused him to avoid any direct mention of the college at Fort Valley in his anti-race-mixing crusade. The governor did manage, however, to fire Cocking and another administrator at a white college on grounds that they had advocated racial "mongrelization."[7]

These moves backfired. The dismissals caused Georgia's university system to lose its accreditation with the Southern Association of Colleges and Secondary Schools, and this, in turn, was a major factor in Talmadge's defeat by Ellis Arnall in the 1942 gubernatorial election.[8] With Talmadge out of the way for at least the next few years, the regents moved to spend some money on the state's black colleges, confident that they would not suffer reprisals from the governor's office. This was the context for the upturn in state funding for Fort Valley State College that took place during the later years of Bond's presidency.

Statewide politics was not the only arena in which Bond had to be active. As president of the newest public college in the state of Georgia, he had to confront the competition for state funds among his own institution and the state's two other black colleges, the Georgia Industrial College, located in Savannah, and the Albany Normal School. At times, the presidents of the three institutions had to work together in the interest of educating the state's entire black population; but at other times, they each tried to influence the chancellor of the university system, the members of the board of regents, state legislators, and other local and state political figures in the interest of their individual colleges. When Bond arrived in the state, he approached his brother presidents carefully. The president at Savannah was a member of an old Georgia black family that had some influence in the state. The president at Albany was a supporter of Governor Talmadge who could possibly exert some influence on state-level decisions. Bond had few connections and little influence with the politicians; he could, however, look for support from the regents and chancellor who had hired him,[9] and they, in turn, were interested in the financial help the system could receive from the Rosenwald Fund and the General Education Board, agencies which had been and were heavily involved in sponsoring Bond's career.

Ostensibly at least, a division of labor existed among the three black colleges. Savannah had the major responsibility for trade, industrial, and agricultural education. Albany played a major role in teacher education for blacks in the rural regions of the state. Fort Valley was brought into the system with a mandate to do progressive work in teacher education for rural blacks. This arrangement put Bond's school in potential conflict with the other two institutions. Agricultural study would be involved in any genuinely experimental approach to teacher education for rural blacks, while innovation in rural teacher education was at least an implicit criticism of the program at Albany. The location at Fort Valley of a state supervisor of vocational education, who had a long history of conflict with the president of the college at Savannah, aggravated the situation. Bond tried initially to smooth over matters by stressing that Savannah would maintain all the teacher certification and degree work in vocational agriculture while Fort Valley would concentrate on "practical" agriculture. In home economics, Bond let the other two schools offer the only teacher-certification programs in the field. Fort Valley maintained a noncertification, degree program in home economics, thereby responding to the practical desires of many of the college's female students, who wanted to study something they would use in their later lives. This degree program also qualified Fort Valley for federal support in home economics.[10]

One might conclude that Bond was navigating through a political swamp in which dangers lurked at all times in all places. Yet he managed to steer Fort Valley successfully through the swamp, avoiding collisions and succeeding in building his college's financial support, enrollments, and faculty. To do this, he cultivated local Fort Valley whites who could be helpful to the college in state political battles, Rosenwald trustees who might have influence with such politicians as Governor Talmadge, and officers at the Rosenwald Fund who might be able to persuade the regents or the chancellor of the legitimacy of the college's claims.[11]

The fortunes of Fort Valley's college and its president improved after Governor Talmadge's defeat. His successor, Ellis Arnall, had promised that he would remove political influence from the board of regents, and Bond expected him to give the regents and the chancellor more autonomy in their conduct of the state's academic affairs. Immediately following Talmadge's defeat, the regents dismissed the Albany college's president, a Talmadge supporter, and installed in his place the registrar of Fort Valley State College.[12] Bond was thus free of the wily machinations of one of his most astute competitors; in addition, the successor to that individual owed his position, at least in part, to the influence of his superior at Fort Valley.

Bond had still another potential political rival in Rufus Clement, the president of the privately sponsored Atlanta University. The particular issue over which this competition might arise was graduate education. The *Gaines* v. *Canada* Supreme Court decision of the late 1930s forced the state of Missouri to provide separate professional education in the state's black college for a black plaintiff, rather than pay to have him educated out of state. This marked the beginning of southern states' realization that, if they wished to maintain their segregated systems of higher education, they would have to increase their support of black colleges so that black students could obtain graduate and professional degrees. Atlanta University, a private, graduate institution in the state's capital city, was the likely recipient of increased funding, although the state's public black colleges might be expected to bid for upgrading their programs to compete for more state dollars. Bond, however, thought that Atlanta, with its proximity to black liberal arts colleges and its existing strengths, was the obvious place for graduate study in the arts and sciences; in the areas of home economics and agriculture, the state colleges could be expected to develop graduate programs. Thus, when Atlanta University moved to offer more courses in home economics, Bond objected; generally, however, relations between the private institution and the public college in Fort Valley were cordial, a situation that could not have been hurt by the fact that Bond's brother Max was married to Clement's sister.[13]

By 1945, Fort Valley had built on its efforts in rural education to the point that it also offered degree programs in agriculture and home economics and looked forward to offering graduate programs in these fields, and Bond used the developing programs to rise to a position of influence in the organization of presidents of black land-grant colleges. Though Fort Valley was technically not a land-grant institution (that status belonged to the college at Savannah), its work in these two fields qualified its president to be a member of the group of presidents of black land-grant colleges. He quickly ascended to the presidency of the organization, a testimony

to his popularity among his fellow presidents as well as to the influence
he exerted through his connections with the Rosenwald Fund and the
General Education Board.[14]

Though he was frequently involved in the political intrigues that bedeviled
a black college president in the South, Bond did not allow these activities to deflect too much of his energy from the purpose for which he
came to Fort Valley State College. That purpose, in conformity with the
Rosenwald Fund's emphasis on rural education, was to institute innovative
teacher-education programs in rural Georgia.

  Bond's own experience in higher education, both as a student and as
a faculty member, had largely been in traditional institutions that emphasized the liberal arts. Lincoln University, the University of Chicago,
Dillard University, and Fisk University all shared a commitment to traditional studies. However, Bond's field — education — sought to distinguish
itself from traditional academic fields, in part by encouraging ideas and
programs that deviated from the norm and thus could be labeled as "progressive." Also, while working with the Rosenwald Fund in the 1930s,
Bond had had significant experience in rural educational experimentation.
Thus Bond came to Fort Valley as both a traditionalist and an innovator.
His actions in changing the curriculum and other aspects of the college at
Fort Valley would fortify both of those images.

  Shortly after accepting the presidency at Fort Valley, Bond was able to
persuade the board of regents to change the name of the school to one
that suggested more academic prestige. Not satisfied with the name Fort
Valley Normal and Industrial School, as the school was then named, Bond
proposed that the name be changed to Fort Valley State Teachers College.
Perhaps responding to the imperative of a post-*Gaines* world, the regents
went the president one better and approved the new name of Fort Valley
State College.[15]

  Whatever the new school was to be called, it was clear to all concerned
that the top priority for Bond's administration was to upgrade teacher
training. The chancellor of the university system stated this goal in a letter
to Bond on May 5, 1939, and the black educator's reply indicated both
his agreement and his desire to avoid "the training of specialized teachers . . . in the trades and industries." This latter emphasis was consistent
with Bond's own educational priorities; it also allowed him to avoid both
stepping on the toes of the college at Savannah, which stressed industrial

education, and conjuring negative connotations in the black intellectual
community of an approach that smacked of the accommodationism of
Booker T. Washington.[16]

Bond recognized the need to improve the training of the state's black
teachers. Shortly after coming to Georgia, he noted that the state's existing
complement of 6,500 black teachers was 3,500 short of the number needed
to educate all of its black children adequately. Further, those 6,500 possessed an average of considerably less than two years of college training.
Yet teacher training would not be the only objective of Bond's college: he
also wanted his graduates "to be able to find employment in a variety of
other occupational endeavors." He believed that the way to achieve this
versatility was, not to train students for particular jobs, but to pursue the
liberal goal of producing "young people of character, balance, intelligence,
and preparation. Fort Valley exists to discover such persons, and to help
them develop these and other personal qualities."[17]

In a speech to students, he stressed teacher education as the major objective of the college, while noting that work in high school teaching
and administration would also be offered. Preparation for subject-oriented
high school teaching, with its concentrations in teaching fields that were
also academic disciplines, meant that a distinctly more traditional program of study would be taking place alongside that of training elementary
teachers for rural areas. Also accompanying the work in teacher education
would be nondegree work in home economics as well as expanded coursework in English, the natural sciences, and the social sciences. What Bond
was suggesting was a range of studies wide enough to allow the college a
modest curricular diversification and its students a range of nonteaching
objectives. One might conclude that, within his teacher-training school,
Bond was creating a liberal arts college.[18]

From the beginning, however, Bond also sought to publicize the work at
Fort Valley as genuinely experimental and as fitting in with the programmatic priorities of the Rosenwald Fund. As he told one prospective faculty
member, "I envision the work as including a program of community study
integrating with the institutional instructional plans." And he took serious
steps to find out about the college from its constituents' point of view: a
little more than a year after becoming president, he developed a lengthy
questionnaire that explained the goals of the college and invited recipients' comments and suggestions on how those goals might be modified.
Bond sought respondents' opinions on the place of vocational training and

home economics in the curriculum as well as how the college might best train teachers for the rural schools. In addition, respondents were asked to answer two open-ended items that called on them to criticize, suggest, "or write anything about our program that you think we ought to make stronger, or give more stress to."[19]

The questionnaire noted that the college would strive to achieve the seven objectives that had been promulgated by Georgia's educational authorities in 1937: "Health, earning a living, citizenship, using what's around you, ability to make yourself understood by others, the spiritual life, educating others." These objectives intentionally deviated from subject matter, a change that was thought of as educationally progressive in the 1930s and 1940s. The deemphasis of subject matter could also be used to differentiate educational needs for blacks and whites. For example, Bond told Governor Talmadge's son, Herman, that science studies in black colleges should stress "the common health problems of Georgia Negroes such as Malaria, Tuberculosis, Syphilis, and the like," while in home economics the goal should be to "try to teach the students to use cheap and native materials for dress, furnishings, food, and the like; how to care for babies, how to prepare and select healthful food, etc." Bond also referred to a difference between blacks and whites in applying the objective of earning a living: "Inasmuch as Negroes are a very poor people, our concern here must take notice of this fact." Thus one sees how Fort Valley's education could simultaneously serve the rhetorical needs of educational experimentalism and the claims of white racism.[20]

Bond's experimentalism leaned heavily to the emphasis on efficiency and measurement then pervasive in the field of educational administration; it was largely silent on other parts of the progressive agenda, such as innovation inside of the classroom. Bond doggedly pursued the delineation and measuring of objectives at Fort Valley. He not only specified administrative and subject-matter objectives but also broke down the state's seven curricular objectives into 180 "activities objectives," which were to be achieved, for the most part, outside of formal courses. He made attainment of these objectives a requirement for graduation, and he vigorously publicized this innovation as "a genuine contribution to American educational administration" that "in the not far distant future will be widely adopted." He claimed that it represented a "unique approach to a fundamental problem," and he further noted that it was a key part of the school's response to the need for "life adjustment," a catchphrase of educational innovators in the 1940s.[21]

Bond also emphasized that, by living and farming together on campus, students at Fort Valley were learning practical skills in areas of study
such as agriculture. He gave this approach a catchy title, "Education for
Production," and publicized it widely in the state and elsewhere. He told
an official of the General Education Board that the program of education for production had been "a decisive factor in winning the support
of such people as the Governor, or certain key members of the Regents
and of other important public officials." Their support meant a substantial increase in state funding for the college in the last few years of his
presidency.[22]

Of course, it seemed that Bond was telling the whites that blacks wanted
to stay on the farm and in their places, a distinctly conservative message. It is not clear, however, that Bond believed completely in his own
rhetoric. Rather, he seemed to be a genius at packaging what he was
doing in ways that appealed to diverse audiences and constituencies. What
seems obvious in retrospect is that neither the activities objectives nor the
practical-agriculture experiences were the momentous accomplishments
that he touted them as being. They did illustrate, however, that he was not
a slavish devotee of traditional liberal arts education, just as he was not
a simpleminded advocate of the industrial education that southern whites
prescribed for "their" blacks.

At Fort Valley Bond resisted attempts to make the college into a trade
school or a "fancy pants liberal arts college." Instead, he tried to use innovative ideas to make the school speak to the students' life problems and also
to raise their expectations. He used the college's focus on teacher education
as a base from which to enlarge its curriculum, including its range of academic subjects, to allow students to get the benefits of study in the natural
sciences, humanities, and social sciences in addition to their occupational
focus on teaching. Yet he also stressed agriculture and home economics in
an effort to help his students survive and prosper. One might be tempted
to see in this last focus at Fort Valley a resemblance to Tuskegee Institute. However, this would be a misunderstanding of Bond's approach. He
never saw agriculture as the single viable path for all blacks, or even for all
of Fort Valley's students. The teacher-training focus of the school meant
that agricultural study was to train students in skills that they would use
in the rural schools in which they would work. Bond's reference several
years later to Fort Valley as "my little hick college in Georgia" reflected,
not so much a disdain for the college or its students, as a realization that
the college was not the center of the black educational universe.[23]

It was, however, Bond's own place in that educational universe. He turned all of his considerable abilities to making it a better institution than it had been when he arrived, according to both traditional and nontraditional criteria. While his commitment to progressivism and innovation might have meant a propensity for setting a myriad of objectives and organizational tinkering as well as a distinct facility for promoting these "innovations," it also reflected a real attempt to make the college responsive to the needs of its constituents. In addition, his vision for the school was one that would raise the sights of its constituents. In 1943, he responded to the regents' request for a plan for the future by sketching out a design for an institution that would accommodate fifteen hundred students in a variety of fields. The plan called for a college of services composed of five schools (health and physical education, business administration, rural life and education, agriculture, and home economics), a college of arts and sciences also composed of five schools (social science, natural and physical science, communication, fine arts, and, in homage to progressive education, the good life), and a graduate school that would offer degree work in rural studies, or education, sociology, and economics, as well as zoology, physical and health education, foods and nutrition, music, and social science. The programs in arts and sciences and in the graduate school testify to Bond's desires to offer more than just practical studies, which tended to confine students to the world of their immediate surroundings. Though Bond did not stay at Fort Valley long enough to see his plans realized, he seems to have left a school that was distinctly improved academically. It offered bachelor's degrees in three fields and the possibility of studying in several academic disciplines, alternatives that did not exist at the two-year institution when he began his tenure.[24]

One personal consequence of Bond's term at Fort Valley State College was a diminution of his research activity. He continued to publish, but the work was usually geared to the purpose of supporting programmatic or administrative objectives of the college rather than to contributing to knowledge in an academic field. Examples of the shift in focus can be found simply by considering the titles of some of Bond's articles from the period. Between 1940 and 1945 his published works included "Seven Aids to Getting a Good Job" and "Ham and Eggs: A History of the Fort Valley Ham and Egg Show."[25]

Bond sought wide circulation in national, professional journals for the innovations he promoted at Fort Valley. He submitted a substantial article on the activities objectives he developed for the college to *School and Society*, a periodical to which he had made several contributions. When its editor, William C. Bagley, turned down the article, Bond was so vigorous in refusing to accept the rejection that the journal ultimately relented and published a two-hundred-word "note" on the program. This compromise satisfied both Bond's desire to see his administrative ideas in print and the editor's judgment that the article was not strong enough to warrant publication in its entirety.[26]

The only book that Bond published in these years was a softcover volume, privately printed by the University of Georgia Press, which touted Fort Valley's innovation in agricultural education promoted in its title, *Education for Production*. The book described in detail the steps taken to involve Fort Valley students in the actual productive processes of farming, a method that was a marked contrast to the traditional mode of abstract learning.[27]

Bond dedicated the volume to the members of the Conference of Presidents of Negro Land-Grant Colleges. This group, made up of presidents of public, segregated colleges from southern and border states, had been much maligned for taking a largely "accommodationist" posture to the racist policies and politicians guiding their institutions and for confining their students to narrow curricula emphasizing vocational agriculture and other practical studies. While Bond was able to plan and produce a curriculum larger than what critics saw as typical of black land-grant colleges, his purpose in this publication was to defend the colleges and their presidents. He mentioned each president by name as well as the name of their institution, and, in the last paragraph of his dedication, he indicated his commitment to the value of the agricultural work at Fort Valley and his dismay at the criticism of the executives of similar colleges: "And so it is to these men and to their great, good works—maligned by many, understood by few, and truly appreciated by none—[that] . . . this book is joyously dedicated."[28]

While he was president of Fort Valley State College, Bond did make a few attempts at continuing his historical studies, though they were oriented to current crises more directly than his previous work had been. Responding to a request from a group at the Army Institute at the University of Wisconsin, Bond set to work on a study of the black soldier in African and American history which could be used in the indoctrination of black troops preparing for combat. He secured a small grant from the Rosenwald Fund to support the work and prepared a book-length manuscript. The army, however, demurred from publication, and Bond was left with a considerable amount of work that had gone for naught. He did manage to publish a portion of the manuscript in the *Journal of Negro Education*. The article, in a manner characteristic of the entire manuscript, did not involve primary research; rather, it depended upon already published secondary works, taking material from several of them and weaving it into a coherent narrative on the black soldier.[29]

Bond also published two other articles in the *Journal of Negro Education* during World War II; both analyzed the war's impact on the prospects of black citizens. As hostilities drew to a close, he spearheaded an attempt by the Conference of Presidents of Negro Land-Grant Colleges to secure funding for a project on the readjustment of black veterans. He wrote a proposal for support for the project, which he submitted to the General Education Board. Officers of the board found the proposal "grandiose, scopy, and [thought that it] would accomplish little," but suggested some changes and a resubmission. Bond complied, but the revised proposal was still turned down.[30]

This was not the first time Bond had been disappointed at a philanthropy's failure to support one of his projects. In 1940, he had asked the Rosenwald Fund for a short-term fellowship to facilitate the writing of his family's history, for he hoped to edit and add to the manuscript that his father had prepared over a decade earlier. The fund declined, however, noting that the request could not be granted under the regular terms of a fellowship and reminding its author of his heavy presidential duties. In 1944, he tried, again unsuccessfully, for a research grant from a Harvard University group that supported the work of promising young scholars.[31]

Though unable to obtain grants for original research in the Fort Valley years, Bond did manage to keep up some ties with the world of scholarship. During most of his residence at Fort Valley, he taught graduate courses in the social sciences at Atlanta University, making the one-hundred-mile trip to Georgia's capital on Saturday mornings to meet his classes. He also approached Charles Johnson to use Fort Valley as a laboratory for Fisk University's research in race relations and other areas.[32]

Also during his residence at Fort Valley, Bond received several offers to take administrative posts at more prestigious institutions. In 1941, the president of the North Carolina College for Negroes in Durham offered

Bond the post of graduate dean, noting that he was seeking a man of national reputation; when Bond turned down the offer, the president further noted that, because it existed in the shadow of Atlanta University, Fort Valley would always be an institution of limited horizons in graduate work. In 1944, when Atlanta University was looking for a graduate dean, both a white member of the board of trustees and the university president sought to entice Bond to take the position; he refused, however, claiming that his combative juices were being stirred by the sparring for funds and jockeying for favor from other black college presidents in Georgia. He stated that, while he did not want the graduate dean's job, he would consider a professorship such as that held by W. E. B. Du Bois, one that involved a significant commitment to research and fewer teaching responsibilities.[33]

While at Fort Valley, Bond did receive an occasional reprieve from his presidential duties, a welcome change of pace. For example, in the summer of 1944, he taught at the Garrett Biblical Institute, a seminary located on the campus of Northwestern University in Evanston, Illinois. Edwin Embree of the Rosenwald Fund had recommended Bond for the position, and, operating under the impetus given to minority studies by the publication of Gunnar Myrdal's *An American Dilemma*, Garrett hired the black scholar to teach a sociology course on the Negro in American life.[34]

The few disciplinary contributions to scholarship Bond made in these years were published in sociology, rather than history, journals. Early in his presidency he published two articles in important sociology journals; even here, however, he emphasized the problems and prospects of his black college and its students. The first of the articles used the emerging sociological terms of *caste* and *class* to analyze the situation of contemporary black youth such as those attending Fort Valley. One message of the article was that the analyst (sociologist) who would illumine the problems of black students must give way to the reformer (teacher) if Fort Valley, or any other black college, were to meet its responsibilities to its students.[35] The second article also focused on problems at Fort Valley and other black colleges. Bond stressed the attitudes that needed to be nurtured if black students were to overcome the environmental handicaps under which they labored. In this essay, he earned the enmity of several black intellectuals by referring to Negroes as a "permanent minority." Bond's critics were concerned that the image of the black minority as "permanent" could reinforce in black students the perception that they could not ameliorate their plight.[36] In his zeal to describe the conditions of blacks in poignant detail, Bond had used language that made these conditions inevitable and irremediable. The cultural utility of religion as a tool that blacks could use to battle their debilitating circumstances was a major theme of this article. This religious emphasis was foreign to the scholars who edited the *American Journal of Sociology*, where the article appeared; in fact, they advised Bond to delete several stories about religious zeal among blacks, because they were not "in keeping with the spirit of scholarship" that animated the other contributions to the issue. The journal had agreed to publish the essays offered to celebrate the seventy-fifth anniversary of Fisk University. One wonders if the commitment to Charles Johnson, editor of the volume, precluded the journal from turning down any of the contributions they deemed inappropriate, such as Horace Bond's essay.[37]

A religious emphasis was a staple of many of Bond's writings and speeches during his Fort Valley years. As mentioned earlier, however, Bond was not a particularly religious man. Though a minister, James Bond had undertaken the myriad secular duties demanded of black clergymen of his day, and, despite close ties between father and offspring, none of the sons followed James into the ministry. Horace was clear about his own lack of a formal religious commitment. Once, in a letter to Edwin Embree wherein he discussed his summer teaching position at the Garrett Biblical Institute, he remarked that he hoped to "conceal [his] lack of religion from the Theologs for at least five weeks."[38]

Despite his lack of a religious faith, Bond appreciated the positive outcomes that religion seemed to encourage in his young black students. He noticed that those at Fort Valley who were members of the "Sanctified," a local fundamentalist sect, refrained from alcohol and exhibited a strong personal discipline that carried over into their academic pursuits, for these religious enthusiasts were disproportionately represented among the better students at the college. He also remarked that the best reader in the elementary school at the college was one of the "Sanctified" and attributed this young man's ability to the rigorous regimen of Bible reading that characterized his home life. In short, religion fostered several cultural characteristics that were linked with academic success.[39]

There was also a psychological dimension to the positive outcomes that came with black religious faith. Mentioning William James, the empiricist philosopher who had written *The Will to Believe*, Bond described the special utility of faith for an oppressed people. Blacks, who were severely circumscribed in their present conditions, had a special faith in the future that was much harder for whites, who did not experience such privations, to experience. This special faith spilled over into the political arena. The principles enunciated in such phrases as "all men are created equal and are endowed by their Creator with certain inalienable rights" were attractive to religious blacks, fortifying their faith in a nation that refused to live up to them in practice. White recalcitrance on issues of racial equity could be interpreted by blacks as evidence that black citizens were the true Americans, while their white brethren were backsliders.[40]

Bond sought to build on these religious views by writing a book on the philosophy of education for minority groups. In it he attempted to foster in all of his students the strong religious faith that animated some of them. Though he never published this work, its emphasis was evident in an outline for a course on the philosophy of education that he taught at Fort Valley. The assigned readings for the class included several of the books of the Bible. Prefatory items noted two important aspects of the Bible: first, the King James version was "the foundation of our language. Read it and help yourself become literate"; second, Bible reading was important because "the Old Testament is the history of a minority race that has survived and flourished under endless oppression for three thousand years. Negroes ought to study the secret of their survival." This exhortation to study the Scriptures highlighted the religious connotation of Bond's term *permanent minority*. The course outline went on to mention other reading material that could be found on library reserve, including Bond's own "Five Essays toward a Philosophy of Education for Negroes."[41]

While these essays have not survived in the Bond papers, several speeches he gave during this period help us to understand his ideas. In them he makes explicit the parallel between the Jewish people of the Bible, who were and who remained a permanent minority, and American blacks. The story of the exodus of the Hebrews from their long Egyptian bondage was the theme of one of these speeches, wherein Bond addressed theological students and told them that their mission was to lead their own people out of Egypt. Yet the land that twentieth-century American blacks should leave was not a geographical place, but a psychological state: the despair that dominated many of them. They could combat this despair through a renewal of faith in themselves and in their future; they could will a better future by reinvigorating their faith in themselves and their future.[42]

In another talk, Bond concentrated on the Book of Job. He utilized the travails Job endured as examples analogous to what his own people were then facing. By studying the faith of Job and emulating Job's commitment to the Lord, blacks could find a basis for their own faith and overcome the evils then being foisted on them. Faith would prevent them from being overwhelmed by adversity and help them prepare for a better future. Without faith, blacks were almost sure to be overcome with bitterness and resentment at the conditions under which they were forced to live.[43]

In still another address, Bond expanded on what blacks could gain from faith in themselves. He urged students at Paine College in Augusta, Georgia, to concentrate, not on the slings and arrows whites aimed at them, but on their own failures of spirit and will. Only by faith in their own abilities could blacks prepare the ground for individual and racial achievement. Concentrating on discrimination would lead only to a fatalistic acquiescence in the current state of affairs; concentrating on positive achievements was the way to change things in the present and the future. Faith, then, the religious faith of the Old Testament Jews, was a proper model for American blacks.[44] And Horace Bond attempted to instill that faith in his students at Fort Valley through his classes in the philosophy of education, for he believed that, if future teachers could be imbued with the proper faith, they would in turn pass it on to their students. In this way, black youth would be taught a message of hope and saved from the counsel of despair.

Implicit in Bond's views was a profoundly conservative message. Ignoring white discrimination to focus on blacks' psychological health was a form of fatalism that condoned discrimination by making it seem an inevitable part of the world. And this seems to be the real issue behind the dispute Bond had with other black intellectuals over the term *permanent minority*. He utilized the phrase because it furthered his analogy between blacks and Jews, while his critics pointed out that his term fostered the perception that inferior status was ineradicable. Views such as Bond's provided evidence for Marxists who saw religion as the people's opium, a narcotic that numbed their awareness that their condition might be ameliorated by social and political activism.

Bond's position was understandable given the situation faced by the blacks of Fort Valley and the rest of Georgia, who could see no sign of respite from discrimination. In this case, we can say that the environment clearly shaped Bond's views. He genuinely empathized with the situation of Georgia's black citizens and tried to use their strong religious faith as a balm against the disease of racism. Had he not been in Georgia, it is unlikely that he would have propounded such a program.

For the first few years after Bond had left Fort Valley for Lincoln University, a Presbyterian institution in Pennsylvania with a theological seminary, he continued to use religious imagery in his speeches. However, the intent and execution of the message were distinctly different. In New York City in 1947, for example, in an address at a black church pastored by a Lincoln alumnus, Bond spoke on the theme of freedom, using a text from the New Testament book of the Acts of the Apostles to defend the activism of Lincoln students who were challenging segregation in the nearby town of Oxford, Pennsylvania.[45]

Even while he was still at Fort Valley, Bond could become politically aroused about racial issues in other parts of the nation. To a query from some black parents in Trenton, New Jersey, who were attempting to end segregation in that city's schools, he responded with a vigorous and sophisticated defense of integrated schools. In another instance, he lobbied the United States attorney general to appoint a Georgia judge who had a reputation for being a liberal on racial issues. He also wrote to Governor Dewey of New York to praise that state's passage of a law guaranteeing fair employment practices.[46] He undertook all of these activities, however, out of the public eye. As long as he was in the limelight in Georgia, he felt compelled to behave in a way that would not bring personal harm to him or his family or retaliation against his college.

In his role as president of Fort Valley State College, Bond acted as a practical college administrator, and it seems that his presidency altered his intellectual orientation toward the pragmatic and the practical and away from the scholarly. Though he had not embraced the role without some reservations, he did function quite successfully in the position. To amplify this point, let us consider the vicissitudes of his own attitude toward his presidency.

After less than a year in office, Bond betrayed his ambivalence in a letter to the president of Lincoln University. He remarked that he found the presidency "interesting," but full of a lot of "messy details" such as student discipline, and he regretted having "no time for 'scholarly' work of any kind." He added that he was working extremely hard, but, on the whole, he was enjoying his duties. He concluded that he had openings for several faculty and would be happy to fill those positions with qualified Lincoln graduates.[47]

Many black college presidents of this period earned the enmity of their faculties by the "dictatorial" nature of their governance. Though Bond

seems to have avoided such a reputation, he was not above commiserat-
ing with his colleagues: in a letter to the president of Albany State College, Bond remarked that the "no-good teachers" on a staff could make
life distinctly uncomfortable for the chief executive of a black college.[48]
The documentary record of Bond's Fort Valley presidency, however, indicates little antagonism between Bond and the faculty. This may be a
testament to his identification with the faculty's role and responsibilities,
even as he took on the duties of full-time administrator. He continued
to teach while he was president of Fort Valley and, later, of Lincoln, and
in Georgia his frequent interactions with faculty seemed pleasant. When
Fort Valley expanded its enrollment and degree offerings, he was able
to hire the instructors needed to handle the new loads, and he was thus
able to handpick a substantial number of the new teachers. Special problems did exist in hiring faculty in such nonacademic areas as agriculture
and home economics because of the state and federal agencies' interest
in these fields and who would teach them; here again, though, he managed to satisfy the outside agencies without unduly compromising his own
priorities.[49]

Bond often spent a great deal of time working on obtaining Rosenwald
or GEB fellowships so that his faculty could pursue graduate studies. This
was a pleasant task, since he could be reasonably confident that the philanthropies would follow his recommendations, and faculty members' success
in obtaining graduate degrees helped them, their president, and their institution. Shortly after arriving at Fort Valley, he spearheaded the adoption
of a set of statutes, modeled on the statutes at the University of Georgia, by
which his institution would be governed. He claimed that it was because
of the statutes, which codified the "rights, privileges, and limitations" of
faculty and administration, that he could report no disputes over tenure,
promotion, or salary in his six years there.[50]

Despite his success as president, Bond frequently seemed ready to give
up administration if he could find a faculty position that would enable him
to fulfill his scholarly desires without suffering an economic setback. As
already noted, he turned down the graduate deanship at Atlanta University,
seeking instead a chaired faculty position with research responsibilities. In
the summer of 1944, while teaching at Garrett, he responded to a request
for nominations for a faculty position in North Carolina by remarking
that he himself would be interested in the job, provided that it would give
him time for research and pay him a salary close to what he was making
as a president.[51] But teaching positions of that type and level of income

were not available at black colleges. Given this depressing fact, he decided that he would make his way in the administrative world for most of his academic career.

In 1945, when it came time for Bond to evaluate his Fort Valley presidency for the board of regents, as he was poised to take a similar position at Lincoln, he was able to provide facts and figures that documented the extent of his success in Georgia. The total income for the college had more than doubled since the first year of his presidency, increasing from $66,000 to $135,000. More importantly, especially in light of his concerns about a lack of state support early in his tenure, the state appropriation had increased more than threefold, from $21,000 to $67,000. Also, while the Rosenwald Fund's contribution had decreased by a third, an outcome that had been specified in the original agreement between the philanthropy and the state, income from student fees had quadrupled from $11,000 to $44,000. Given this jump, it is not surprising that enrollment almost quadrupled, rising from 114 in the year before Bond became president to 404 for the 1944–45 academic year.[52]

In his report, after recounting faculty activities in graduate study, publication, and professional organizations, Bond turned to the number of bachelor's degrees annually awarded, noting that graduates had doubled from 22 in 1941, the first year in which degrees were awarded, to 48 in 1945. He added that, in the next academic year, two new degrees would be offered, one each in agriculture and agricultural education, complementing the existing bachelor's programs in education and home economics.[53] In discussing the library, Bond stated that the number of volumes on hand had more than doubled from the 5,000 available at the beginning of his presidency in 1939 to 12,000 in 1945. He then detailed the substantial grant income that had been received from the Rosenwald Fund and other philanthropic agencies. He ended this discussion with an account of a $1,500 fund for student loans, a fund made up of contributions of one cent from each black schoolchild in the state. The point was that the college received support from both the largest and the smallest of potential givers. Bond closed with what must have seemed a staggeringly bold request for over $1 million in building funds for the college. He also requested $51,000 in new operating funds to support the new degree programs in agriculture, to hire new faculty, and to bring existing faculty in line with a recently adopted salary scale.[54]

Bond's report was the work of a confident college president who knew that he had done a good job with his institution. Its statistics testified to his command of the data needed to impress regents and other outside agencies. The language was crisp and clear; the plans for the future were set out in a factual, but subtly intimidating, manner. Bond observed that southern states had moved in recent years to shore up their black colleges, adding to their facilities and increasing the qualifications and salaries of faculty. Though he did not mention it, the legacy of the *Gaines* decision was being attended to throughout the South. If Georgia were to keep pace with other southern states and to avoid legal cases similar to *Gaines* (this was not stated, but the implication seems clear), Georgia would have to continue to increase its support for its black colleges. To stop now would ensure a troubled future.[55]

Given the record of success and the bright prospects for the future outlined in the report, Horace Bond's decision to leave Fort Valley State College deserves careful attention. He did not easily abandon a presidency where he was confident in his relations with philanthropists, state officials, faculty, and students.

Lincoln University was Bond's alma mater. At numerous times during his career, he indicated his affection for the institution where he had gone as a mere boy of fourteen and left as a young man of eighteen. He had also kept up a correspondence with Lincoln faculty and administrators as he pursued his doctorate and rose through the ranks of southern black colleges. He had negotiated for a faculty position at Lincoln during the 1930s and had been apprised of the coming vacancy in the Lincoln president's office early in his Fort Valley days. He had also received an honorary doctorate from Lincoln in the early 1940s. Further, Lincoln University's academic reputation meant that its presidency was more prestigious than that of a public teachers college in rural Georgia. Thus Bond had ample personal and professional reasons to want to return to Lincoln. The fact that Lincoln had never had a black president added to the challenge of the position and the prestige that would accrue to the first black who would hold it.[56]

Despite these many attractions, moving to Lincoln would mean that Bond would have to break his close ties to the Rosenwald Fund and the General Education Board. These two philanthropies made grants mainly to black colleges in the South, not usually to northern institutions such as Lincoln. Bond knew that. But he also knew that the Rosenwald Fund, in conformity with the directive of its founder, Julius Rosenwald, was to spend all of its assets and to liquidate its operations by 1948, twenty years after it was founded. Four years later, the GEB would cease its philanthropic efforts.[57]

Robert Labaree, one of Bond's former professors at Lincoln, had retired but had stayed in close touch with the school, and he urged Bond to leave Fort Valley to "escape the tyranny of the educational foundations."[58] This may have been an overly harsh judgment of the philanthropies' influence on Bond's career, yet it also seems to be true that the mid-1940s were an especially propitious time for a black scholar and administrator to declare his independence from his white philanthropic benefactors.

Relations with the Rosenwald Fund were still close, but a blot on the landscape had begun to appear in 1944. Fred Wale, the director of rural education for the fund, became concerned by what he perceived as an insufficiently practical bias on the part of President Bond and his faculty at Fort Valley. Bond had recommended only faculty for Rosenwald fellowships for graduate study, while a white Georgia college that also received Rosenwald support recommended rural teachers for such aid. In general, Fort Valley staff seemed reluctant to go off campus in their teacher education activities. To Wale this lack of community involvement was related to Bond's emphasis on developing a full collegiate program at Fort Valley. To drive home his displeasure, Wale told Bond that funds for faculty fellowships would be taken this time from existing Fort Valley accounts and would not be financed with new money.[59]

Later in that same year, Wale expressed his dissatisfaction with Bond to Edwin Embree, noting the need "to move him [Bond] and his staff off the college campus" and into the rural community surrounding the college. Wale added, "When this has been done, we shall begin to realize the investment we have already made in that institution." Fort Valley evidently did not heed Wale's recommendations, and he reiterated his criticisms in a lengthy report to Embree, recommending, "We [should] think of no more funds for Fort Valley than those remaining in the original grant." Wale also voiced his displeasure directly to Bond. He denied Rosenwald support for a salary supplement for a new faculty member brought to Fort Valley to begin degree work in agriculture, noting that the individual was not in the field of rural education. The conflict here was between Wale, a Rosenwald official with a distinct preference for the field over academic studies, and Bond, the Fort Valley president who wished to develop the collegiate, as well as the practical, side of his institution.[60]

Bond's difficulties appear to have been largely with Wale rather than with Embree, with whom relations remained cordial throughout the Fort Valley years. In 1942, when Embree was approached by Lincoln University about nominations for its forthcoming presidential vacancy, he named Bond and two others. He noted that Bond had done an outstanding job at Fort Valley and added, "Personally, I hope that nothing will take him from his present important post." When Bond did accept the Lincoln presidency in 1945, he took the position with Embree's final blessing. He had notified the Rosenwald official when he had received the offer from Lincoln, and Embree wrote to him, though briefly, to congratulate him when he accepted the job.[61]

Despite this amity, it seems likely that Embree shared at least some of Wale's displeasure with Bond. There is no evidence that he countermanded any of Wale's punitive financial directives, and Bond's unsuccessful attempt to secure Rosenwald support for Lincoln's building fund in 1946 may have been due, at least in part, to a chill in his relations with Embree. An exchange between the two men in the next year supports the notion that they had grown apart. In January 1947, Bond wrote to Embree seeking support for a Lincoln University student who had lost out on a Rhodes scholarship to study at Oxford. Bond suggested to Embree that racism was behind the student's rejection and sought Rosenwald funds to prove that a black could do as well as a white at the prestigious British university. Embree's answer both denied a grant for the young black and disputed Bond's contention that racism had influenced the Rhodes committee's decision.[62] The documentary record of their fifteen years of association before Bond's leaving Fort Valley reveals no exchange as sharp as this one.

However, potential or actual difficulties with the Rosenwald Fund and its officers do not seem to have been the only determining factor in Bond's decision to go to Lincoln. Two other factors were of the utmost importance in persuading him to leave Fort Valley. The first was concern for the future of his children. His daughter, born in 1939, and his first son, Horace Julian, born in 1940, were of school age. Shortly before receiving the offer from Lincoln, he and his wife had just had their third child, another son, James. The educational opportunities for the children in rural Georgia were inferior to those available in Pennsylvania, and Bond was reluctant to see his children handicapped in the beginning of their lives. He and his siblings had been schooled in the South, but at private institutions attached to universities near where his father worked; Fort Valley provided no such haven for the Bond offspring.[63]

There was also an issue of self-respect involved in the decision. Horace Bond was raised in the South and accustomed to southern race relations. But he also had lived in the North, where a black man did not face the routine possibility of physical violence and psychological intimidation at the hands of whites. The editor of a black Philadelphia newspaper explained to his readers that Bond left Georgia to escape "the heels of the oppressors constantly on his neck." Lincoln University, though certainly not set in an area free of racial problems, offered Bond "freedom" from "the chains which bind his mind and body in the sovereign state of Georgia." The article concluded that the South was "a veritable hell where few white men and no Negroes can live and keep their self-respect." The editor sent Bond a copy of the article, noting that it was also being sent to the governor and members of the Georgia Board of Regents. Bond replied to the editor that the article had had its desired effect, causing much consternation among the ranks of the Georgia officials who had received it.[64]

Bond's Fort Valley years contained several painful instances where he had to deal with racism in Georgia. He wrote a bitterly humorous account of Governor Talmadge's visit to Fort Valley that reveals the psychological twists and turns he underwent to get through that event. In that same year, he wrote a letter to his wife, who was spending the summer in Nashville, in which he described a black woman who had had the temerity to violate segregation by refusing to go to the rear of one of Fort Valley's shoe stores for service; she had remarked that it was cooler in the front of the store, a decidedly relevant consideration in middle Georgia in July. After being forced to leave, the woman met her husband, who returned to the store to investigate the situation. The husband discussed the matter with the store's clerk and then left. Shortly thereafter, the black man was accosted in the street by a policeman, who asked the clerk, "Is this the nigger?" The officer handcuffed the black man, dragged him "by his belt buckle" to a paddy wagon, took him to the police station, beat him, and placed him in a cell. The black man was booked for disorderly conduct and released after posting bond; his wife and child were also detained and brought to jail, though they were not charged. Bond ended this depressing account to his wife by noting: "This is our life."[65]

And so it was. The possibility that incidents such as this one could happen at any time to any black in Georgia was quite real. This reality was enough to entice any self-respecting individual, particularly one with a family to protect, to escape from the situation when a good opportunity presented itself. Lincoln University was just such an opportunity.

Chapter 8

Lincoln Again

When Bond accepted the presidency of Lincoln University, there were several reasons to be optimistic about his future there. An alumnus, he had made a name for himself as a scholar and educational leader since his graduation over two decades earlier. He had been a successful president at Fort Valley State College, and he was expected to continue that success at Lincoln. Further, and perhaps most importantly, he loved Lincoln University and had both a deep regard for many of its faculty and a clear appreciation for what it had accomplished for black people. In fact, he would write the university's history while he served as its president. Yet the twelve years Bond spent at Lincoln were, on the whole, not successful. After a few relatively placid years, he became embroiled in disputes with faculty and alumni groups, with whom he kept up an intermittent struggle until his departure in 1957. This chapter seeks to account for the discrepancy between the high expectations Bond and others set for his presidency at Lincoln University and the nagging controversies that marred his years there.

The story of his presidency is perversely complicated. This account of it is based mainly on the documentary record left by Bond himself, and thus it is subject to the weakness of presenting evidence primarily from his point of view. Interviews with faculty and others who served at Lincoln under Bond have provided some insight into the viewpoints of those who opposed him. While I do not claim a complete understanding of the events and forces that separated Bond from his opponents, I do think it is possible to understand the complexities of personality and belief that hampered Bond in his functioning as Lincoln's chief executive.

Until Bond's election, Lincoln had had only white presidents. Its board of trustees did not hire its first black member until the late 1920s, and its regular faculty was all white until 1932. Both the board and the faculty appointments were made at least partially in response to a 1920s student strike over the lack of blacks among the faculty and trustees.[1] In the early 1940s, with the retirement of president Walter L. Wright imminent, it became clear to Lincoln's alumni that the time was due—or, rather, over-due—for the appointment of a black president. The individual who would be chosen for the office would embark on a journey unprecedented in the history of Lincoln; however, the honor and prestige that would accrue to the first black president was expected to counterbalance the unknowns of his situation. Lincoln's historic status as a pioneer in the education of the black elite made it likely that its first black president would immediately be thrust into a leadership role in black higher education, and Bond was therefore not the only academician who found the position alluring.[2] Some of the black faculty already at Lincoln were particularly interested.

As Bond's name moved to the top of the list of presidential candidates, supporters of other contenders moved to head off his selection. Backers of a Lincoln faculty member, Laurence Foster, began to circulate among the members of Lincoln's board of trustees a rumor that Bond had a drinking problem.[3] Lincoln's historic relationship with the Presbyterian church, the Presbyterian seminary at the university, and the presence of many ortho-dox Presbyterians, most of whom were teetotalers, on the board of trustees as well as in both the college and seminary faculties, all meant that any presidential candidate who had a reputation as a drinker would not be acceptable.

A board member close to Bond who supported his candidacy apprised him of the situation, and the two men consulted on how to counter the rumor. They agreed on the strategy of having the board write directly to Charles S. Johnson of Fisk University and ask if Horace Bond had a drinking problem. In reply to this inquiry, Johnson first noted that rumors about personal problems were often a ploy that opponents used to prevent a particular individual from attaining high administrative office in black colleges. Johnson reassured the board that Bond was "not an alcoholic"; while he may have had a drink on occasion, in no sense could he be said to have a drinking problem.[4] Johnson's letter, along with some further lobby-ing on Bond's behalf by supportive alumni and board members, carried the day.

Lincoln's tenuous financial situation, a marked contrast to the healthy state of its academic reputation, presented a stiff challenge to the individual who assumed its presidency in 1945. The university lived from hand to mouth. Though tuition was low, many students stretched to pay even these fees. While endowment had once been substantial, it was raided over the years to cover deficits and had considerably eroded. Although the Presbyterian church was making a small contribution to Lincoln, it could not be expected to increase its support in the future. The state of Pennsylvania had recently begun to contribute some funds, but only on condition that the school admit Pennsylvania students on scholarship, and the expense of supporting these students consumed most of the state appropriation. According to W. E. B. Du Bois, Lincoln needed to raise substantially over $100,000 per year in new funds to do its work effectively. The main source for these contributions had to be the alumni.[5] Thus Bond's identity as a Lincoln graduate and active member of its alumni group was a factor in his election. His reputation as one who was well connected to philanthropic foundations also surely worked in his favor.

Bond was aware of these institutional difficulties when he accepted the Lincoln presidency. He told a fellow alumnus that although Lincoln's physical plant, faculty, and academic reputation clearly were superior to Fort Valley, the budgets of the two institutions were not very different; furthermore, faculty salaries at Fort Valley compared quite favorably with those at Lincoln. While Fort Valley was clearly on the upswing, the future of Lincoln was cloudy. State support for public black colleges was rising in the aftermath of the *Gaines* case, but private schools such as Lincoln faced an uncertain future as they searched for the funds with which to continue their work. Lincoln, like many other private black colleges, received support from the recently established United Negro College Fund (UNCF), but these funds were minimal. UNCF support was awarded on the basis of number of students; Lincoln, a men's school, had been hit much harder by enrollment losses during World War II than had coeducational colleges.[6]

When Bond described Lincoln as more "sophisticated" than Fort Valley, he surely was referring to differences in the level of preparation of both students and faculty.[7] Lincoln's students were much more likely to have come from urban, northern, and middle-class backgrounds than the youth who attended Fort Valley. Members of Lincoln's faculty were also likely to be better prepared academically and more experienced than their counterparts in Georgia. The faculty at Fort Valley, like that at Dillard, was completely black; in contrast, the Lincoln faculty was biracial. Further, while many of Fort Valley's faculty had owed their positions and their relatively good salaries to President Bond, the Lincoln faculty was largely in place when he arrived. Several of its white members had been his teachers when he had been a student there over twenty years earlier. These men especially were not likely to see President Bond as their leader; in fact, they were quite likely to feel paternalistic toward their new president. Also, black faculty members who had unsuccessfully competed with Bond for the office of president had reason to be cautious in dealing with their new superior.

Lincoln's curriculum, unlike Fort Valley's, was relatively fixed. Lincoln was a liberal arts institution with a course of study modeled on the nineteenth-century liberal arts college. Though it might be modified in part, it was likely to continue unchanged in its basics and its direction. The addition of new areas of study and graduate study, which had provided opportunities for the expansion of the faculty and the student body at Fort Valley, could not be expected to take place at Lincoln.

The seminary at Lincoln was also in some difficulty; the Presbyterian church had recently recommended against continuing its support, then gone back on its recommendation. The increasing secularization of American society in the years after World War II meant that theological study would become more and more tenuously related to the mainstream of American life, and even black American life, where clergymen had long been dominant. Black clergy were about to enter into an era of social and political activism, neither of which was a priority at Lincoln's seminary. The propriety of the church continuing to fund a seminary at an institution that received state funds was another problem both for Lincoln and the Presbyterians. The place of the seminary at Lincoln University was thus an issue that would plague Bond throughout his presidency.[8]

In short, Lincoln was a troubled institution when Horace Bond ascended to its presidency. Though he was aware of most of the troubles, Bond was young (he was not yet forty-one), vigorous, and experienced; he expected to meet successfully the challenges that Lincoln presented. Unfortunately, he was not able to overcome the myriad obstacles to success that both circumstances and individuals placed before him.

At first, however, Bond enthusiastically threw himself into his presidential duties and achieved considerable success. He managed to raise substantial funds from alumni, no doubt building on his own friendships and acquaintances, and in 1946 he reported that Lincoln had been able to raise $83,000 from alumni. In addition, enrollment was buoyed by the

surge of World War II veterans who came to the college to study with
the help of the GI Bill; Lincoln had to obtain buildings from the army
to help it deal with its increased enrollment. The army veterans were a
mixed blessing, however; their presence intensified needs for dormitories
and academic buildings at Lincoln, as well as for more faculty and housing
for their teachers.[9] While white faculty could easily reside in the area surrounding Lincoln, blacks were forced to live on campus, for the rural area
of southeastern Pennsylvania, where Lincoln was located, was lily-white.
Neither finances nor faculty, however, provided the earliest sign that the
new president might not have smooth sailing. That came from the alumni,
a group from which President Bond might have expected support. Shortly
after his acceptance of the position was announced, and three months
before he would arrive on campus, Bond received letters from alumni
complaining about the athletic program at Lincoln. One went so far as to
advocate firing the head football coach, since he had produced losing sea-
sons, though blessed with good material.[10] Bond responded that while he,
too, "had an abiding enthusiasm for athletics, especially for football and
track," he could not assess the state of the athletic program until he arrived
on the campus. He added that he knew that Lincoln's ability to recruit
good athletes was hampered by its high academic standards and that he
was not interested in tampering with those standards; he also opined that
competitive athletic teams would result without a lowering of standards or
an increase in scholarship aid if enrollment could reach and stabilize at the
level of four hundred students.[11]

This assessment and prediction proved to be overly rosy. Bond was
dogged by alumni complaints about the athletic program throughout his
presidency. The teams compiled mediocre records, a far cry from the glory
days, early in the twentieth century, when Lincoln had been a power in
black athletics. The situation seems not to have been due to a failure in
coaching or presidential leadership; Lincoln had to compete athletically
with schools such as Morgan State College in Maryland and Virginia State
College, public institutions with large enrollments and increased support
for their athletic teams from their state governments.[12]

Athletics was not the only arena in which Bond ran afoul of alumni.
He heard from several alumni who complained that their sons, or the
sons of close friends, had been denied admission because of poor academic
records.[13] In fact, through Bond's entire term as president, Lincoln alumni
felt free to write the president, and to expect an answer, regarding any

aspect of the university's life in which they were interested or any policy or personnel that they felt needed changing.

A few years into his presidency, Bond came into direct conflict with the alumni association through a dispute with a group of alumni wives. The ladies' auxiliary of the alumni association wished to construct on campus a guest house for visiting alumni, for the dearth of off-campus establishments where blacks were welcome meant that an on-campus social facility was sorely needed. The women, however, evidently proceeded with their plans without consulting the president. Annoyed, Bond attempted to stop the guest house project, but he was not successful. He also tried to suggest other possible areas of concern or activity to the women's group, but here, too, he failed to shape an agenda that would have had the group work under his direction.[14]

In the midst of the controversy, Bond explained to one of his closest friends, who was also an alumnus, that the problem stemmed from the tradition of independence from the college's administration on the part of both the alumni association and its women's group. The desire for independence dated back to the earliest days of the college, when black alumni confronted a succession of white presidents who refused to accede to their demands for black faculty and board members. Bond thought that, now that alumni had considerable representation on the board of trustees and had influenced the selection of a black man to head the school, their official body should be incorporated into the institution's formal chain of command. And the ladies' auxiliary, a sister organization to the alumni association, ought not to proceed with plans without the approval of the college president.[15]

Bond was not opposed to the guest house itself; in fact, its completion meant that functions formerly held at the president's house could now take place at the new facility, a considerable relief for the president and his wife. However, Bond was not able to distinguish the building from the threatening organizational context in which he located it. He also seems to have been naive to expect an alumni association in the well-established habit of intervening in the college's affairs to refrain from doing so now that Lincoln had a black president.

Three years after this episode, the ladies' auxiliary was still a thorn in the president's side. This time, discontent among the women was fueled, according to Bond, by the wife of a black faculty member who had presidential aspirations. Bond did his best to placate the ladies' auxiliary, but never with any substantial success. His own wife, burdened with three young children, felt little inclination to get involved in the affairs and intrigues of the alumni wives, and he was supportive of her desires. While some of the trouble may well have been due to ambitious faculty wives, part of the difficulty must also be attributed to President Bond's inability to persuade the ladies' auxiliary to support his leadership.[16]

Bond's early problems with alumni and their wives were echoed in his relations with the Lincoln faculty, and particularly with its older members. Lincoln's teachers were experiencing the ravages of significant inflation in the post–World War II years, and Bond's failure to raise their salaries accordingly caused resentment. When he instituted a yearly letter of annual appointment, even for tenured faculty, senior professors questioned the president's motives. He also clashed with faculty over the issue of summer pay, claiming that their regular contracts already covered the summer months and that they therefore should teach without additional pay.[17]

Bond's own analysis of his friction with the faculty ignored these economic problems and focused on race. From that perspective, he insightfully analyzed many of the problems faculty had in dealing with their new black president. He noted that the faculty itself was going through a period of adjustment, as it metamorphosed from an almost completely white body to one almost evenly split between blacks and whites. For whites this meant meeting black colleagues as equals, a situation that presented difficulties even for those who had professed their long-term commitment to black betterment by staying at Lincoln throughout their academic careers. Having to deal with the beneficiaries of one's largesse was a new situation that tested the white faculty's commitments and beliefs. Black faculty, on the other hand, had to face the isolation of living in a predominantly white area, which, despite the presence of a black college, was intent on maintaining segregation in its public schools and other aspects of its community life. Since most Lincoln faculty, and all of its blacks, lived on campus, potential for racial strife was exaggerated by the continued proximity that inevitably turned little incidents into major problems.[18] Bond's analyses of these situations were invariably astute and subtle, but his attempts to ameliorate them were too often ineffective.

For example, he, along with other black faculty members, vigorously pursued a school desegregation suit against the village in which the Lincoln University community was located. They did so, however, without realizing that some white Lincoln faculty were not as concerned about the school desegregation issue as they were with the resentment of the community's whites who saw white faculty members as allies of the black agitators. While winning the lawsuit meant that black faculty could send their children to desegregated public schools, white faculty faced the loss of long-standing personal relationships with some whites in the local community.[19] This is not meant to justify the position of the white faculty, but rather to point out the unpleasant ramifications that issues of race could provoke both on and off the campus.

The main point to be made, however, is that Bond allowed his very real concerns about racial dynamics among faculty and between town and gown to obscure larger economic realities. Black faculty were suffering just as much as whites from economic problems. While some of them might still be coveting the president's job, as Bond believed, they were also as upset as their white colleagues with their president's failure to address their economic grievances.[20]

Harold Fetter Grim, a professor who had taught Bond biology in the early 1920s, was one of the most severe critics of his presidency. Grim had come to Lincoln at a very young age, shortly after his graduation from nearby Lafayette College. The Lincoln University class of 1923, Bond's own class, dedicated its yearbook to the vital young biologist, who was extremely popular among the many students who took his biology classes as a prerequisite to subsequent studies in medical school. By 1945, Grim had become an institution at Lincoln, having served on its faculty for almost four decades. His prominence was recognized when Lincoln University made him secretary to the board of trustees and President Bond had him appointed to the largely honorific office of dean of the university.[21]

Grim took in the affairs of Lincoln University an almost proprietary interest, one that was intimately related to his long-term efforts as a benefactor of the black race. Grim was not averse to lecturing Lincoln students and alumni on the appropriate ways for them to behave. For example, in late 1947, he sent to Lincoln alumni a letter alerting them to be on their best behavior at the upcoming Lincoln-Howard football game, to be held at the stadium of Temple University in Philadelphia. He told alumni that they, along with their Howard counterparts, would be "on trial" during the game and that their citizenship would be evaluated by officials from the state of Pennsylvania as well as those from Temple University and from Philadelphia. Provoked, alumni protested Grim's letter to the president, and Bond assured the alumni that the dean of the university spoke only for himself and that he had recently been asked to clear all public statements about the university or to the university community with the president. But Grim was not likely to be restrained by a slap on the wrist from a president who had been one of his students. As Bond's presidency wore on, he came to perceive Grim as an implacable opponent.[22]

In addition, other faculty, mostly older men, felt just as free as Grim did to go over the president's head in a variety of ways, which distressed Bond throughout his presidency. He was not opposed to faculty involvement in the institution's affairs; in fact, early in his tenure, the university passed its first set of statutes, in which relationships and prerogatives of faculty were directly addressed. But, less than three years afterward, Bond expressed his dismay to the board of trustees at the tendency of deans and faculty members to approach the board directly, rather than through the president.[23]

By the beginning of the 1949–50 academic year, Bond's difficulties were aggravated by a decline in enrollment as the number of veterans returning to school diminished. He continued to be plagued by problems with faculty and discontent among the alumni and in the ladies' auxiliary. He attributed his alumni problems to faculty at Lincoln who sought support for their own presidential aspirations; however, even Bond's supporters among the alumni told him that the problems were greater than the desire of some faculty to succeed him.[24]

After his first four years at Lincoln, Bond's frustration surfaced in an exchange of letters with Harold Grim in late 1949. No doubt motivated by the salary grievances he and other professors harbored, Grim wrote to Bond, questioning the profligacy of the travel expenses of the president as well as another black administrator. Trying to conciliate Grim, Bond echoed Grim's concern over the university's financial situation. The president noted that he had personally absorbed a significant amount of university-related expenses, which had left his own financial situation considerably worse than it was when he had come to Lincoln. He then related how his efforts to regularize Lincoln's various expense accounts had led to charges that he was "a busy-body, a tyrant, a slanderer." He concluded that, while he had always been meticulous in accounting for his own expenditures, "four years of continued criticism—suspicions—etc.—from certain trustees, faculty members, students—alumni—have of course taken something . . . out of me."[25]

Bond's early problems with alumni and faculty contributed to a distinct sense of unease in his presidential role at Lincoln. In February 1949, in the fourth year of his presidency, he spoke of his ambivalence about administrative work and his desire to return to teaching. Later in that same month, he told an old friend from undergraduate days that he was dissatisfied with administration. He again expressed a desire to return to teaching and summarized his experience at Lincoln in the following plaintive note: "There is no percentage in administration. You work like the dickens—for nothing—and then all you can expect is a lot of griping from day to day and finally some nut or accumulation of nuts puts you out on your ear." However, Bond did not now act on his desire to abandon the presidency and seek a faculty position, perhaps because he was aware that he would have to shoulder a substantial cut in salary if he were to teach.[26]

Later in 1949, instead of moving to address the issues raised by his alumni and faculty critics, Bond made plans for the first of many trips to western Africa. He would make at least ten more visits to Africa in the next eight years. These trips provided an outlet for Bond, a way to escape from internal problems at Lincoln, but they did not provide a solution for these problems. In fact, his interest in African affairs and African students, increasing numbers of whom would come to Lincoln during his presidency, were resented by some Lincoln faculty and students. They felt that his affinity for African students and African studies pulled his attention away from very real problems that existed for faculty and American students on campus. This resentment increased when, in 1950, Bond established an Institute of African Studies at Lincoln and encouraged more African students to come there to study. In fact, African studies would be the one area at Lincoln in which substantial curricular additions were made during Bond's presidency. Thus, although Bond's interest and activities in African affairs helped him to avoid being consumed by his Lincoln problems, they did nothing to alleviate these problems, and eventually they exacerbated them.[27]

The last seven years of Bond's Lincoln presidency, from 1950 to 1957, proved even more harrowing than the first five. He continued to run up against faculty and alumni, particularly Harold Grim. Bond's problems with different segments of the Lincoln community were intensified by the marked decline in enrollment that struck the institution during the Korean War. As it had during World War II, Lincoln University experienced a decrease in overall enrollment that far exceeded the decline in coeducational colleges.

Though Bond's worst problems with the faculty often emanated from older members who had been at Lincoln when he arrived, at times he also managed to alienate younger members through his bluntness and reserve. For example, in a letter to a professor who was on leave, Bond began by informing the young teacher that he had a job for the coming year but added that, since he had complained so much about campus conditions, he was hurting the morale of the students and should seriously consider whether or not he wanted to come back to Lincoln. The faculty member's eventual decision not to return could not have surprised Bond. Presidential actions such as these, combined with Bond's lifelong difficulty in developing easy and relaxed personal relations, quite likely intensified ruptures between the faculty and the administration.[28]

In 1951, several faculty members sent to the board of trustees a petition seeking faculty representation on that body. A letter from an older white faculty member to one of the alumni on the board explained the impetus behind the petition, including the allegation that twenty-eight teachers had resigned in the past three years because of the high-handed ways of the president. A new note also crept into the battle between the president and dissident faculty when there surfaced a rumor that Bond was anti-Semitic, since several of the faculty who had left were Jewish.[29]

It is difficult to judge how much each of these issues contributed to general faculty disenchantment. Bond himself attributed the discontent to the usual cabal of a few older white men who had had it in for him since he came to Lincoln. They had managed to make ordinary instances, such as the comings and goings of part-time faculty or faculty hired temporarily to replace permanent faculty who were on leave, into examples of presidential tyranny. As for Bond's anti-Semitism, the fact that he was the first Lincoln president to hire a Jew and that he hired several more Jews during his presidency lends credence to his denial of the charge and his contention that it was simply one more weapon wielded by his opponents.[30]

Late in 1950, the board of trustees, smarting under financial and enrollment reverses, voted to release the president from his on-campus duties. Bond was to devote considerable time to writing his history of Lincoln and to fund-raising among alumni for the Lincoln University centennial, which was to be celebrated in 1954. The board simultaneously approved a proposal to hire a vice-president to manage on-campus affairs. Bond, after initially agreeing to offer the vice-presidency to a white former faculty member, vetoed the plan when the candidate decided not to accept the position. Bond attributed the proposal for a vice-president to his spending too much time away from campus, thus enabling the few but powerful dissidents to foment unrest and enlist recruits in their vendetta against him. In his mind, the vice-presidential plan was strictly the result of the disaffected group's lobbying; it did not relate to any deficiencies in his performance as president.[31]

Bond was at least partially correct. Yet his treatment of black faculty, even some whom he had no cause to consider enemies, fed the fires of faculty dissidence. In 1953, John A. Davis, a black who had served as a professor of political science at Lincoln since the 1930s, was surprised to find President Bond urging the board of trustees not to grant an extension of his leave of absence. Davis had been away from campus for several years, but returned in 1952–53. When he sought leave for the next year to try out a faculty position at a white New York college, the president urged the board to refuse, and it did. Bond surely had institutional reasons to recommend against Davis's taking another leave, but his personal loyalties to Davis and his awareness of the political reaction that might come from other faculty members should have cautioned him against opposing it publicly. But straightforward, blunt language and public recommendations were Bond's style, a style that did not endear him to many of his faculty.[32]

Bond also made little progress in solving the faculty's salary and employment grievances, which had plagued his presidency from its earliest years. In 1952, he had to urge Lincoln's dean to make sure that recommendations on faculty performance be turned in soon so that the previous year's "accusations that appointments and announcements of reappointments had been delayed for too long a period" might not be repeated. Later in that same year, the Lincoln University faculty sent a note to the head of the board of trustees and sought $200 that President Bond had withheld from the $500 raise approved by the board. Even if he had good reasons for not disbursing the money, the president did not communicate them successfully.[33]

By the 1952–53 academic year, the board of trustees had approved the election of two Lincoln faculty to its membership. Bond had objected to this because he thought that the faculty pushing it were recalcitrant whites who were against the best interests of the black students of Lincoln University. Once the plan was approved, faculty-administration wrangling shifted to Bond's new plan to substitute, for the vice-president that the board had earlier endorsed, an assistant to the president. This individual would be mainly responsible for raising funds for the centennial campaign from alumni, and he therefore would most likely be a black alumnus. Bond had in mind for this position a Lincoln graduate who was then on the faculty of a black college in Missouri, and he wanted to include faculty rank in the English department as part of his offer. Faculty objected to this stipulation, but Bond had his way with the trustees.[34]

In 1953–54, the focus of faculty-president bickering shifted to the library. Bond proposed to pay two faculty wives who were employed in the library $500 less in salary, since they resided with their spouses in university-subsidized, on-campus housing. Bond persisted in this seemingly harebrained scheme until the weight of faculty objections, or, perhaps, fundamental fairness, caused him to reconsider. Jobs in the library for wives of faculty members were one perquisite that Lincoln faculty could point to as a compensation for their geographic isolation and economic burdens. The fact that one of the two wives in question was the spouse of one of his bitterest enemies on the faculty may have had something to do with Bond's doggedness in the matter. Even as he rescinded the plan, Bond claimed that he was correct in principle and that he gave in only because he had no chance to prevail.[35]

In May 1952, in the midst of his continuing difficulties with the faculty, Bond's problems with the alumni resurfaced, this time sparked by a resolution, emanating from the Detroit chapter, that attributed the ongoing difficulties between the president and the faculty to the "dictatorial policy" of the Lincoln administration. The president of the Detroit alumni chapter, William Molbon, a minister, had recently been invited to the campus as part of a program on religion, and while there he delivered a speech in which he criticized the state of religion at Lincoln and bemoaned the decline of Lincoln's seminary.[36]

The Lincoln University of the 1950s, supported much less by the Presbyterian church and much more by the state of Pennsylvania than before, was a distinctly more secular school than it had been twenty or thirty years earlier. Moreover, President Bond did not share the commitment to sectarian religion of his white predecessors, almost all of whom were ordained Presbyterian ministers. In fact, in 1945, before coming to Lincoln, he had tried to persuade his predecessor that the compulsory chapel program at Lincoln, a clearly denominational Presbyterian enterprise, could be turned into a more secular educational experience. Four years later, Bond sought to institute for Sunday mornings an earlier chapel service characterized

Horace Mann Bond (courtesy of Mrs. Julia W. Bond)

Bond, circa 1930, at work for the Rosenwald Fund, a philanthropic foundation
that supported the establishment and improvement of southern black colleges
(Archives, University Library, University of Massachusetts/Amherst)

Bond with sociologist Robert Park (center) and Lewis Wade Jones (right), circa 1935, at Dillard University, New Orleans (courtesy of Mrs. Julia W. Bond)

Bond with Governor Eugene Talmadge (third from right) and entourage, May 1941, Fort Valley State College, Fort Valley, Georgia (Archives, University Library, University of Massachusetts/Amherst)

Above: Horace Bond, W. E. B. Du Bois (left), and E. Franklin Frazier (center)
with Bond's children Julian and Jane. This photograph was occasioned by the
induction of the Bond children into the "estate of the Scholar," March 14, 1942.
Facing page: A reproduction of the document signed during the ceremony
pictured above. (Archives, University Library, University of
Massachusetts/Amherst)

KNOW ALL MEN BY THESE PRESENTS—

That the estate of a Scholar is an ancient and honorable one, known of olden times, and in each generation, even in the times of distress and human misery and wretchedness, a refuge and a haven for the souls of men—
And that for the good of humankind such an estate should not be allowed to perish from the earth, but that each generation of Man should find among their number some who shall cleave unto that honorable estate—

AND IN TESTIMONY WHEREOF WE HAVE TODAY

consecrated Horace Julian Bond to the high and noble estate of the Scholar, to the end that he may in all of his life diligently seek the truth, and worthily set himself to communicating truth to his fellow man—

And this we have done by breaking with him a common bread in representation of the humble fare which a Scholar needs must partake that he may give himself without stint to his high calling—

And this we have done by drinking with him pure water in representation of the purity and self-denial to which the Scholar must pledge himself

So have we also consecrated Jane Marguerite Bond that she may be a scholar and a mother of Scholars for the benefit of future generations, to the end of time.

IN WITNESS WHEREOF WE HAVE AFFIXED OUR HANDS THIS FOURTEENTH DAY OF MARCH, IN THE YEAR OF OUR LORD NINETEEN HUNDRED AND FORTY TWO

[W. E. B. Du Bois (PhD. Harv.)]
Scholar

[E. Franklin Frazier (PhD. Chicago)]
Scholar

[Julia W. Bond]
Witness

[Horace Mann Bond]
Witness

Above: Bond (second from left) and Fort Valley State colleagues at a radio broadcast devoted to the Fort Valley program of studies, March 10, 1945 (Archives, University Library, University of Massachusetts/Amherst)

Right: Bond in Africa, October 1949 (Archives, University Library, University of Massachusetts/Amherst)

Bond (right) with Robert Park (left) and Charles S. Johnson, sociologist and editor of *Opportunity*, the official organ of the Urban League (Archives, University Library, University of Massachusetts/Amherst)

The Bond family: Julia, James, Julian, Jane, Horace (courtesy of Mrs. Julia W. Bond)

Above: Bond with John A. Davis (left) and Nnamdi Azikiwe (center), Lagos, Nigeria, 1961. Bond and Davis, former Lincoln University colleagues, were cofounders of the American Society for African Culture; Azikiwe, a Lincoln alumnus, became the first president of the Republic of Nigeria in 1963. (Archives, University Library, University of Massachusetts/ Amherst)

Right: Bond (left) and President Kwame Nkrumah of Ghana, circa November 1963 (Archives, University Library, University of Massachusetts/Amherst)

by a more "flexible" approach, such as his own Congregationalism. The existing eleven o'clock service would remain the property of the orthodox Presbyterians.[37]

Despite his religious liberalism, Bond failed to meet head on the sectarian orthodoxy that dominated certain parts of the campus, and particularly the seminary. He would not dispute Presbyterian control over the main chapel service, just as he could not bring himself to discontinue the seminary, which had become a financial drain on the university as well as a possible legal problem for an institution that accepted state aid. Bond's failure to act decisively on the seminary issue may have clouded his vision of the Detroit alumni resolution. Although the resolution did not refer to the religion issue, Bond was convinced that religion was in fact behind the resolution.[38]

In Bond's opinion, the main impetus for the Detroit resolution came from the dissatisfied older white faculty, who could find allies among some Lincoln alumni who had always deferred to their white benefactors on the faculty. He spelled out these relationships in letters to various alumni who supported him or were not active in the opposition. He made much of the older faculty who had opposed appointing blacks as teachers in the 1920s and of the poll of the student body conducted in that decade in which a clear majority of the students opposed appointing black faculty. It was these cowardly students who were now active as alumni and who were criticizing constantly, and unfairly, the performance of the first black president of Lincoln University.[39]

Bond vigorously countered the alumni resolution. He distributed it to all faculty and administrators at Lincoln for their response and sought to confront Molbon with the report's errors about the number of doctors of philosophy on the Lincoln faculty. None of this seemed to quell discontent among alumni in the Detroit chapter and in several others. Bond attributed much of the alumni's opposition to the fact that he had refused to certify an insurance document stating that the national president of the Lincoln alumni was two years younger than he actually was, an action that significantly increased insurance premiums for that alumnus.[40]

What seems evident here is Bond's consistent tendency to associate criticism of himself with unrelated issues and thereby to ignore the substance of the criticism. White faculty critics were racists; black faculty critics sought his job; alumni critics were disgruntled sectarians or individuals whose bidding he had been unwilling to do.

Alumni opposition to President Bond culminated in an alumni association study of the university, completed in 1956. Bond initially tried to
cooperate by seeking outside support for a thorough look at the institution.
When he became convinced that the alumni were out, not to study his administration, but to pursue a vendetta against him, he changed his tack and
became a grudging participant. The eventual "study" was a report by only
one alumnus, an official at another black college. Bond condemned the
study for its erroneous conclusions about the quality and the attrition rate
of the student body, and he questioned the ability of its author to conduct
a genuinely objective, scientific analysis of the situation at Lincoln. The
copy of the alumni study preserved in the Bond Papers is peppered with
Bond's notations and circling of such words as *seems, approximately, possibly,*
and other hazy generalities that he thought supported his conclusion that
the object of the study was simply to malign him. He ignored completely
the possible validity of any of the criticisms raised in the report.[41]

Bond continued to be involved in increasingly bitter confrontations with
Harold Grim. The issues that provoked the conflicts shifted from time to
time (in the early 1950s, for example, Grim voiced displeasure with Bond's
fund-raising abilities and his conduct of the athletic program), and as the
years passed by the relationship deteriorated. Despite their difficulties,
however, they were able to work together on occasion, and in early 1952
Bond even wrote to the president of Lincoln's board of trustees to seek
help in obtaining an honorary doctorate for Grim from his alma mater,
Lafayette University.[42]

Grim, however, continued to plague the president and inveigle the board
with communications questioning Bond's performance. The biologist cautioned Bond against hiring new faculty at salaries larger than those offered
to current staff, and he objected to Bond's plan to hire an assistant to help
with fund-raising. Though Grim's objections may have stemmed, at least
in part, from his concerns over the financial status of the institution and
its faculty, Bond thought that they were due to Grim's displeasure at not
being named vice-president two years earlier when that plan was afloat;
now, Bond believed, Grim himself wished to be named alumni fund-raiser.
The two men also clashed over lax collection of monies owed by students
and over the athletic program.[43]

Grim also objected to spending money on Bond's cherished curricular
innovation, the African Studies Institute. He questioned the expenditures
on utilities, supplies, maintenance, and just about every other category

of the university's budget. The dispute between the two men took on a more personal tone when Grim began to question the president's travel and entertainment expenses. Bond was also angered by Grim's tendency to alter the minutes and agendas of board meetings to fit his own interpretation of events. Each disputant could, and did, find alumni to whom he would complain about the conduct of the other.[44]

As Lincoln's centennial year of 1954 drew near, Grim charged that the students' intellectual abilities had deteriorated and that this decline had been abetted by Bond's granting scholarships to Pennsylvania residents who were substandard students. Bond replied that the conditions of Lincoln's aid from Pennsylvania required that these "scholarships" were to go to state residents who were graduates of Pennsylvania high schools, regardless of the students' level of preparation. In support of his position, Grim resigned from the scholarship committee, an action he had taken in regard to other committees in earlier years. Despite Grim's protests, Lincoln University seemed to have little choice but to become more dependent on dollars from the state of Pennsylvania.[45] If this meant some lowering of standards, it could not be helped.

Grim escalated his disputes with Bond by discussing the president and his performance with other faculty members. He also seemed to court direct confrontations with the president by scheduling speakers at times that conflicted with previously scheduled university programs. In 1956, Grim accused Bond of spending laboratory fees paid by science students on nonscientific items, and, later that same year, he objected to the financial problems caused by large numbers of African students who were not paying their full fees. Grim threatened to take his dispute over Pennsylvania scholarships to state politicians and to publish and send his own version of a recent Lincoln self-study to accrediting agencies, foundations, and influential business leaders.[46]

While it is difficult to evaluate Grim's allegations completely, it seems clear that he overstated the extent of whatever presidential transgressions existed and that he was on the verge of taking the institution's linen — linen that may not have been as dirty as he thought — and washing it in public forums. Grim never carried through on his threats to go public with Lincoln's problems. He did not have to. Within three months of his threat to publish his own version of Lincoln's self-study, the board of trustees voted to seek Bond's resignation.

All of Bond's difficulties — with alumni, with faculty, and with Harold

Grim—played a part in provoking his ouster. However, to fully understand Bond's dismissal, one needs to consider the ostensible, and published,
reason given for his termination: his failure to implement the New Plan
adopted for Lincoln University as it celebrated its centennial in 1954.

The context for talk about a change in orientation for Lincoln was the
progress being made in the early 1950s toward the legal dismantling of segregation in education. As the *Brown* cases were wending their way through
the courts, it was becoming clear to many affiliated with or interested in
Lincoln University that one outcome of a legal judgment against segregation would be a change in mission for predominantly black colleges.
This was especially likely to occur at Lincoln, since it was in a northern
state where, ostensibly at least, defense of segregation was not taken to the
extremes seen in the South.

Bond did not initiate the New Plan; it appears that Lincoln's board of
trustees produced it. In April of 1953, several board members, black and
white, met to discuss the future of Lincoln at a time when desegregation
seemed imminent. The board president concluded, "The day of usefulness
for Lincoln as primarily a Negro college is coming to a close." He went
on to identify six components of the new program for Lincoln: a larger
faculty; a student body doubled to the size of one thousand students; new
board members to enhance chances of achieving the plan; a larger curriculum, which would include a Department of African Affairs; a modernized
physical plant; and the possibility of becoming coeducational. In discussion at a subsequent board meeting, what had been only implied in the
six steps was made clear, namely, that it was time for Lincoln to take on
"a program of recruitment of non-Negro students."[47] Thus an essential
ingredient of the New Plan was that Lincoln University would seek a fully
integrated student body. Despite the invocation of an international student
body in later discussions of the New Plan, it was fairly clear from the start
that Lincoln would move to enroll significant numbers of white students.

This theme had been in the background since Horace Bond assumed
the Lincoln presidency in 1945. At that time a committee on aims had
recommended that the words specifying that Lincoln University existed
for "the education of Colored youth" be stricken from the institution's
charter. This was done with Bond's support. The change reflected two
facts, that Lincoln was open to students of all races and that some whites
had attended and graduated from Lincoln. Bond, however, indicated that
he intended to go no further in inviting white students than stipulating

that the university was open to them. As he put it, "Having done this, have we not done enough? Our self-respect will not permit us to do more." He added that, should white students not come to Lincoln in droves, the institution would not close its doors; rather, it would continue to pursue its historic objective, "the making of Men."[48]

Bond here voiced a principle that he would stand on throughout his presidency, one that put him at odds with white philanthropists who advocated interracial colleges, some black supporters of integrated education, and white Lincoln faculty who sought more white students at Lincoln. Shortly after taking the Lincoln presidency, for example, Bond received a letter from Edwin Embree in which Embree argued that it was time for Lincoln to admit more white students.[49] Bond detailed several reasons why whites were not then coming to Lincoln: neither Lincoln's white trustees nor its white faculty were interested in anything but a college for blacks; the few white students who attended Lincoln were local, and, since Lincoln was in a rural area that was both sparsely populated and socially conservative, the numbers of white students had never been large (there were currently two whites attending). Bond proposed that Embree help Lincoln integrate its student body by asking the American Council on Education to find ten white Pennsylvanians who would come to Lincoln on state scholarships. Though Embree acknowledged Bond's letter and promised to help seek white students, he never responded to Bond's specific request. Perhaps Bond knew that nothing would be done. His actions made clear what he had stated in principle: Lincoln would welcome white students, but he would not waste energy on a task that he considered unlikely to bear fruit.[50]

In 1949, Bond had a sharp exchange with Thurgood Marshall, noted Lincoln alumnus and a leader in the NAACP's fight against educational discrimination, over the issue of an integrated student body at Lincoln. In a speech delivered on Lincoln's campus, Marshall spoke in favor of an interracial student body for the college. Bond replied that he would work to get white students to come to Lincoln, but that he would not make that objective the institution's raison d'être. He went on to criticize Marshall and the NAACP for praising white colleges that had token (two or three) black students but that maintained lily-white trustee boards and faculties, while advocating that black colleges such as Lincoln, which had boards and faculties that were genuinely interracial, seek to enroll more white students. Let those white colleges with token black students hire black faculty and choose black board members; then they might merit being called *interracial*, as I incoln did. Bond added that he was offended at hearing pious white presidents of Pennsylvania colleges with no black faculty or administrators state that they hoped to see the day when the need for colleges such as Lincoln no longer existed. He added that Lincoln stood for something positive: a service to humanity that no white college with a few black students could contemplate.[51] In 1951, Bond responded to an official of the General Education Board who asked why Lincoln did not have white students, and he explained that it indeed had a few, that the number of whites rose and fell in conformity with changes in the business cycle, and that Lincoln would be happy to undertake a study of white enrollment on its own and other black campuses, with GEB support. The philanthropy demurred on financing the proposed research. Later in that same year, Bond wrote to this same official to complain that Lincoln had been left off a list of interracial colleges published by a scholarship service for black students funded by the GEB; why, he demanded to know, were white colleges with token black students and no black faculty put on the list, while Lincoln, with a fully interracial faculty and a few white students, was not? The reply dodged Bond's point by refusing to intervene in the affairs of an agency once a grant had been made.[52]

In 1953, therefore, when the Lincoln board announced its intention to seek more white students, Bond's lack of enthusiasm could have been predicted and did not mean that he failed to follow up on the board's ideas. He announced the New Plan to the faculty, encouraged their ideas on its implementation, and made the matter a subject of discussion at a called meeting. He also intensified his attempts to recruit white students from the Lincoln area. Unlike the trustees, Bond did not expect the numbers of white students to increase significantly, despite the college's efforts. He knew that the mores of Pennsylvania whites were not those of Supreme Court justices. Further, there were many state colleges in Pennsylvania that whites could attend; one, the college at West Chester, was very near Lincoln. Why would whites choose Lincoln over West Chester or other white public colleges? Trustees who expected throngs of whites to come to Lincoln on the heels of the *Brown* decision were deluding themselves. Also, Bond resented having to go out to beg whites to come to Lincoln simply because they were white; he reasoned that Lincoln had always been open, and would continue to be open, to white students. To seek white bodies as if they were some magical resource implied a denigration of the historic mission of the college and of its black students and faculty.[53]

Perhaps Bond gave insufficient attention to recruiting white students. In retrospect, however, it seems doubtful that any amount of effort would have resulted in significant increases in white enrollment. Pennsylvania whites in the mid-1950s were no more eager than southern whites are now to attend predominantly black colleges. The goal of genuinely integrated colleges seems as elusive in the 1990s as it was to Bond in the 1950s.

Lack of enthusiastic support for increased white enrollment, then, appears to have been Bond's major failing in regard to the New Plan at Lincoln University. Policy differences over implementation of the New Plan became the official explanation that both the board and Bond agreed on to explain his departure. Bond, however, was certain that Harold Grim and other old-guard white faculty had engineered his dismissal and had thus betrayed the subtle racism that had always tainted their dealings with colleagues and students. Bond's stated desire that he be succeeded by a black, the selection of one of his white adversaries as interim president, and the ultimate appointment of a white as his permanent successor, all lend strength to his claim that race was a factor in his dismissal.[54]

Yet Bond's tendency to focus on race as the key in explaining all criticism of him must be questioned. That the first black president of Lincoln University should not be succeeded by a black is indeed a sad conclusion to the twelve years Bond spent at his alma mater; however, such an outcome must also be attributed in part to Bond's own inability to maintain productive relationships with his faculty and board.

In a letter to the president of Lincoln's board of trustees, written one month before his departure, Bond summarized what he thought had been accomplished in his twelve years in office. The physical assets of the institution had increased by more than twofold. Long-needed maintenance, which had to be put off by his two immediate predecessors because of the Great Depression and World War II, had been accomplished. Faculty housing had nearly doubled, and some housing had also been provided for staff, which enabled Lincoln to continue to add black faculty members and, for the first time, to add blacks to its secretarial staff. Without on-campus housing, black faculty and staff would have faced the gravest difficulty finding a place to live near Lincoln.[55]

Bond also argued that the quality of students had improved during his tenure. This was a particularly important point for him, since the charge of a decline in the quality of students had been a staple in the arguments of his faculty and alumni detractors. He admitted that student quality had reached a high point in 1948, because of the competitive standards that could be maintained during the enrollment rush caused by the GI Bill. The falloff since then was real, but the Lincoln students of the 1950s, when judged by such indexes as standardized test scores and class rank, were still superior to the students of the presumed good old days of the 1920s and 1930s. Bond concluded that Lincoln's students had never been average or better than average when judged by national norms; rather, Lincoln now, as it had in the past, took students who suffered from environmental deprivations of one kind or another and taught them. This was Lincoln's mission—to teach students who made up for their deficiencies with high motivation to succeed.[56]

Although Bond's analyses of student quality during his tenure, as well as his conclusions about black students in general, seem on the mark, his conclusion that Lincoln students of the mid-1950s were superior to students of his own (and his alumni detractors') day cannot be confirmed. Changes in the meaning of class rank and test scores from the 1920s to the 1950s as well as changes in the geographical and socioeconomic status of Lincoln's student body over the decades, make comparisons of students in the two periods difficult, if not meaningless. Here again, Bond let differences with his opponents cloud his assessment of a situation.

Bond next mentioned the significance of the desegregation of the public schools of the community surrounding Lincoln University, which had taken place in the late 1940s, mainly because of a suit he had filed with two other black faculty members. In addition, segregation in the nearby village of Oxford, in its hotel and its movie theater, had stopped because of a suit filed by Lincoln students. He added that these actions had incited the lasting enmity of many whites in the area and that this enmity accounted for the small number of area whites who enrolled at Lincoln. Bond here ignored the fact that few whites had attended Lincoln before the surrounding area was desegregated. He proceeded to contrast the paucity of white students at Lincoln with the relatively large numbers of whites at the former black public college in West Virginia, arguing that since that institution, unlike Lincoln, had never challenged community mores, it was now able to enroll more white students. Missing from his analysis was an obvious difference between the schools that did not serve Bond's argument: the West Virginia college was the only public college in a major metropolitan area in the state. Perhaps in defiance of the vocal advocates of Lincoln's New Plan, Bond concluded, "I do not regret the part I played [in desegregating the area surrounding Lincoln]." He added that the situation in race relations would ultimately be, and indeed was now becoming, healthier in the Lincoln area because of the civil rights activities at the university.[57]

Bond then described his hiring practices in building Lincoln's faculty, noting that he had always operated on a strictly nondiscriminatory basis in choosing the best-qualified applicant regardless of race or creed. He had hired the first Jew at Lincoln, and his had been the first presidency during which a Jew and a Catholic had been granted professorships. In addition to bringing the best-qualified teachers he could find to Lincoln, Bond had improved the intellectual life at Lincoln by doubling the number of volumes in the library and significantly improving the library building itself. The policy of not offering athletic scholarships, which had been adopted by the board and scrupulously adhered to, was still another indication of commitment to intellect. Though this may have caused discontent among alumni who thought that one of the objects of Lincoln University was to produce winning teams, the student body had found that athletics was not the key to maintaining campus morale. Bond did not point out here that the athletic problems had festered unsolved for most of his presidency. The board seemed to have acted on stopping athletic scholarships without a strong lead from the president, so Bond's taking credit for resolving the issue is disputable.[58]

In addressing finances, Bond mentioned Harold Grim by name as one who had perpetuated a false picture of Lincoln's status. In contrast to Grim's image of financial ruin, Bond pictured a fundamentally healthy Lincoln University, with a budget that had increased more than threefold, from $220,000 in 1940–41 to $750,000 in 1956–57. Particularly significant was state assistance, which rose almost tenfold in the same period, rising from $25,000 to $240,000. Bond stated that the deficits, though long-running, were small, particularly when compared to the size of the budget, and were a condition of receiving the increases in state support. In concluding his assessment of Lincoln's financial health, Bond stated, "This is, comparatively, a wealthy operation. The money is here for what needs to be done; and during the next biennium, there will be even more." None of these particulars directly confronted the contention, made by Grim and other critics, that Lincoln's fiscal picture had worsened substantially during Bond's tenure.[59]

Bond then described Lincoln University's international stature, particularly in Africa. He attributed this prestige to notable Lincoln graduates, such as Kwame Nkrumah of Ghana, and also to his own efforts to add to Lincoln's reputation in Africa. He added that Lincoln's standing would be enhanced by recent graduates who had obtained or were about to obtain their doctorates. The production of scholars such as these was the goal of any university, and Lincoln, since 1945, had sought to turn out scholars, not the "money-grubbing" preprofessionals from earlier eras who distorted the meaning and mission of a liberal arts college.[60] This last statement seems to be a gratuitous attack on his detractors, most of whom had studied at Lincoln in preparation for their careers in medicine, law, the ministry, and other prestigious occupations.

The final accomplishment Bond recalled was the wedding of the daughter of a Jewish faculty member in the campus chapel. He claimed that the fact that this wedding took place at all and that the faculty member invited all of his colleagues, black and white, testified to the strides in interracial contact made during his years at Lincoln. This event also served as Bond's final answer to those who wished Lincoln to recruit white students. Interracialism was real at Lincoln, along with its commitment to the betterment of its largely black student body. Whites were welcome and were well treated. Anything more than this was bound to be harmful to the institution's historic commitments.[61] Bond's defense of integration on the Lincoln faculty was certainly warranted. It should also be pointed out, however, that the faculty was interracial before he arrived and that it would remain interracial after his departure.

The particulars Bond gathered in defense of his presidency contained some genuine accomplishments and some self-justifications. However, more objective indicators of Lincoln's progress during Bond's presidency do exist. In 1953, an accrediting team from the Middle States Association of Colleges and Secondary Schools came to Lincoln for an evaluation visit, and its report gives the student of Bond's presidency an unbiased view of the institution. The report seems to have been basically positive without being uncritical, about both the institution and its president. In its opening paragraph it described Lincoln as follows: "It is plagued with the economic difficulties which beset its people — and beset all colleges to a distressing extent — but it is in many ways a sound, strong institution." In speaking of the president, the report characterized his performance of his duties as "satisfactory." It added that "he gives educational leadership to the faculty, that he is cognizant of the basic problems of the institution, and that he is concerned with the selection of the best faculty members available." The report also commended the president for his stance against scholarships for athletes. It noted that morale on campus was generally "high" and concluded that "the institution operates in a democratic manner, and while there are normal conflicts and grievances, administration-faculty-student relations are, on the whole, satisfactory."[62] These remarks certainly seem to be at variance with the picture of the college painted by dissident faculty and alumni.

Other parts of the report, however, echoed some of the criticisms of Bond's management. The visitors disapproved of the president's frequent absences from campus, the underused college library, the lack of institutional self-study, and the unbalanced nature of choice of major by the students; of these particulars, the only one that seems pointed specifically to the president is the first one. In what seemed to be a direct criticism of the president, the report concluded that "some administrative procedures, particularly in the area of budget formulation and control, are carried on in too informal a manner," which apparently led to "some misunderstandings between department heads and the administration, as there is presently no systematic procedure for presentation of needs, or procedure to advise responsible officials as to budgetary decisions." The fact that the accumulated deficit for Lincoln had reached $82,025, the latest yearly deficit was almost $9,000, and there was no plan for reducing the deficit also raised eyebrows. Further, endowment had shrunk by $67,000, the total amount that had been used to supplement income to meet expenses in the recent past; the report advised that "endowment funds should remain inviolate."[63] This list seems to give at least some credence to Harold Grim's and others' concerns about the finances of the university.

The report's criticism was not strident, however, in the budgetary or any other area. It concluded that Lincoln "is accomplishing what it sets out to do": "producing the kind of men and fitting them for the kind of opportunity and citizenship, it [d]eclares it intends to do." In short, while less than a ringing endorsement of the accomplishments of President Bond, the report largely approved of Lincoln's affairs and, at least implicitly, of its presidential leadership.[64] Bond was perhaps unduly proud of the report; he ignored its criticisms and used its positive points to counteract rebukes from both faculty and alumni.

In 1955, two investigators from the Middle States Association of Colleges and Secondary Schools came to Lincoln specifically to address the issue of the seminary. The investigators found the seminary facilities adequate, but observed that there were too many weak students among the twenty or so enrolled and that the faculty of the seminary was too small, as it had to be supplemented by instructors from the college. In projecting the seminary's future, the evaluators noted that the president had pledged to continue the seminary, even if the Presbyterian church followed through on its threat to cut off all support. The evaluators concluded that the president's pledge was "unrealistic. The College simply can not afford to forego a dollar of its income." The future of the seminary, then, should be dependent on the Presbyterian church's willingness to fund it.[65]

This report exposed Bond's mistake in maintaining his support for an institution that had long outlived its usefulness to Lincoln University. That the church that helped to fund it was aware of the problem, while the president of the university refused to acknowledge it, suggested Bond's obstinacy or at least unwillingness to confront reality. The seminary's demise, which occurred shortly after Bond left Lincoln, clearly indicates that he erred grievously in not reconsidering his position.

As a counter to critics of his fiscal stewardship of Lincoln, Bond cited one generally acknowledged accomplishment of the latter years of his presidency: a sizable grant from the Ford Foundation in December 1955. The Ford grant, totaling $139,200, was made in two parts. The first $92,800 was made to increase teachers' salaries; the same amount was given to each of 625 colleges throughout the country. The second part, $46,400, went only to 125 of the 625 colleges, those which "have led the way in their regions to improving the status and compensation of faculties." Bond was proud that Lincoln recieved the second part of the grant, and he pointed to the grant when defending himself against the charge that Lincoln faculty were underpaid.[66]

Still another area in which Bond contributed to Lincoln in both the short and the long run was his relationship with Albert Barnes, the Philadelphia art critic and philanthropist. Bond's cultivation of Barnes enabled Lincoln's art students to experience personally the paintings held in Barnes's extensive private collection. Though Bond did not succeed in getting Barnes to make a significant financial contribution to Lincoln, the university has recently benefited from the relationship by being placed in control of Barnes's art collection.[67]

The accreditation reports and the Ford Foundation grant showed that Lincoln University under Horace Bond was hardly the autocratic, irresponsibly managed institution that his critics described. Yet one can also conclude that some of the critics' points, particularly the problem of the budget deficits, were indeed valid. Moreover, the budgetary procedures at Lincoln evidently reflected a looseness that was uncharacteristic of the thoroughness and meticulousness with which Horace Bond addressed his own scholarship and many of his personal endeavors.

In fact, it is this thoroughness and meticulousness that faculty and others who were not his adversaries have pointed out as one of the major reasons for his downfall. Many people have mentioned how his great powers of intellectual concentration led him to focus on a problem so completely that he could blot out all other distractions, and frequently did. He could walk across the campus, lost in thought, and not even notice those who crossed his path. This contributed to an image of aloofness that many misunderstood as a disinterest in others. Another generally acknowledged aspect of Bond's personality—his excessive formality—also contributed to his being viewed as unsympathetic. Finally, Bond's straightforwardness presented still another handicap in interactions with faculty and others. One former faculty member thought that Bond was "unable to 'suffer fools gladly,' and [was] too blunt (untactful) to make faculty with whom he differed feel mellow about him." It seems that these personal dimensions, as much as any weaknesses in his administrative actions, were instrumental in the unhappy end of the second college presidency of Horace Bond.[68]

These characteristics of Bond's personality seem to have been in place well before his Lincoln presidency, according to individuals who knew him as early as the 1930s. At Dillard University, he was unhappy in the role of academic dean, but not because of problems related to his aloofness or formality.[69] Bond's clash with Dillard's business manager over control of campus affairs, however, foreshadowed some of his problems at Lincoln. At Fort Valley State College, problems with faculty did not surface. The poison of race relations in Georgia and the rest of the South, however, may well have contributed to his problems as president of Lincoln University. His penchant for seeing racism at the root of all his conflicts with white faculty meant that he was blinded to some very real grievances.

Certainly, Bond's maladroit handling of dissidents among the faculty and alumni cannot be attributed to southern racial mores. It may have been due simply to his unfitness for the intrigues and machinations that seem to bedevil twentieth-century American higher education, white or black. In many ways, Bond was too honest. He could not hide his attitudes toward individuals, even as he was forced to deal with them from day to day. His problems were also aggravated by his inability to forget a grievance once it was lodged as well as by his tendency to go after his opponents with a tenaciousness that surely was unproductive in the ever-fluid world of campus politics.[70]

One should not conclude that Bond was unpopular with all of Lincoln University's faculty and students. He seemed to have quite good relations with faculty whom he hired: they described him as straightforward, fair, and courteous. Similarly, a Lincoln student who went on to excel in graduate school remembered the high regard he had for Bond, enumerating the ways in which the president helped him prepare for his scholarly career.[71]

Those faculty members who were present when Bond was hired were not as partial to the chief executive. Although not a vocal critic, one of them had trouble with Bond, and his account of Bond's actions as president supports the impression of a deep fissure between the president and his senior faculty, mainly over the issues of salaries and finances.[72]

Intellectual and personal habits such as thoroughness, meticulousness, and formality, while perhaps not always key attributes for an administrator, seem well suited to the roles of scholar and teacher. Ultimately, then, what we may have in Bond is the case of a scholarly mind trapped in an administrative role. He had excelled in scholarship, publishing two books before he was forty years old. Like other black scholars of his day, however, he had nowhere to go as a scholar. Having a family to support and desiring recognition, he took the path open to ambitious black academics of his day: the road of the college president. After serving an apprenticeship at Fort Valley, he came home to Lincoln as its first black president. His difficulties in this post seem rooted in a combination of institutional obstacles and personal characteristics that made him constitutionally unfit to manage the Lincoln situation.

Perhaps understanding his predicament from the beginning, Bond, early on in his presidency, wrote several letters asking about teaching or research jobs. Afterward, from time to time he sought academic positions as a possible alternative to administration.[73] It should be added that Bond was happiest in his presidency when he was working on projects, such as writing Lincoln's history, that were largely unrelated to his administrative duties.

Bond's work as president of Lincoln University was doomed from the beginning. The antagonisms of certain faculty members and some alumni fueled each other. The personality and orientation of the president were such that he could not, or would not, perform the ministrations necessary to soothe the dissidents and curry their favor. This was not Bond's style. Rather, he had the scholar's habit of searching doggedly for and proclaiming the truth. In administrative situations, where the truth was never as reachable as it seemed to be in scholarship and where some smoothness and indirectness were often the requisites of success, Horace Bond was not up to the task.

Chapter 9

Africa

Horace Bond had learned about Africa from his earliest childhood, mainly from his Aunt Mamie, who had served for a time as a medical missionary there and who had instilled in her nephew an enduring love for that continent and its people. Young Bond's affinity for Africa was enhanced by his reading, in the pages of the *Crisis*, of the accomplishments of his race and the nobility of his African ancestors.[1]

As a student at Lincoln University, Bond had several African classmates and learned more of his African heritage from teachers such as Robert Labaree. In graduate school, he took several courses on Africa and Africans in sociology and anthropology as part of his master's and doctoral programs.[2] For the first two decades of his academic career, however, his interest in this field of study was put on the back burner as the young scholar made his way in the world of black higher education in America. In 1945, when he returned to Lincoln as its president, he soon rekindled his interest in Africa and Africans.

In his inaugural address as the university's first black president, Bond noted that Lincoln University had been founded for "the redemption of Africa by American Negroes." During his presidency, as he studied Lincoln's history, he learned more about the Africans who had attended Lincoln and returned to their homelands to minister to their people, and he did whatever he could to ensure that the number of African students at Lincoln increased.[3]

Of course, Bond's efforts in this last regard would not have borne fruit if political conditions beyond the control of Lincoln and its president had not been favorable. During the late 1940s and 1950s, the time of Bond's presidency, Africa emerged from the colonial yoke of Western Europe. As it became clear that a new order would be established in the "dark" continent, various government and private agencies in the United States sought to aid African students who wished to study in America, to spread the message of American democracy in Africa, and to promote American business and political interests in the emerging African colonies. Bond became involved in all of these aspects of American relations with Africa.

He vigorously promoted the cause of scholarships for African students in America; as Bond knew, this activity was a natural extension of the missionary thrust that had characterized Lincoln University since its founding. He was also an apostle of things American in Africa; in particular, he sought to enlighten Africans on the accomplishments of their African-American brethren. Similarly, he recommended the cause of the new African countries to African Americans, seeking to foster in them an affinity for the continent of their ancestors. In all of these activities, Bond tried to serve the cause of brotherhood between Africans and African Americans and the goals of the emerging African nations. However, in his pursuit of these relatively uncontroversial goals, he sometimes took positions that exaggerated the affinities between the two groups.

In conjunction with paying considerable attention to the development of American business and political interests in the new African nations, Bond sometimes advocated plans that Africans would have considered against their interests. On the economic front, he tended to pursue development of African natural resources that could benefit him personally as well as the American and other corporations that backed his activities. On the political front, he tended to follow an ideologically pro-American and anti-Communist course that was not adhered to by many Africans. When called on to discuss the political path that Africa should follow, Bond sometimes evinced a cold war mentality and a concern for only those African nations that fell in line with the American approach to issues.

Beginning in 1949, Bond made more than ten trips to Africa. Most of his energies were devoted to improving African education and to strengthening the ties between African educational institutions and Lincoln University. His first trip was sponsored, in large part, by the African Academy of Arts and Research. This agency, headed by a Lincoln alumnus from Nigeria, cooperated with other African sources to pay half of Bond's expenses; he agreed to raise the other half from Lincoln or from other sources, such as black newspapers for which he would write articles about his trip. Bond's itinerary called for stops in the Gold Coast (now Ghana), Nigeria, Liberia, Sierra Leone, and French West Africa. Lincoln had had students enrolled from most of these areas, particularly from the first three. It had conferred an honorary doctoral degree in 1947 on Lincoln alumnus Nnamdi Azikiwe, leader of the Ibos in eastern Nigeria, and would soon confer an honorary doctorate on Kwame Nkrumah, leader of the emerging nationalist movement in the Gold Coast.[4]

Most of Bond's first African trip was taken up with visits to institutions of higher education and officials in the education ministries of the various colonies. His sponsorship by indigenous African interests meant that, ostensibly at least, he would be free from the political and economic motives that might ordinarily be expected to taint such a trip. As he told a black American newspaper editor, "Since I go on the invitation of the Africans, and not through either philanthropy or colonial governments, I would be able to write from the viewpoint of the people—here and there—interested in the people, and not in their material resources or the exploitation of them." Yet in the same letter, Bond indicated that he was aware of the economic issues and interests that might also be seen as relevant to African-American educational interchanges. He remarked that "Africa is the chosen land both for European and American hopes for investment" and described "the vast sums being poured into West Africa, both by the British, and by American capital—the Stettinius interests; Republic Steel; Firestone, and the like." He indicated that his own desires were to become informed about education there and to develop "a system for providing scholarships for African students," but he added that he also wished to learn about politics, colonial reform, industrialization, "exploitation generally," and progress in business.[5]

Bond's visit, like most international affairs, did involve political considerations. While the colleges in Nigeria and the Gold Coast reflected the organizations and values of English universities, new colleges would be founded and existing institutions might be reorganized to benefit African Americans and the United States. In a letter written after his trip, Bond described to a black doctor the lack of "race consciousness" reflected in the English education then received in African colleges and by Africans studying in England and commented on how this lack was remedied by educational contacts with American blacks. Enhancement of these contacts would benefit both the Africans and the African Americans.[6]

In his early trips to Africa, Bond was able to enlarge the stature of his university in African educational circles as well as in his own circles. For example, he was able to establish the African Studies Institute at Lincoln

University in the early 1950s and to increase the number of African students studying at Lincoln and elsewhere in the United States. He also managed to help his brother, J. Max Bond, to become president of the College of Liberia.[7]

Although some benefits did accrue to Bond, his friends, and his family, Horace Bond nevertheless worked tirelessly, through a variety of individuals, government agencies, and private organizations, to further the cause of Africa and Africans in the United States. He also sought to promote the African-American image as well as the image of the United States in Africa. He wrote letters for African students who sought enrollment at such prestigious American institutions as Barnard College, labored mightily on behalf of an African student who was enrolled at Lincoln University and whom immigration authorities suspected as a subversive, served on the boards of several associations devoted to increasing the numbers and improving the living conditions of African students in America, and sought to involve Lincoln and other Pennsylvania colleges and universities in helping to establish a new Nigerian university. After leaving Lincoln University and going to Atlanta University in 1957, Bond worked just as assiduously to cement ties between the latter institution and Africa and Africans.[8]

As he pursued these goals, Bond found himself becoming a valued friend of the emerging leadership in Nigeria and Ghana (the African name that Kwame Nkrumah adopted for the Gold Coast colony). He was invited to both countries for ceremonial occasions marking the installation of the new national leadership and was consulted about educational affairs in these and other African nations. His advice was sought on the appointments of Americans to African colleges, and he himself was offered high-level jobs in African higher education.[9]

In his African activities, Bond constantly sought to enhance the image of Africa and Africans in the minds of African Americans. He especially tried to correct the impression that American blacks had little appreciation for or interest in their African roots and African brothers and sisters. In several published articles he spoke movingly of the flowering of his personal connections to Africa as the result of his trips. Shortly after his first trip to Africa in 1949, for example, he published an article in which he spoke of seeing a woman in Nigeria who looked to him exactly like his grandmother. His official hosts, Africans trained by the British and imbued with British notions of the propriety of class distinctions, could not understand why their honored American guest insisted on talking to and touching this ordinary African woman. In his anecdote, Bond skillfully blended American democratic sentiments with descriptions of the physical resemblance between Africans and African Americans into a story that sought to reinforce the strong affinities between the two groups.[10]

In several other speeches and articles, Bond echoed these themes and the need for these ties as he became a tireless apostle of better relations with Africa. In religious forums, he couched his message in terms of the positive outcomes that had been gained and that could still be enhanced by missionary activity in Africa. In more secular forums, he stressed familial, cultural, and political aspects of the African-American experience that would be enhanced by contact with Africa and Africans.[11]

In most of his speeches and writings for American audiences, Bond was unfailingly upbeat about developments in Africa. He wanted African Americans to understand that considerable strides were being made in the emerging African nations. For example, in a discussion of the All-African Peoples Conference, which took place in December 1958, he stressed the "rare courage of the African people," the "great adaptability of Africans" who were exchanging village life for modernity, the "great wisdom of the contemporary African leadership," and the enormous educational accomplishments of African nations. In education, he singled out Ghana, which had increased its enrollment of school-age children from 10 percent of the eligible age group in 1949 to 90 percent in 1958. He marveled at the rapid educational progress that had occurred in the nine years since he had started his visits to that continent. What those years had taught him was "new respect for black men." This message was intended to stir American blacks as they, too, were emerging from the stigma of racial segregation. Bond invoked African accomplishments to spark pride in African Americans and to urge them on in their own quest for social justice. He used the accomplishments of black Americans, in turn, to support the American message in Africa.[12]

At times, Bond's constant advocacy of the African cause in America and African-American interests in Africa bordered on hyperbole. This may well have been because his message was not getting through in the way that he intended. Evidence of this can be found in Bond's vigorous critique of two white authors, Harold Isaacs and Russell Howe, who in 1961 published articles claiming that black Americans did not feel warmly toward their African brethren and that this unfriendly feeling was reciprocated. In rebuttal, Bond recounted his own positive experiences with Africans and disputed the authors' assertions that African heads of state did not want black diplomats from America as representatives to their countries. He also disagreed vigorously with their contention that Africans did not wish to use the term *Negro*. Bond's use of anecdotal evidence to contradict points that the authors made with similar evidence meant that the dispute could not be satisfactorily solved on any objective basis.[13]

The conflict between Bond's views and those of Howe and Isaacs as to how African Americans saw Africa was similarly unresolvable. To Isaacs's report that interviews with African Americans showed them to be suspicious of Africa and Africans, Bond responded with an attack on the interview methodology; a charge that Isaacs had misused the interview data; an account of his own interview with Isaacs, including Bond's stipulation that the interview could not be published; and a claim that blacks would not tell the truth to a white interviewer, such as Isaacs (instead, they would tell him what he wanted to hear). When Isaacs published an account of his interviews with blacks in *Phylon*, the journal of Atlanta University, he responded by disputing Bond's contention that a white would want to hear a negative view of Africa from a black American. Isaacs argued that his black interviewees had no more cause to hide their true views from their interviewer than white interviewees would.[14]

It seems that the views of Isaacs and Howe were more obnoxious to Bond than they were to the black intellectuals who originally published them in *Phylon*. It also seems that the authors' interpretations of their evidence were as plausible as Bond's critique. This is not to say that Bond did not believe every word of criticism that he spoke and wrote. It is to say, however, that his unwavering advocacy of interchange between Africans and African Americans may have been as decisive in the formation of his views as any objective critique he could make about these articles.

Bond's exhortations about the promise of Africa were designed both to lift the spirits and the visions of African Americans about Africa and to spur on African national development. Unfortunately for Bond, these efforts brought results that were as mixed as the affairs of the African nations.

Bond's African activities even proved to be a factor in his dismissal from the office of president of Lincoln University in 1957. In fact, it was while he was away on a trip to Ghana that the Lincoln University Board of Trustees decided to seek his resignation. The decision was provoked by several factors related to Bond's African interests. Some faculty resented his frequent absences from campus while he traveled to Africa. Financial deficits at the college were aggravated by the frequent failure of African students to pay all of their fees and the tendency of the president to overlook their shortfalls. Bond, of course, knew that Lincoln had forgiven the debts of needy students, both African and African-American, at many times in the institution's history, and he saw no need to stop the procedure now. Some African-American students resented what they perceived as their president's tendency to favor African students, to give more attention to them than he did to other students. While it certainly would overstate the case to claim that Africa was the source of Bond's downfall at Lincoln, it is true that his devotion to Africa, at the expense of other interests dear to the heart of some Lincoln faculty and students, was one factor in creating the on-campus climate that led to the unfortunate conclusion of his presidency.[15]

Despite the negative ramifications of his African pursuits, Bond did not stop making trips to Africa and advocating educational and cultural exchange between Africans and African Americans. Bond's resolve stemmed in large part from his convictions and dedication to his cause. However, there were other factors, factors not related to education and black advancement, that also influenced Bond's advocacy.

From the first of his several trips to Africa, Bond faced the problem of how to finance his travels. African governments, Lincoln University, and the African-American press, all sources of funding for his initial African hegira, could not afford to underwrite yearly ventures. Bond therefore came to rely on businesses, foundations, and government agencies for funding, and it seems fair to say that these sources of funding introduced a shift in focus in his efforts.

In 1952, L. E. Detwiler, a white American promoter and middleman, approached Bond and asked him to intercede with Gold Coast leader Kwame Nkrumah on behalf of American interests seeking to develop mineral deposits and other natural resources in that colony. In the early 1950s, Americans' major competitors in this economic development were the British, who had colonized the Gold Coast and were in the process of giving up their colonial power. Nkrumah, a fervent nationalist, had been jailed by the British for his political activities. Detwiler hoped that Nkrumah's resentment toward his captors could be used to help American developers gain the advantage. The American promoter sought and received an introduction to Nkrumah from Bond.[16]

Detwiler started Bond on a decade of promotion of economic development in Africa. For most of that time, Bond was associated with groups set
up by Detwiler which also included such noted American political figures
as Senators Millard Tydings of Delaware and James H. Duff of Pennsylvania; Johnston Avery, the former deputy director of the Point Four
program; Donald Richberg, a former official in the National Recovery
Administration; and numerous other high-level lawyers, engineers, and
businessmen. Bond was associated with several agreements by which the
Americans were granted concessions to mine iron ore and develop other
natural resources in Liberia.[17] American corporations involved as players
in the various development schemes (or which contemplated such involvement) included Reynolds Metals, the Anaconda Copper Mining Corporation, Bethlehem Steel, and others. Groups with which Bond was involved
also cooperated with British, Canadian, and Swedish interests and clashed
with German-backed ventures.

The context for all of these ventures was Ghana's and Nigeria's coming
independence from Britain as well as the emerging nationalism in other
West African colonies. From one perspective, Bond's activities can be
viewed as participation in American economic (and government) interests'
attempts to interject themselves into the development of the new African
nations—that is, economic colonialism. It is difficult, however, to see Bond
as simply a colonial agent. He was careful at almost all times to ensure
that the activities he supported had, as at least one of their goals, the pros-
perity of the host nations. For example, he attempted to make sure that a
fair share of the profits from any proposed ventures would go to the African countries involved. He also frequently emphasized his desire to serve
emerging Africa in his economic enterprises, trying to make it plain that
he was looking for American interests "who would play square with the
Africans, and at the same time make money."[18]

Bond also attempted to connect his economic ventures to activities that
would benefit the interests of both the host countries and black Americans.
For example, in conjunction with the concessions the Liberian government
made to his group, he pushed hard for an American-funded educational
exchange and development plan which involved Lincoln University, the
Tuskegee Institute, and West Virginia State College. He also arranged it
so that a large part of any financial gains he received would go to Lincoln University: a significant portion of his interest in the International
African-American Corporation, a group that was involved with most of his

African business ventures, went to Lincoln University, despite the Lincoln board's willingness to allow him to be the major beneficiary.[19]

It should be stated, however, that in his African ventures Bond was also pursuing personal economic gain. His initial agreement with the American sponsors of his African economic activities called for him to receive a monthly salary of one thousand dollars and expenses while he was on his African business trips. Though he assigned stock from his ventures to Lincoln University, he also kept some for himself. And he also provided his friends with information about the prospects of the stock if they were interested in purchasing shares. When he left Lincoln, with considerable bitterness, in the summer of 1957, he attempted to regain from the university the stock he had given to it. He reasoned, at least somewhat disingenuously, that the purpose for which he had granted the stock to Lincoln — the promotion of African students at the college — would not be fulfilled, for Lincoln had chosen a white faculty member and Bond opponent as his interim successor. After leaving Lincoln, he continued his African undertakings by heading up a new group that competed with ventures sponsored by his former associates.[20]

One must conclude that Bond pursued his economic activities with a mixture of motives, most of which were geared to serve the African countries, though through the agency of American economic and government interests. At the same time, however, he served the institutional interests of his college as well as his own financial interests. Bond was thus a bit of a middleman promoter between American capital and developing African nations, and he sometimes behaved in ways typical of the breed. He became quite negative, for instance, about other black Americans who competed with him for influence with both Africa and American capital, and he easily agreed to serve as an agent for friends of Lincoln University trustees who sought to do business with the Africans, without worrying much about the qualifications or interests of these friends.[21]

It is difficult to evaluate this aspect of Horace Bond's African activities. On the one hand, it seems that he was simply taking advantage of the post-colonial situation, which enabled him to pursue his own educational and cultural interests in Africa. Yet, as time passed, economic ventures came to absorb a larger and larger part of his agenda. For example, an itinerary for a two-day trip to Nigeria in September 1954 shows that only one leg of the trip was devoted to a visit to an educational institute; the rest of the trip was spent at trade institutes, a cashew plantation, a power station, and a meeting with a government official.[22]

In and of itself, this division of labor means little. Bond was regarded as a famous black American; he was not pigeonholed as only an educator, so his visits to noneducational settings should not seem unusual. Yet the reader of Bond's personal correspondence is drawn to the plethora of letters regarding economic ventures, the vigor with which he pushed his own enterprises at the expense of those of competitors, and his seemingly constant concern for his own financial prospects. These seem to be the letters of an international businessman, not of an African-American college president attempting to serve Africa and African Americans.

There is a distinctly ironic twist to Bond's activities in economic development. From the beginning, he was suspicious of L. E. Detwiler and several of the other promoters with whom he became involved in African economic ventures. After being approached by Detwiler, Bond tried, through a variety of sources, to check the integrity and qualifications of the man, and the response he received was decidedly mixed. Therefore, Bond was always cautious in dealing with Detwiler, and he encouraged the African governments to be wary of Detwiler and his schemes. Later, in 1962, when Detwiler attempted to gain economic concessions in the Congo, an exposé in *Newsweek* described the many failed schemes of this promoter, so Bond's care in dealing with him seems prudent. What seems questionable is the zeal with which Bond simultaneously embraced the activities led by the very person whom he distrusted. Bond's practices in 1957, when he set up his own African development venture and competed with others who were promoting various schemes, seemed to indicate that he had joined the ranks of these dubious characters.[23]

Bond's own financial situation was certainly one reason that he promoted economic development in Africa that might result in his own personal gain. His salary at Lincoln was not particularly generous; four years after his arrival, his salary was raised from $6,000 to $7,500. By 1957, the end of his Lincoln years, he had received no other significant raise. Two of his children attended expensive private schools: Jane was at the West Town school in Maryland, and Julian attended the George School in Philadelphia. He had no savings or investments. In short, though not financially uncomfortable, he was in no sense well off. However, his economic ventures in Africa did little to alter the situation. He was able to sell some of his stock on at least one occasion: he sold shares of stock in an African venture for $3,500 in June 1958, one year after his dismissal, when he had children in college and had taken a pay cut to come to Atlanta University.[24] It is very difficult to argue, then, that Bond made much money from his African activities.

In the political realm, Bond was, from the beginning, a vigorous advocate of the emergence of African nations from the yoke of western European colonialism. He also was a forceful spokesman for the cause of Africa and Africans in the United States and a passionate supporter of America and American interests on the African continent. As his experience in Africa increased, his links with American political and economic interests, through a variety of organizations, also increased. The times when Bond's devotion to American causes in Africa conflicted with goals pursued by the emerging African nations are of particular importance for this discussion; before looking at these conflicts, however, an overview of Bond's African political activities and their relationship to his participation in domestic political affairs is in order.

The earliest years of Bond's African visits constituted a most exciting period. Nigeria and Ghana were gaining their independence from Great Britain. Two of their most famous leaders in the nationalist movements, Azikiwe in Nigeria and Nkrumah in the Gold Coast, were Lincoln men. Bond cultivated contacts with both and empathized with them as they trod the thorny path toward independence. As the Gold Coast became independent Ghana, Bond rejoiced in Nkrumah's accession to power. He was also pleased with Azikiwe's ascendance in the eastern region of the Nigerian federation, which developed as Nigeria's first independent government. Similarly, he paid close attention to developments in the Republic of Liberia, as that ostensibly democratic nation was watched by numerous black and white Americans who hoped that it would be the showcase of democracy in Africa.

As independence from Great Britain loomed for Ghana and Nigeria, the cold war between the United States and the Soviet Union was intensifying even as Communist ideology swiftly moved to the forefront of the political reflections of Bond and the black American intellectuals with whom he associated. In American political life as a whole, the cold war climate of the 1950s fed a fervent anticommunism that was particularly virulent in the part of the Republican party that supported Senator Joseph McCarthy of Wisconsin. Bond found himself caught in the middle. His ties to Republican politicians were based on the relatively liberal attitude of Pennsylvania Republicans on racial as well as other issues. His Republican contacts also meant that he could pursue an influential role in whatever plans and programs for Africa that were developed by the Eisenhower administration from 1953 to 1961.[25]

Bond was not shy about adopting extreme anti-Communist rhetoric, however, particularly if it helped him to curry political favor for his African plans. For example, one month after President Eisenhower's inauguration, he wrote to a federal official to obtain support for proposed endeavors in Ghana and Liberia. Bond began:

> In the life and death struggle now in process in the world, the natural and human resources of Africa are the prizes for which the two principal protagonists now contend. For the moment, the control of the natural resources of the Continent seem securely held by allies of the United States. Our antagonists, however, are satanically fore-minded in their estimate of the situation, and in their planning for the future. Radio Moscow sows daily seeds of disaffection everywhere in Africa; indigenous and European agents are already active on the uneasy soil; and cadres of young Africans go quietly, but in increasing number, to Moscow, and to Prague, to be indoctrinated in the Universities and to participate in demonstrations and parades of the fanatic Young Communist hordes in East Berlin and elsewhere.[26]

While the hyperbole of this statement seems obvious, it is typical of much of what was said about Communists in many parts of American society as well as in many government circles at the height of the cold war in the 1950s. Whether this statement represented Bond's true views, or whether he sought to use contemporary rhetoric in which he did not believe to advance his own interests, is a question that deserves attention.

Bond invoked the Communist menace many times in these years. In 1955, for example, at a conference of educational administrators, he proposed that, although America had lost much of Asia to communism, this would not have to be the case in Africa. Yet he also often dissented from knee-jerk anticommunism, particularly when charges of communism were directed at his African friends. In 1954, for example, he wrote a stinging rebuke to an Oregon newspaper editor who had alleged that Nkrumah of Ghana was a Communist.[27]

Before reaching any judgment as to the place of anticommunism in

Bond's activities, one must look closely at the government channels he utilized and the two major organizations he served in pursuit of African relations with America. Bond often contacted various government agencies and Republican politicians on behalf of Lincoln University's African programs and his own reputation in Africa. The African desk in the State Department, the United States Information Service, and the Foreign Operations Administration were frequent contacts. He also kept up a steady correspondence with Val Washington, director of minorities for the Republican party. He used these interactions to foster Lincoln's African exchange programs as well as to promote his own candidacy for such influential positions as ambassador to Ghana.[28]

Bond's political activities can be examined in greater depth through an analysis of two organizations of Americans devoted to African affairs. The first, the African-American Institute, was founded as the Institute for African-American Relations (IAAR) in 1953. Just before the IAAR's inception, Bond corresponded with a white who was interested in Africa about the points of view that the proposed organization might take. The two agreed that blacks in the IAAR might follow a more avowedly pro-African, nationalist line, while whites could be more "objective" and entertain ideas that might not be inimical to colonial influence in Africa. This sort of balance was a characteristic that both men considered to be necessary in order to receive funding from foundations and government agencies.[29]

The goals of the IAAR included the promotion of study by African students in America, the enhancement of understanding of Africa in America, and the improvement of the image of America in the African countries. The IAAR was involved in a variety of projects, such as Africa House, founded in Washington, D.C., as a clearinghouse and funding agency for African students. This aspect of the IAAR program was particularly important to Bond in his pursuit of a larger African enrollment at Lincoln University. The IAAR's funding of his own trips to Africa was also important. In 1958, the name of the organization was changed to the African-American Institute (AAI), and the statement of purpose was redrawn in accordance with the wishes of Alan Pifer of the Carnegie Corporation.[30]

After this alteration, the AAI appears to have taken a new direction. Early in 1959, Bond received a letter from a black employee of the AAI who charged that it did not really have the interests of African students at heart and that it was also removing blacks from any meaningful role in the group. A black newspaper in New York also published an editorial, titled

"Gentle Imperialism," that was critical of the AAI. The directions taken by the AAI distanced Bond, though he would continue as an inactive board member of the group for several more years.[31]

An organization devoted to African-American interests that did not allow whites to usurp the prerogatives of blacks was the American Society for African Culture (AMSAC). AMSAC was born in 1956 during a trip by a delegation of African-American intellectuals, including Bond, to an international conference in Paris sponsored by the Society for African Culture. AMSAC developed initially as the American affiliate of the larger organization, although it clearly saw itself as a mainly independent group. From its inception, AMSAC made sure that blacks would not lose influence in its organization; whites were welcomed as associate members of AMSAC, though they could not hold the privileges and responsibilities of full members, who were black. As this policy became clear to all members, it caused some controversy and several defections. The historian John Hope Franklin was the most notable black member to leave AMSAC because of its racial exclusivity. Bond supported the membership restrictions of AMSAC, perhaps because of his and others' experiences in the African-American Institute. He concluded that, if an organization were not clearly controlled by blacks, they might well serve only as figureheads, as was happening in the AAI.[32]

The American delegation to the Paris conference of the Society of African Culture included Bond, John Davis, formerly of Lincoln University and then of City College; another former Lincoln professor, William Fontaine of the University of Pennsylvania; John Ivy, editor of the *Crisis*; and Mercer Cook, a professor at Howard University who was then living in Paris. Later American members on the international board included such cultural figures as Duke Ellington and Langston Hughes, the black writer and Lincoln University alumnus. The inclusion of musical figures and writers was in keeping with AMSAC's stated mission as a group of "scholars, artists, and writers" whose purpose was "to examine, record, and cultivate the culture of the emerging African continent, to study the contributions of African culture to American life, and to help Western and more particularly American culture sweep away the prejudices that would deny the contributions of African culture."[33]

This largely nonpolitical statement of positive goals was followed by a phrase indicating some things that AMSAC opposed: AMSAC existed "to defend the great cultural contributions of man against the perversions of political, economic, and national movements." The particular perversion that seems to have been in mind here is communism. From the first conference of the Society of African Culture, its American affiliate was embroiled in a fight against communism, both in the United States and in Africa. For example, W. E. B. Du Bois could not attend the first conference because he was refused a passport by the United States Department of State. Du Bois, by this time clearly on his way to becoming a Communist, wired the Paris group to warn them of his own situation and to cast doubt on the credibility of any American blacks who could obtain official clearance to attend the meeting.[34]

AMSAC needed to be careful to avoid taking an obviously political stance. As a cultural organization that sought to exert influence in Africa, it could not take an openly pro-American position. AMSAC was largely funded, however, by a group that did not have to be ideologically neutral in its public statements and positions: the Committee on Race and Caste in World Affairs (CORAC) could be more open about its orientation because by channeling its activities with Africans through AMSAC, it did not have to deal with Africans themselves. In the plans and activities of blacks who served both organizations, such as John Davis, the distinctions between the two seem to have been largely formal. Bond was also active in both organizations, serving as an early president of AMSAC and as a board member of CORAC.[35]

Bond's own view of communism as a competitor of American democracy for influence in the African context, though generally negative, was not without complexity. In his report to CORAC on the first conference of the Society of African Culture, he included a section called "The Communist Line," which recounted a vociferously antiimperialist speech by a black Communist from Martinique. Bond attributed the favorable response to this speech to the fact that the audience was stacked with Communists. He delightfully described his leveling the charge of "hooliganism" (which he said was "Pravda's favorite epithet") against the Communist-dominated audience, who reacted negatively to speech by a young non-Communist from the Cameroons. Later, in describing another international conference of the Society of African Culture, Bond was somewhat more balanced about communism and American democracy, though he still made his loyalties clear: "The two great ideologies in conflict in the world, each in its way, tend to pervert, I think, free creative expression, by the very nature of their conflict; I am 'American' enough to believe that the United States is much the less a culprit in this, and to believe that any compulsive system like that of the Soviet Union cannot produce a great art." In discussing with a chief of the Kikuyu tribe the relative appeal of America and the Soviet Union to blacks, Bond exhibited still another aspect of his position: acknowledging that the Russians voted with the new African nations in the United Nations, while United States tended to favor the colonial powers, he cautioned the African to remember that "they [the Russians] too were white; and . . . [that he had] heard that African students were mistreated in Russia." Bond concluded the conversation by stating his own theory: "The black man was his own best friend." [36]

These three points of view are not mutually exclusive. In the first case, Bond was speaking to a funding group and telling it what it wanted to hear as well as what he probably believed. In the second case, he was reporting to a white academic and responded with a "balanced" point of view that still favored the American position. In the third case, he was speaking to a black African and, no doubt, telling that individual what he wanted to hear. Anticommunism is evident in all three cases, though the degree of consideration for alternatives other than simple anticommunism increases in the second and, even more, in the third instances.

It is clear that Bond was comfortable with taking a "government" sponsored anti-Communist line on African affairs. For example, in 1963 a United States Information Service official in Africa wrote to Bond and asked him to respond to the statements in Ghanaian circles that attacked African Americans in that country as "spies" and stooges. One week later, Bond wrote a letter to the editor of the *Ghanaian Times* to defend African Americans against charges that they were imperialists linked to the designs of the Central Intelligence Agency (CIA). Bond recounted the history of twentieth-century cooperation between American blacks and Africans and defended AMSAC against charges of imperialism. He noted that ambassadors from America and Western Europe were the only black ambassadors to African countries and reminded the paper that Mercer Cook, the black American ambassador, had been active in AMSAC from its beginnings. He concluded that Ghanaians should take all this into account before "slamming the door on American Negroes." [37]

The relatively constant opposition of Bond and his African-American colleagues in AMSAC to Du Bois deserves some discussion. Du Bois had had a long and productive career as a professor at black colleges, editor of the *Crisis*, and spokesperson for blacks in the United States, yet the personal rebuffs and political attacks to which he was frequently subjected, as well as his own changing views of the relationship between capitalism and racism, drove him late in his life to embrace communism, renounce his American citizenship, and become a citizen of Ghana. Before his official renunciation of his American homeland, Du Bois, along with such left-leaning black figures as the actor Paul Robeson, had been heavily involved in the Council for African Affairs (CAA).[38]

Bond and his AMSAC colleagues competed with Du Bois and the CAA for influence on the African continent. In this context, Bond's vigorous opposition to communism and his willingness to respond to requests from government agencies seem to be both the voicing of a message in which he basically believed and the counteracting of a group whose major goal was to neutralize the influence and sully the reputation of organizations with which he was involved. Bond's personal regard for Du Bois's accomplishments dated back to his childhood, when he first read the *Crisis*, and the two men had collaborated on several occasions.[39] Yet Bond did not allow his regard to soften his opposition to Du Bois's communism and anti-Americanism in the 1950s and 1960s.

Another aspect of Bond's pursuit of quasi-official anticommunism was his need for funds for his educational and economic ventures in Africa. CORAC was a constant sponsor of various of his activities, and he knew that praising America to African audiences would stand him in good stead when he sought more funding from CORAC, other foundations, and government agencies. There was a certain cynical realism apparent in Bond's pursuit of funding, at least as evidenced in some of his correspondence. For example, in responding to a letter from the AMSAC office regarding an unnamed "confidential" project, he told John Davis whom to contact and added, "As always, I am willing to sop up any 'gravy,' if any is available."[40]

Bond's papers do not reveal whether he saw any real conflict between his personal advocacy of both the cause of African emancipation and the interests of the United States government. When given an opportunity to speak to these questions, he declined. In 1962, for instance, as AMSAC president, he received a communication from an African-American woman in Nigeria who criticized a recent AMSAC-sponsored concert for having performances in areas, such as modern jazz, that did not appeal to Nigerian audiences. She also chastised AMSAC for reserving too many seats for VIPs, a typical American tactic that she said did not sit well with African audiences. Instead of responding, Bond passed the letter on to John

Davis, who answered defensively and without dealing with the criticisms specified.[41] The writer's complaint that Africans did not have much in common with certain African-American cultural accomplishments was one that might be generalized politically and economically. Genuinely common interests are hard to imagine between Africans in developing nations and African Americans who were, comparatively speaking, reaping or aspiring to reap the material benefits of capitalism and participating in a culture that was becoming separated from its African antecedents.

The issue of genuine allegiance between Africans and African Americans represented by such groups as AMSAC was also poignantly raised in an exchange of letters between Martin Kilson and John Davis. Kilson, who had been a student of Davis and of Bond at Lincoln University and who later studied Africa in the Department of Political Science at Harvard, became Harvard's first regular black faculty member. Gently but firmly, Kilson accused AMSAC and Davis of imperialism, of considering the interest of America over the interest of Africans, and of not being vigorous enough in advocating African development when that development clashed with the desires of capitalism or the procedural conventions of democracy. Kilson also wrote to Bond, inviting his opinion on the issues he raised. Bond, however, demurred, preferring to remain on the sidelines in the dispute.[42] Thus Bond turned down an opportunity to put himself firmly at one or the other end of a spectrum in which valuing American interests would be one extreme and valuing African interests would be the other. He preferred, instead, to keep his views blurred and impossible to pin down.

AMSAC's demise began in the first half of 1967, when it was exposed, along with the African-American Institute, as organizations supported by funds or trusts that were secretly financed by the CIA. Clandestine government funding of such overtly nonpolitical cultural and intellectual groups as AMSAC was a shocking revelation in American academic circles, where many of the members of these groups were employed. Again, Bond left no record in his papers of his own reactions to these revelations. What has survived, however, are the frantic, but unsuccessful, attempts of AMSAC to find funding alternatives to CORAC, its major CIA conduit.[43]

One issue that merits mention is whether or not Bond knew of the ties between the CIA, and AMSAC and the AAI. The record cannot definitively answer that question, yet there is ample evidence for concluding that, if he did not know, he did not want to know. First, Bond's papers contain for both groups financial records that list the largest portion of income as coming from "Contributions"; the sources of these contributions are not identified. Second, Bond's published response to Ghanaian charges, including an allegation that AMSAC was CIA-funded, involved, not a direct rebuttal, but a recital of historic affinities between African Americans and Africa. Third, Bond had connections with other individuals associated with still other CIA-linked organizations: for instance, Mercer Cook, a cofounder, with Bond and John Davis, of AMSAC, became an official of the Paris-based Congress for Cultural Freedom, an international group of liberal intellectuals also exposed as an agency supported by the CIA,[44] and Bond's defense of AMSAC to Ghanaians included the laudatory identification of Cook as *the* black American ambassador to an African nation. In short, if Bond did not know of the links between his own groups and the CIA, he should have known.

The real question, however, is not whether or not Horace Bond knew of the ties between AMSAC and the CIA. It is, instead, how to interpret most fairly his actions as a representative of African Americans in Africa and as a friend of Africa in the United States of America.

Isolating a single thrust for Horace Bond's activities in Africa is an elusive task. The educational aspect of his African visits seems to track with his work in American educational circles. His African educational interests were extensions of his desire to increase educational exchanges between the two continents, to the mutual benefit of all parties. His economic and political pursuits, however, raise the issue of whether or not his drive for economic gain and political influence at times put him at cross-purposes with the interests of Africans.

Although this is a difficult matter to evaluate, Bond's views can be characterized as inhabiting a spectrum. In three examples taken from his speeches and writings to illustrate different positions on that spectrum, Bond was, respectively, one who dissembled with Africans; one who advocated a pointedly pro-American position in African affairs, even though he knew that it was not a complete answer to African problems; and one who had the interest of Africans completely at heart.

Bond's discussions of the agenda of AMSAC seem to have involved some stretching of the truth. In a presidential address given at an early meeting of AMSAC, Bond stated, "Our aims are not political." Similarly, in a letter to Kwame Nkrumah wherein he sought an invitation for AMSAC members to a conference in Accra, Bond remarked that the society is "concerned

with intellectual studies and artistic attainment. It is not a political organization." This chapter shows that that characterization was not completely
true. A distinct part of AMSAC's agenda was the pursuit of the political
goals of American foreign policy, and AMSAC cooperated closely with
government organizations devoted to that policy. Further, it had secret
funding from the CIA, the foreign intelligence arm of the United States
government. Bond's claim that he and his organization were not political
was therefore not candid.[45]

While Bond seldom publicly disavowed American interests in his dealings with Africa, he on several occasions admitted that these interests were
not wholly devoted to the improvement of Africa and that criticisms of
America's activities by her ideological opponents were not without foundation. In a 1961 speech to a church group in Washington, D.C., Bond
acknowledged that one reason that the United States was not winning the
cold war in Africa was that the West had much more to gain from the exploitation of African raw materials than did the East. Thus Africans could,
at least in this sense, see the East as a less threatening power. In another
part of the speech, he discussed W. E. B. Du Bois's recent advocacy of
Russia and China in Ghana as being based on Du Bois's experiences with
race riots while he was in Atlanta, with "lynchings, the disfranchisement,
the denial of simple human dignity; and, at the last, the humiliation of
arrest and handcuffing, and the denial of a passport"; Bond added, "If you
treat an intelligent and sensitive man like this for 93 years, what would
one expect but a relentless opponent in the Cold War?" Although Bond
was disappointed at the anti-Americanism gaining strength in Africa, he
understood the reasons behind Africans' advocating that point of view and
sensitized his audience to the debilitations of official American actions for
both Africans and African Americans.[46]

Finally, Bond could at times be completely devoted to African interests.
In a letter to Nnamdi Azikiwe, a Lincoln graduate who was then prime
minister of eastern Nigeria, Bond discussed the best possible educational
arrangement that that state might adopt. He described aspects of English,
Australian, Scottish, and American systems as desirable, but he thought
that none of them should serve as a model: "I think the new system should
be neither English, nor Scottish—American, or Antipodean—but African;
and that those who plan it should be open to imaginative willingness to
borrow from whatever source seems promising, but nonetheless, feel free
to improvise."[47]

It seems understandable that Bond would exhibit his most generous and least ideological side in discussing educational affairs, for that is what he knew best. He understood the strengths and weaknesses of American and other approaches to educational institutions. If one concludes that, in the economic and political realms, Bond may have understood both the benefits and drawbacks that American approaches would have for Africa, one can also conclude that he at times failed to act consistently on that understanding, choosing instead to act in ways that advanced his own personal interests and those of his country in preference to those of the Africans he sought to serve.

From the 1960s to the present, the history of the African nations, including those in which Bond was active, is one that gives little evidence of the effectiveness of the efforts of Bond and his colleagues. In Ghana, Nkrumah was deposed by a coup in 1966 and died in exile in 1972. Ghana has since been ruled by a succession of military governments, none of which has delivered on the promises of democracy and development made to its people at the time of independence. Nigeria came apart in the 1960s. After achieving independence with Nnamdi Azikiwe as governor general of the federation, it then became a republic with Azikiwe as its first president. The Republic of Nigeria, however, was soon overthrown by a military regime and then suffered a hideous civil war that followed the eastern region's secession from the federation and declaring itself the Republic of Biafra. The collapse of Biafran resistance to the federal forces meant that Nigeria once again had its eastern territories. The world was haunted during and after this civil war by the photos of starving Biafran children. At the federal level, a succession of military regimes was broken only for a brief period by a democratic interlude from 1979 to 1983, after which military rule resumed and continues to this day. Thus the Nigerians, like the Ghanaians, know neither political freedom nor economic development. Finally, Liberia, a showcase of democracy and American influence in Africa, failed to become either an economic or a political model for the rest of the continent. While until recently it maintained an ostensibly democratic government, its economy stagnated, ensuring that the bulk of its citizens did not escape poverty. In the last decade it fell under a military dictatorship, with its representative politicians executed by the new rulers as traitors to the nation. Most recently, it has lapsed into civil war, with two groups of rebels pitted against the government forces (aided by troops from other West African nations) and, sometimes, against each other.

Bond was bitterly disappointed by these kinds of developments. In a letter to Nkrumah shortly after he was deposed and expelled from Ghana, Bond remarked that the happenings in Africa had been "shocking," adding that the "African world that I have known has fallen apart." But he was not completely unprepared for the downfall. He had been well aware of both the personal weaknesses of the African leaders with whom he was friendly and the tenuous nature of their hold on power.[48]

In the United States, developments in African-American attitudes toward Africa and Africans were not much more palatable to Bond than were developments in Africa. The Black Muslim religious movement was certainly distant from the Christian missionary work in Africa and in the post–Civil War black South, which Bond frequently defended. While the phenomenon sparked by Alex Haley's *Roots* might have been amenable to Bond's love for things African as the source of much of value in American black life, that book's publication and the television series based on it came long after Bond's death.

In terms of tangible positive results, little remains that could testify to the success of the efforts that Bond and other black intellectuals expended on behalf of Africa and Africans in the 1950s and 1960s. Yet, for Bond himself, his African activities provided an outlet by which he could satisfy his own need for discovering the antecedents of his people, could pursue with other African Americans the objectively noble goal of the self-determination of nations emerging from colonialism, and could take himself away from the turmoil he was enduring in performing his administrative duties at Lincoln.

Chapter 10

Still a Scholar?

During and after his tenure as president of Lincoln University, as in his years as president at Fort Valley, Bond did not steadily produce the scholarly work he had learned to value early in his academic career. At Lincoln, administrative responsibilities and African affairs were major concerns, often to the detriment of his scholarship. In spite of these obstacles, he continued to write on academic subjects; still thinking of himself as primarily a historian of education, he made most of his contributions in this field.

In this chapter I consider two of Bond's scholarly efforts, both undertaken during the Lincoln years. The first is a piece of historical research done for the National Association for the Advancement of Colored People. Bond's effort was part of the NAACP's legal campaign against school segregation, which culminated in the 1954 decision on *Brown* v. *Board of Education*. The second is a history of Lincoln University which, though not published until 1976, four years after Bond died, was substantially completed by the time he left Lincoln in 1957.[1] In addition to discussing Bond's works and focusing on their contributions, I will highlight the intimate relationship between his historical research and the contemporary situations in which he found himself. In both cases, this relationship was allowed to affect and undermine Bond's scholarship. In the case of the Lincoln University history, it even appeared to contribute to his problems as a president.

It is a rare occasion when a historian is called on to participate in the framing of an important public policy. Such an occasion presented itself in 1953, when the NAACP put out a call to several noted historians and social scientists to help prepare a brief on school segregation. In June 1953, the NAACP lawyers and opposing counsel were requested by the United

States Supreme Court to prepare answers to five questions. The first two required answers dependent upon historical scholarship:

1. What evidence is there that the Congress which submitted and the State legislatures which ratified the Fourteenth Amendment contemplated or did not contemplate, understood or did not understand, that it would abolish segregation in public schools?

2. If neither the Congress in submitting nor the States in ratifying the Fourteenth Amendment understood that it would require the immediate abolition of segregation in public schools, was it nevertheless the understanding of the framers of the Amendment a) that future Congresses might, in their exercise of their power under Sec. 5 of the Amendment, abolish such segregation, or b) that it would be within the judicial power, in light of future conditions, to construe the Amendment as abolishing such segregation of its own force?[2]

To help answer the questions, the NAACP Legal Defense and Education Fund, under the leadership of Thurgood Marshall, sought the advice of some of the best academic minds in America. Those who worked for the NAACP included C. Vann Woodward, the southern historian, then of Johns Hopkins University; Howard Jay Graham, a legal historian and a law librarian in Los Angeles; John Hope Franklin, a black historian, then of Howard University; and Alfred H. Kelly, a constitutional historian who was also the chairman of the history department at Wayne University (now Wayne State University).[3]

The NAACP asked several other historians and constitutional experts to serve as the fifth member of this group, but they declined. (Among them were such established scholars as Henry Steele Commager, Carl Swisher, and Robert Carr.) Consequently, another historian had to be found. One of Horace Bond's colleagues at Lincoln, John A. Davis, had been named director of nonlegal research for the NAACP just as it was called on to prepare its answers to the Court's questions, and Davis knew that Bond would undertake the task with the dedication and thoroughness that the NAACP desired. When the invitation to join the NAACP effort was extended, Bond accepted with alacrity, though he had undertaken little historical research relevant to the issues addressed by the Court since the publication of his doctoral dissertation in 1939. However, the topic of that study—black education in Alabama after 1860—was directly related to the questions the Court had asked.[4]

The Supreme Court presented its questions to the contending parties in the school segregation cases on June 8, 1953; by early July, Bond was hard at work on relevant historical study. He was assigned to research the issue of how the states that ratified the Fourteenth Amendment understood its provisions with regard to school segregation. In addition to his own study, Bond coordinated the work on this topic of Marion Wright of Howard University and Mabel Smythe of the NAACP: Bond, through memoranda to the NAACP staff, suggested readings and research strategies for his two coworkers.[5]

Bond and his colleagues were only one part of the group working for the NAACP on the historical evidence relevant to the Court's questions. C. Vann Woodward and John Hope Franklin were studying the development of post-Reconstruction policies regarding race relations in the South. Based on their work, the NAACP hoped to show that the segregation that finally was countenanced in the *Plessy* v. *Ferguson* decision of 1896 represented a backing away from the commitments imposed on the South by the Fourteenth Amendment and other Reconstruction measures. Alfred Kelly and Howard J. Graham were working on the attitudes and intentions of the framers of the Fourteenth Amendment. As a result of their research, the NAACP planned to show that the radical Republican congressmen who proposed and approved the Fourteenth Amendment clearly intended to abolish segregation in schools and other areas of public life. In September 1953, the NAACP held in New York a conference that featured four seminars: three discussed, respectively, the work of Woodward and Franklin, Kelly, and Bond, and one was devoted to nonhistorical questions asked by the Court.[6]

The assignments of Kelly and Graham, and Bond and his collaborators, were in a particularly controversial area. What the framers and ratifiers of the Fourteenth Amendment intended regarding the issue of race and schools was by no means a settled historiographical issue. When Henry Steele Commager declined the NAACP's invitation to participate in the work, he reasoned that it was doubtful that the historical record would support the argument that the NAACP wished to make. Recent analyses of southern schools during and immediately after Reconstruction have revealed conditions that validate Commager's skepticism: while the freedmen had white friends in Congress, their friendship often stopped well short of their contemplation or enactment of full equality in education or in other realms.[7] To prove or substantiate the assertion that the framers of the Fourteenth Amendment and the state legislators who ratified it intended outcomes that were in conformity with the NAACP's position was an extremely complicated and demanding task.

Bond had little difficulty, however, embracing the NAACP's objective of desegregation. He had been involved in the debate among black educators about race and the schools at least since the late 1930s, when the *Gaines* decision sparked the beginning of the drive to desegregate graduate and professional education in the South. He had participated in a 1952 conference at Howard University to discuss the direction that court challenges to segregated schooling might take. There, he had urged the NAACP to push ahead with a constitutional challenge to segregated schooling itself, rather than to take the more timid path of arguing on a case-by-case basis that the segregated schools provided for blacks in the South were unequal.[8]

In pursuit of the NAACP's agenda, Bond diligently set out to prove that the states knew that the Fourteenth Amendment forbade school segregation. He was not unaware of the difficulties that existed in making this case; he knew, for example, that some northern states that had ratified the amendment countenanced segregation and that some southern states that had also ratified the amendment moved quickly to establish segregated schools shortly after its ratification. Late in August, he hit on his strategy. He thought that the truest test of the intentions of Congress was to be found in the eleven southern states of the Confederacy, ten of which, under congressional reconstruction, had to ratify the Fourteenth Amendment as a condition of their readmission to the Union. (Tennessee, the one Confederate state that ratified the amendment in 1866, when it was first proposed, was then readmitted and did not undergo the reconstruction process.) These states, after ratifying the amendment, had to submit their new constitutions to Congress for approval as a condition for readmission. Since Congress therefore had the ultimate power over these ten states, close study of their debates over ratification and adoption of their constitutions would provide the best evidence of Congress's intent and the states' beliefs about Congress's intent. According to Bond, "YOUR SOUTHERN RECONSTRUCTED STATES WERE A CREATION OF CONGRESS; AND AN IMMEDIATE TESTING GROUND FOR CONGRESSIONAL INTENTIONS."[9]

No copy of Bond's monograph dealing with this issue has been found. However, a copy of a chart Bond prepared for his work on the *Brown* case has survived. In the chart, Bond noted the constitutional provisions for education, if any, that existed in the eleven Confederate states before Reconstruction; any segregation proposals that were entertained in the state constitutional conventions at the time of Reconstruction; the failure of these proposals to pass their respective state bodies (except for Texas, which had its racially exclusive proposals voided by Congress); the provision(s) for public schools that were embodied in the new state constitutions; and any constitutional provisions regarding education and race that were enacted after readmission. The chart also dealt with statutory provisions regarding race and education before readmission; any actions regarding race and public schools proposed during the readmission process; the statutory educational provisions in the states at the time of readmission; and any statutory actions regarding race and education taken after readmission. In each section of the chart, a finding was presented for every state as well as a reference to the relevant source for the finding. This source was usually the proceedings of a constitutional convention or state legislature; occasionally, however, a secondary source was cited. The key findings of the chart were contained in two columns that showed that, in all of the eleven Confederate states, mixed schools were legal; that is, none of these states prohibited racially mixed schools in their constitutions or in their statutes at the time of their readmission to the Union.[10]

Bond thought that this information would help to make a strong case for the NAACP. In a letter to Mabel Smythe, he drew his own conclusion from this data: "NOW THE WONDERFUL THING ABOUT THESE . . . STATES . . . IS THAT NOT A SINGLE ONE WAS ADMITTED, OR READMITTED, TO THE UNION, WITH ANY PHRASE IN THE CONSTITUTIONS (CONSTITUTIONS DRAWN AND REDRAWN TO MEET THE SCRUTINY OF THE 39TH AND SUCCESSIVE CONGRESSES, AND TO BE IN CONFORMITY WITH THE CONSTITUTION AND THE FOURTEENTH AMENDMENT)—*that sanctioned segregation, or mentioned race, in connection with the public school system.*" He added that the reason for this was that the states knew that if they put any racial restrictions into their constitutions, they would not have been readmitted. "What better proof do you want, of the intent of the 39th Congress, or of the contemplation or understanding of the ratifying states?"[11]

Of course, Bond understood that he was interpreting the evidence in a way that supported the NAACP's case and that there were other conclusions that might be drawn from the same evidence. He alluded to this when he acknowledged that the evidence cited was better proof that Congress did not wish to sanction segregation in the laws and constitutions of the readmitted states than that Congress intended to abolish segregation.[12] Nonetheless, Bond's work provided a strong line of argument for the NAACP to take in its brief for the Supreme Court.

The association did indeed invoke Bond's reasoning in the parts of its brief that dealt with the constitutional provisions for education in the re-admitted states. Of the approximately two hundred pages that composed the brief, some fourteen cover the material developed in Bond's chart and his discussion of his topic. Early in the brief, the NAACP summarized its points, and the eighth numbered paragraph mentioned the states' re-sponses to the Fourteenth Amendment, a topic developed at length later and along the lines of what Bond had claimed to be the case in his let-ters to NAACP officials. The eleven Confederate states had ratified the amendment and, at the same time, eliminated racial provisions in their laws and newly drafted constitutions that had authorized or required racially separate public schools. The ten Confederate states that had to ratify the amendment and adopt constitutions acceptable to Congress before being readmitted "considered that the Amendment required them to remove all racial distinctions from their existing and prospective laws, including those pertaining to public education."[13]

In support of this conclusion, the brief dealt with each of the eleven states separately, giving a short history of race and education before adop-tion of the Fourteenth Amendment, in the constitution passed as a con-dition to readmission to the Union, and after readmission. Close perusal of these state-by-state accounts shows that, for the most part, they utilized the findings and citations included in Bond's chart. Sometimes a secondary source not in the chart appears in the brief, such as Stuart Noble's history of education in the state of North Carolina. However, Noble's work surely was not unknown to Bond; it may well have been that the citation was added by Bond after the chart was first prepared. The bulk of the discrep-ancies between Bond's chart citations and those in the brief are similar additions or slight changes in references. Indeed, there are scarcely any points made in the brief that are not adumbrated in his chart.[14] It therefore seems fair to conclude that Bond was the intellectual progenitor, if not the author, of these fourteen pages of the NAACP brief.

To get a sense of the effectiveness of Bond's contribution, one can com-pare the discussion of state action in the NAACP brief with the discussions in the briefs prepared by the state of Kansas and by the United States government as amicus curiae. Claiming that a single convincing thesis re-garding the understanding of the ratifying states was impossible, given the

wide variety of circumstances in the states before and at the time of ratification, the Kansas brief paid little attention to the actions of the states
in ratifying the amendment. In discussing the former Confederate states,
Kansas noted that they ratified under the pressures of Reconstruction for
one main purpose — "to regain their representation in the national Congress" — so their assenting vote was not a true indication of sentiment in
these states. The relevance of Kansas's argument here is doubtful, since
the Court sought information, not on sentiment in the state, but on the
"state legislatures which ratified the Fourteenth Amendment." [15]

Kansas went on to claim that any conclusion regarding the sentiment
in the states could best be reached by examining their actions regarding
race and schools contemporaneous with the ratification of the Fourteenth
Amendment. Kansas stated that, "of the 37 states that comprised the Union
at the time of adoption of the Fourteenth Amendment, 24 of them maintained legal segregation in the public schools at the time of adoption or
subsequent thereto"; this meant "that none of those 24 states considered
that segregation was abolished by the Fourteenth Amendment." [16] On this
last point, the Bond-inspired part of the NAACP brief, which discussed
the actions of the states, provided a strong counterargument. The NAACP
showed that 10 of the 24 states that had segregated schools after the enactment of the Fourteenth Amendment were the southern states that provided
for segregation only after they were safely free from the scrutiny of Congress. While under Congress's eye, these states dared not segregate their
public schools, because they thought it would prevent their readmission to
the Union.[17]

The United States government had officially entered the *Brown* case at
the time of its first hearing, when it filed a brief favorable to the claims
of the NAACP. On the answers to the Court's historical questions, however, the federal government did not make an argument compatible with
that of the NAACP. Regarding the issue of sentiment in the states at the
time of ratification of the amendment, the United States contended that
the materials relevant to ratification were too sparse and the references to
education in these same materials too few to "justify any definite conclusion that the state legislatures which ratified the Fourteenth Amendment
understood either that it permitted or that it prohibited separate schools."
In support of a contention that the states did not consider that the amendment prohibited segregation, the United States noted, as did Kansas, that,
simultaneous with or subsequent to ratification, "some of the Northern

states had and continued segregated schools and some of the Southern states, in providing for the first time for public education for Negroes, established separate schools."[18]

The NAACP brief also provided some answers to the contentions of the federal government. First, the NAACP undoubtedly would have responded that the question of intent as reflected in the states' ratification processes should be answered on the basis of the best evidence available, not dodged, as the government seemed to do. The NAACP brief, relying on Bond's work, provided such an answer—and it was that Congress intended not to allow school segregation. Interestingly enough, despite its contention that the evidence regarding the states' ratification processes was scanty, the government provided approximately 230 pages of appended material related to this very topic. Like the portion of the NAACP brief devoted to the ratifying states, the government's appendix was organized by state. Each section had a brief opening statement and then a recounting of the states' constitutional and legislative actions relating to race and schools. Close study of the sections on the eleven southern states reveals little disagreement with the NAACP brief on questions of fact; the discrepancies that exist are in the interpretation of the facts.[19]

The government contended that the fact that the southern states established segregated schools shortly after readmission called into question the argument that the states understood the amendment to prohibit school segregation. The NAACP contended, to the contrary, that the fact that the southern states waited until after readmission to establish segregated schools meant they clearly understood that Congress intended that segregation was not to be in the constitutions or laws of the readmitted states. As for the northern states that had segregated schools at the time of ratification, the NAACP's interpretation was that Congress did not have the power to prohibit segregation; that Congress could not act to end the segregation in the northern states did not mean that it agreed with that segregation. The NAACP argued that, when Congress encountered the opportunity to keep segregation out of the constitutions and laws of the states, as in the case of the southern states, it did so.

None of this is to say that the section of the NAACP brief which was based on Bond's analysis of the ratification process in the eleven southern states provided the final answer to the Court's questions. Its weaknesses, however, were not clearly noted in the Kansas or the federal government brief. One weakness was the claim that the actions of the Congress and the eleven states did establish that the Congress wished to "abolish segregation in public schools," the precise wording used in the Court's question. The NAACP showed, not that Congress intended to abolish segregation, but that Congress did not allow a state to place school segregation in the constitution it submitted as part of its process of seeking readmission to the Union or to place school segregation in the laws it enacted under that constitution while still subject to the congressional oversight of the reconstruction process.

A second problem with the Bond-NAACP argument was that the evidence regarding the intent of Congress was not direct evidence. Instead, the NAACP brief made an inference on the basis of actions taken, not by Congress, but by the eleven southern states in response to their understanding of the intent of Congress. This indirect evidence, no matter how strong it may have been, was subject to counterevidence, both indirect and direct, about the intent of Congress.

What emerged from the various briefs was more a puzzle than a picture. The Court had asked for historical evidence on the intent of the Thirty-ninth Congress. In contexts much less complex than those surrounding that session of Congress, historians have struggled mightily with the problem of the motivations of historical actors. It would be an overstatement to say that the Court asked for the impossible; but, clearly, it asked for a relatively simple answer to an immensely complex question. One should not be surprised, then, that the justices did not find the historical answers of any of the contending parties completely convincing. Speaking for the Court, Earl Warren, chief justice of the United States, called the historical evidence "inconclusive." Describing evidence offered by all sides in response to the historical questions, Warren noted:

> It covered exhaustively consideration of the Amendment in Congress, ratification by the states, then existing practices in racial segregation, and the views of proponents and opponents of the Amendment. This discussion and our own investigation convince us that, although these sources cast some light, it is not enough to resolve the problem with which we are faced. At best they are inconclusive. The most avid proponents of the post-War Amendments undoubtedly intended them to remove all legal distinctions among "all persons born or naturalized in the United States." Their opponents, just as certainly, were antagonistic to both the letter and the spirit of the Amendments and

wished them to have the most limited effect. What others in Congress and the state legislatures had in mind cannot be determined with any degree of certainty.[20]

That the Court was not persuaded by the historical argument proffered by the NAACP did not mean that the work done by its consultant historians played no role in helping the Court to reach its ultimately favorable decision. Alfred Kelly, one of the historians who aided the NAACP, noted that the Court's verdict that the historical evidence was "inconclusive . . . does not mean that the historical argument was without meaning in the Court's opinion." Kelly thought that the historians were able to help the NAACP obtain a draw in the matter of answering the historical questions, which was all that Thurgood Marshall really wanted from the voluminous historical record. What this accomplished, according to Kelly, was to allow the Court to back away from the flat statement, in the *Plessy v. Ferguson* decision, that Congress condoned segregation and to look to other areas for guidance on the issue. Without the historical draw, Kelly speculated that the Court would have been unwilling to deviate from the *Plessy* precedent. Casting aside *Plessy* enabled the Court to speak for "the American conscience."[21]

As for Bond's role in the case, when his participation in the historical research done for the NAACP brief is considered alongside his forthright advocacy of the NAACP's frontal attack on school segregation in 1952, he appears to have played a significant role in the struggle for integrated schools that was successfully culminated by *Brown*. Rita Norton, one of the librarians involved in organizing the Bond Papers, has contended that these activities represent one of the major accomplishments of Horace Bond's career.[22] It is hard to argue with her conclusion.

Yet it must also be stated that the accomplishment illustrates Bond's political advocacy better than his scholarly work. Bond's historical research for the NAACP was certainly competent enough for the purposes for which it was intended—helping the association to build its case in answer to the questions of the Court. That the information supplied by Bond was used in the NAACP's brief is testimony to its value. The overlap between his sources and those cited by others involved in the case testifies further to his competence as a historical researcher.

To have made a primarily scholarly contribution of this work, however, Bond could have published his findings in a forum that would have made them accessible to other historians and educators. This is exactly what Alfred Kelly, C. Vann Woodward, and John Hope Franklin did. Kelly published several articles related to the work he had done for the NAACP. Woodward published a now-classic book, *The Strange Career of Jim Crow*, which was based in considerable part on the research he did for *Brown*. Franklin expanded upon his work on the *Brown* case to write *Reconstruction*.[23] In Bond's case, the scholarly community never had a chance to evaluate his contribution, since he published nothing related to it.

There are several explanations for Bond's failure to publish. His time was taken up by the myriad presidential duties in which he was engaged, including intricate infighting with faculty and alumni critical of his administration. Planning for and taking lengthy trips to Africa and working on behalf of various educational, economic, and political interests related to Africa also took up large segments of his time. This left little time for the pursuit of scholarly research and publication. When an emergency call from an old colleague such as John Davis came, Bond answered, and he threw himself into the work of helping to prepare the NAACP brief. Yet it is also true that he spent, at most, parts of three to four months on the work, and then he moved back to his more immediate concerns, running his college and working for and in Africa. The important goal, for Bond and for the NAACP, was to win the case. That accomplished, Bond quickly removed himself from the historical world of Reconstruction and post-Reconstruction South to pursue the practical concerns of college president and international advocate.

The desire of the NAACP to win the case also did not necessarily mesh with scholarly concerns. While an academic historian such as Alfred Kelly pondered the relationship between his scholarship and his advocacy, Bond revealed no such qualms. Kelly worried in print over whether or not he allowed his political allegiance to the NAACP to distort his scholarly judgment. In contrast, Bond was content to let his political goals drive his scholarship and was unconcerned about difficulties in reconciling the two. Although he did not think that advocacy and scholarship were identical, Bond argued that the historian who made his political position known at the time that he wrote or spoke about an issue had discharged his professional obligation to the truth.[24] The problem in Bond's argument here is that, while disclosing one's political position is clearly better than hiding it, this is no guarantee that good history will result.

In June of 1954, Bond received from the NAACP a congratulatory letter acknowledging his contribution to the successful pursuit of the *Brown* case. Shortly afterward, he wrote to Thurgood Marshall, thanking him for the opportunity to participate and praising Marshall and the NAACP for carrying on the civil rights struggle that "radicals" at Lincoln University had carried on starting in 1875. In that year, black alumni had begun to agitate for black representation on its all-white faculty.[25]

The history of Lincoln University was the major scholarly effort on which Bond would labor during the years of his Lincoln presidency. He began work on the project in 1947, two years after he was appointed chief academic officer at Lincoln. He pursued the research avidly, working during the night and any other free hours that he could steal from his busy schedule. He often regaled old friends who visited him at Lincoln with accounts of what he had found in his research.[26] Bond planned on finishing his history in time for the celebration of Lincoln's centennial in 1954. However, he missed that deadline and in fact never completed the history to his own satisfaction or that of a publisher during his lifetime; publication of his manuscript did not take place until after his death.

Probably the first thing that strikes the reader of the published version of Horace Bond's history of Lincoln University is its size. The text runs to some 550 pages, with 30 pages of notes (though the notes to two of the book's twenty-six chapters are missing) and several pages of photographs as well as prefatory material and an index, all of which add up to a volume of well over 600 pages. Almost from the beginning, the project was formidable in size. At different times while he was working on it, Bond remarked that the length of the volume was 150,000 to 180,000 words, with several chapters still to be written.[27] The manuscript was overly long, particularly for a volume that covered only one hundred years of the institution's history. In fact, Bond really stopped his account with the inauguration of his own administration in 1945, so these 180,000 words covered fewer than ninety years of the college's development (1854–1945).

Bond did not discuss the founding of Lincoln University as the Ashmun Institute, which took place in 1854, until over 200 pages had elapsed. Clearly, then, Bond included in his volume more than what was typically included in an institutional history, and he explained this by noting that he was writing the history of an idea as well as an institution.[28] The idea that Bond chronicled was that the black man should receive a higher education. Lincoln University was the first institution to provide for the higher education of blacks in America—in fact, anywhere in the world. Bond felt that this unprecedented accomplishment required an examination of the ideas and events that led to the founding of the Ashmun Institute.

That examination stretched over twelve chapters, or 207 pages of text, that chronicled the intellectual and spiritual roots of John Miller Dickey, the founder of the Ashmun Institute. As Bond described them, these roots were "ancient," for he saw Lincoln's founding as one of the most propitious outcomes of the Judeo-Christian ethic that animated western European culture for at least a thousand years. The Presbyterianism of John Miller Dickey as well as the Quakerism of the founder's mother, Jane Miller, were the most important illustrations of that ethic for Lincoln.[29]

Bond discussed still another facet of the prehistory of Lincoln: the development of political thought in Pennsylvania, particularly the ideas of Benjamin Franklin and Benjamin Rush, a young physician from Philadelphia whom Franklin befriended. Rush possessed a "humanitarian" zeal inspired by the Enlightenment philosophers and their passionate conviction of the rights of man. The idea of humanitarianism was crucial to Bond's account of Lincoln, as it had been to many of his other historical works. In Bond's history, it was defined as "the idea of instant and vigorous response to any claim by the poor or oppressed for fair treatment; the idea that all men are the children of one God, and thereby are brothers who owe to each other the readiest and most generous response when a need becomes apparent."[30]

In addition to detailing the various white humanitarians who opposed slavery and advocated black education, Bond devoted a number of pages to the free black community in Philadelphia, a group particularly important to Bond's formulation of the idea of Lincoln University, because they were the forerunners of the Lincoln students and alumni who would lobby for a greater black presence in the faculty and administration of the school. Black Philadelphians also played a large part in supporting Lincoln, with both dollars and enthusiasm, almost from the beginning of its history.[31]

However, Lincoln University was not completely a product of the humanitarian ideas that Bond so loved; rather, Lincoln was founded by colonizationists, men who opposed slavery but eschewed the radical step of abolition in favor of the much less controversial measure of colonizing American slaves and free blacks in Africa.[32] As Bond saw it, the cautiousness of the colonizationists clung to the white leadership of Lincoln University from its inception, through the time of his own inauguration in 1945, and afterward. In Bond's history, black students and alumni who chafed under paternalistic white rule could see the seeds of their own commitment to black liberation, not in the white leaders who founded Lincoln and led it in its formative years, but in the Quaker, abolitionist, and Enlightenment traditions that influenced the climate of opinion in Pennsylvania and the rest of the North in the pre–Civil War era. The few white faculty who supported the desires of black alumni for black faculty and administrators were seen as acting in the true humanitarian spirit.

Bond's two hundred pages of prefatory material, then, were needed so that he could construct for Lincoln, the college of colonizationists, a history that could speak to the activist black members of the Lincoln community, who sought an institution that reflected an authentically black agenda, rather than the agenda its white founders and their successors had prescribed for their charges. In a sense, Bond constructed for Lincoln a history that had not really existed—one that served his own personal vision of what the university should be.

When Bond finally did get around to dealing with actual events in the history of Lincoln University, his work resembled the more typical institutional history of a college or university. Three chapters examined the administrations of the presidents who had preceded Bond, and four chapters addressed, respectively, curriculum, administration, support, and finances.[33] The chapter on curriculum was particularly significant, for it showed how the agendas of paternalistic white administrators and those of black activists reinforced each other. The white Presbyterian ministers, who maintained their influence into the time of Bond's presidency, valued a liberal arts curriculum that would prepare students for the colonizationist-inspired task of service to their black brethren, be it through teaching, the ministry, or such fields as medicine. This emphasis put Lincoln squarely at odds with Booker T. Washington and his allies, who stressed industrial education for black schools. Lincoln's anti-Washington orientation was admired by activist blacks who did not want the school to submit to the political and economic accommodationism that characterized Washington's work. Bond showed how Washington's influence in helping institutions obtain funding from the philanthropies he favored influenced Lincoln's decision to announce a program in scientific agriculture in 1909 (the program never got off the ground). Lincoln, like other black liberal arts colleges, was not above appearing to cater to the program of the noted Tuskegeean in order to obtain funding; it did not, however, deliver on its promises. Bond's readers could therefore conclude that Lincoln had used Washington for its own purposes.[34]

Bond's treatments of such topics as organization and administration, finance, and donors to the college were less interesting and less significant than the discussion of curriculum. They mimicked traditional institutional histories in their detailed concentration on the internal and external forces that contributed to Lincoln's development. Bond examined the various departmental and other organizational plans as well as endowment, tuition, scholarships, and other aspects of Lincoln's financial development. The chapter on donors detailed the contributions made by Presbyterians, philanthropic agencies (such as the General Education Board), and members of the Lincoln community (such as faculty and alumni). All of this material, while of importance in accounting for the college's development, was as inert in Bond's discussion as it is in most institutional histories.[35]

More lively were the descriptions of various presidential administrations as well as of other aspects of campus life. Here Bond painted the individuals who drove the institution and the ways that the student body related— or, rather, did not relate—to the white ministers who led Lincoln in its early years. Later, Lincoln's white presidents came from the faculty and were somewhat more approachable, but they still stood at arm's length from the students. Indeed, student life proceeded almost independently of the administration. Bond surveyed the rise and fall of such student groups as the debating societies and the coming to prominence of the athletic program and the Greek-letter social clubs in the first few decades of the twentieth century, when he had been a student.[36]

The real drama in Bond's history, however, was contained in two chapters and other sections devoted to disputes between black alumni and the white leaders of Lincoln. In the 1880s, Lincoln alumni began their campaign for black faculty. Notable names in black American history involved in this effort included Frederick Douglass and the Grimké brothers, Archibald and Francis, who attended Lincoln, and their white aunt, Angelina, who supported them and the college. Bond detailed both the zeal of black advocates for an integrated faculty at Lincoln and the intransigence of the white minister-presidents who refused to accede to the demand. In discussing later administrations, he again returned to the issue of the alumni's goal of an integrated faculty and, later, administration. Resolution of the dispute would not come until the 1930s, when the first black faculty member was hired, and 1945, when Horace Mann Bond was hired as Lincoln's first black president.[37]

In accounting for administrative opposition to a biracial faculty, Bond cited the geographical situation peculiar to Lincoln. It was difficult to introduce black professors into a white faculty that lived close together in a rural Pennsylvania community whose racial mores were more southern than northern. The theological views of the Presbyterians who led Lincoln until 1945, however, were most important in accounting for the failure of Lincoln to add black faculty. In explaining the opposition of Isaac N. Rendall, president of Lincoln from 1865 to 1905, to blacks on Lincoln's faculty or board, Bond cited Rendall's theology of mission as the animating force. The notion of "Xarisma" (hereafter discussed as charisma) was the critical element in this theology. For Rendall and many of the other Presbyterians who worked at the college, charisma was their biblically based, special mandate from God to work among the black race. To admit blacks to the faculty would be to deny these white men the opportunity to work at their divinely appointed task of ministering to their black brethren.[38] . Bond's discussion of charisma, without acquiescing to the racial exclusiveness in which it resulted, was sympathetic. Here he was the historian at his best, empathizing with the person whom he was studying and coming to an understanding of the forces that drove men like Isaac Rendall. Linking this episode to the early caution of the colonizationists, Bond skillfully explained how Lincoln came to seek its student body in the South, where blacks were in dire need of education and also where blacks were much less likely to exhibit the independence shown by the northern alumni who had sparked the controversy over a racially mixed faculty.[39]

When it came to describing the situation in the 1920s and thereafter, however, when the issue of black appointment to leadership roles again arose, Bond made little effort to empathize with the opposition. Instead of describing charisma in detail, he simply remarked that the white trustees who refused to seat a black from the alumni association on the board were relying on "the ancient dogma that Lincoln University was 'the white man's work for the Negro.'"[40] Of course, the situations were not truly comparable. In the earlier case, a man who was the president of Lincoln University for forty years was commenting on the work to which he and most of his faculty colleagues had seriously committed themselves. The 1920s board was dominated by fundamentalist, white Presbyterian ministers, many of whom had little experience in or genuine commitment to black education. In 1926, the board tried to fill a presidential vacancy three different times with men who were unacceptable to alumni, faculty, and student activists; the board finally chose a president who came from the faculty and was acceptable to alumni. Smarting from this setback, the trustees were more determined to thwart alumni efforts to have a black alumnus sit on the board. The alumni association had petitioned for black representation on the board as an added measure to the grievances it was pursuing over the choice of the next president.[41]

Bond also did not highlight the differences between the larger social and political climate in the 1880s and that of the 1920s. In the earlier period, Lincoln was one of several black colleges that had no black participation in its faculty and administration. In the 1920s, on the other hand, many black colleges were being swept by a movement to redress the inequities of not having any black teachers, trustees, or administrators at colleges conducted for the black race. The agitation on black campuses over this and other issues has been described as the campus equivalent of the New Negro movement of cultural and political awareness that was then taking place in the larger black community. Bond did not highlight the turmoil in the black intellectual community or the unrest on other campuses in his discussion of Lincoln University in the 1920s; he did, however, describe the unfavorable attention that the Lincoln board's intransigence was gaining in the black press as well as in some liberal white religious papers.[42]

The board's miscalculation of the strength of alumni feeling, the support among some white faculty, and the embarrassment that some trustees felt at the unflattering newspaper descriptions of their activities resulted in the appointment of the head of the alumni association to Lincoln's governing body. That shifted the battle to the issue of a permanent black faculty member, and here, again, the board was in opposition to black alumni who supported the move. The black trustee, however, chose to support his white colleagues' opposition rather than the wishes of those who had supported his appointment. Even more perplexing was student opposition to the selection of a black teacher. Bond explained the situation by noting that these students were largely from working-class homes, had worked at menial jobs for whites, and therefore would not be likely to challenge the authority structure that pervaded their personal as well as their academic lives.[43] He ended his account of this episode by showing how persistent alumni pressure, along with the liberal attitudes of the new president and several of his faculty colleagues, finally resulted in the appointment of Lincoln's first black professor in 1932.

Bond's criticism of Lincoln's blacks in the 1920s seems excessive. A careful reading of his analysis of Lincoln's student body and alumni, particularly of their southern origins and their penchant for safe conduct and for avoiding political controversy, should have led him to some understanding of their point of view. One can only speculate as to why he did not internalize his own analysis. Perhaps it was because the situation in the 1920s too closely resembled the debates and disputes that surrounded his own hiring as Lincoln's president in 1945 and the racial animosities that flared between him and a few of the diehard faculty members and that dogged his presidency.

The last two chapters of Bond's history were devoted to Lincoln's continuing relationship with Africa and Africans, and they reveal one reason for Bond's affinity for the colonizationists who founded Lincoln, even though, with regard to ideology, he clearly preferred the abolitionists of that day. What the colonizationist impulse allowed Bond to find in Lincoln's history was a long tradition of interest in Africa that he was building on in his own presidency.

This discussion of Bond's history of Lincoln University leads to the suggestion that he wrote it to speak directly to the political issues that had arisen in his own presidency. The main dispute in which Bond was embroiled was with alumni and some older white faculty members who, as he saw it, sought to thwart his direction for Lincoln. The understanding Bond showed in dealing with Isaac Rendall's desire to maintain a white faculty did not extend to his discussion of student, faculty, and alumni who opposed the selection of a black faculty member in 1932. Bond's attitude toward this instance of black opposition may well have been influenced by the memory of black opposition, mainly from alumni, to his own candidacy for Lincoln's top post in 1945. His mention by name of a white faculty member who opposed blacks on the board or the faculty in the 1920s and who was also a leading critic of his own presidential actions in the 1940s and 1950s can also be interpreted as an instance of how his current political battles shaped his views of Lincoln's past.[44]

Self-justification seemed to underlie some of Bond's history. His elaborate construction of a more radical, Quakerly, abolitionist past for Lincoln allowed him to use it to compete with the conservatism that accompanied the colonizationist orientation of the school's founders—and that he himself was still fighting in the faculty. If this explanation is not adequate, certainly one needs some other description that accounts for his spending two hundred pages on the prehistory of Lincoln University. Similarly, highlighting the African connections in Lincoln's history served Bond's need to answer critics who claimed his own stress on African students at Lincoln and his personal activities in Africa were harming his presidency.

I have thus far focused on the ways in which Bond may have interpreted Lincoln's past to suit his presidential priorities. But his concentration on the particulars of Lincoln's past may also have prevented him from acting appropriately in the present. Two examples come to mind. Given Lincoln's enrollment and financial problems in the 1950s, Bond's failure to support coeducation and his desire to hang on to the seminary need explanation. From the beginning of his presidency, he consistently refused to consider the admission of women students in any but token numbers, despite frequent suggestions that he do so.[45] It may well have been that his allegiance to the all-male student body, the makeup that had characterized Lincoln throughout its history and that he remembered from his own days as a student, kept him from understanding that coeducation would certainly be a way to even out Lincoln's roller-coaster enrollment cycles. On the issue of the seminary, the economic drain it imposed on the rest of the university was clearly described in the accreditation reports made at Lincoln in the 1950s, yet Bond did not choose to try to abolish the seminary. His own sense of the importance of Presbyterianism to Lincoln's historic role of missionary to Africa as well as the cultural depth of his own historically conditioned religious commitment seems to have contributed to his refusal to see the handwriting on the wall. Whatever the reasons behind Bond's stubborn allegiance, within two years of his departure the seminary was closed.[46] Increasing secularization was occurring at Horace Bond's Lincoln University. This process began with the initial grant of state aid to the school in the 1930s, and it intensified as that state aid increased. Bond understood that Lincoln's future was as a Pennsylvania public institution,[47] and he acknowledged this in his history. But as president he seemed unable to act decisively on the basis of that understanding to alleviate the financial burden that the seminary placed on the institution.

Some of the problems in Bond's history of Lincoln can therefore be seen as the result of his writing it with the present too firmly in mind, and some of his presidential actions can be seen as having taken place with the past too prominent in his thoughts. The condition behind both of these weaknesses is described in historiographical literature as *presentism*, a term that refers to the difficulty historians often have in keeping the past and the present in the proper relationship to each other.[48] It is not that historians do not or should not write their accounts of the past with present concerns in mind. If historical accounts did not in some sense speak to present concerns, they would have little value. However, historians should not allow their account of the past to be distorted by present-day concerns, which, in turn, tempt them to ignore the ways in which the past differed from, as well as resembled, the present. Bond appears to have succumbed to the distorting qualities of presentism in his account of Lincoln's history.

A related problem is the way historical understanding can positively affect the actions of current decision makers. In fact, one recent book details how certain choices made by political leaders have profited from their understanding of parallel circumstances faced by earlier decision makers.[49] Bond's roles as Lincoln's historian and Lincoln's president, however, appear to offer a counterexample. At least on the issues of coeducation and the seminary, his knowledge of and affinity for the past seem to have hampered his ability to make appropriate decisions.

Bond's history of Lincoln University, then, does not appear to have been the escape from the problems of his presidency that some of his acquaintances, and perhaps he himself, thought that it was. Rather, it was a contained, documentary universe wherein he could seek solace, reinforcement for himself in the university's internecine disputes, and guidance for his presidential actions. Unfortunately, his use of the documents appears to have led both to a less than exemplary history of Lincoln University and to a strengthening of his resolve to plow ahead with his presidential priorities in the face of considerable opposition.

For almost fifteen years Bond searched for a publisher for his history with little positive outcome, a testimony to the work's shortcomings. He initially tried commercial publishers. He was for a time involved in a scheme by which a commercial publisher would bring out his book and others under an imprint called Lincoln University Press. At least once he considered publication through a vanity press, and he asked the Pennsylvania Historical Commission if it would publish the manuscript. He also constantly sought subsidies from individuals and philanthropies to underwrite the history's publication.[50] Bond was indefatigable, however: he also attempted, unsuccessfully, to get the manuscript published by several university presses. Gordon Hubel, director of the University of Pennsylvania Press, told Bond that, as it stood, the manuscript could not "make a viable book for a general, or even somewhat specialized, readership." Hubel recommended depositing a copy of the manuscript in the Lincoln University library, where it could serve as a valuable resource for future scholars. For the work to be published, Bond would have to "distill the current manuscript into a less minutely detailed and more straight-forward history of Lincoln University."[51]

By the time Bond heard from the University of Pennsylvania Press, he was sixty-four years old, in failing health, and unable or perhaps unwilling to undertake such a massive revision of the manuscript. Surely this was not the first time he had heard that his manuscript was unwieldy, bogged down in detail, and of little interest to a readership outside the family of Lincoln University. In fact, it was the Lincoln University community that finally arranged for the publication of Bond's work, though this did not come until 1976, four years after he died. While he was still alive, Lincoln University established a committee of staff and faculty to prepare the manuscript and seek financial support for its publication. Progress, however, was slow. Bond was disappointed at the lack of alumni response to a plea for financial support; also, he had to contend with the committee's decision to change the first phrase in the title of the manuscript from what he had chosen, *God Be Glorified by Africa*, to *Education for Freedom*.[52] However, shortly before his death, Bond did learn of the plans that finally effected his book's publication. The Princeton University Press agreed to print the manuscript for Lincoln University (rather than publish it under the Princeton University Press imprint) if a suitable subvention could be obtained. Even this arrangement dragged on for several years, however; *Education for Freedom: A History of Lincoln University, Pennsylvania* finally appeared in 1976 with financial help from the Bicentennial Commission of Pennsylvania.[53]

The relative dearth of published reviews of Bond's book is another clue that it was not a strong work. In a magazine for librarians, a journal noted for its generally favorable, though short, reviews, an unnamed reviewer was ambivalent about *Education for Freedom*, characterizing Bond's work as "a rich, albeit jumbled, book to be read, nay savored, at one's leisure."[54] The reviewer for the *Journal of Negro History* described the first eight chapters of the Lincoln history as "essentially a biography of [Lincoln's founder, John Miller] Dickey in which Bond's major concern is the religious and intellectual heritage of the man and how social forces of the period reinforced or altered these traditions." The reviewer's evaluation began with a discussion of the book's long gestation period as a way of explaining its size. She described the work as "hampered by extensive detailed accounts of individuals and events that have little or no direct relationship to Lincoln's history"; noted "the abundance of undigested information," such as "pages of testimony" from students; decried the overly lengthy quotations from "sermons, speeches, letters, as well as passages from books"; and concluded that the poor organization and unnecessary wordiness often left the reader confused. For this reviewer the book exhibited a tendency to inject contemporary information into the history in a way that confused the reader. However, in spite of its faults, she concluded, "This study is a significant contribution to the scholarly literature on the history of black education."[55]

There seems little doubt that *Education for Freedom* made a contribution to black educational history, but there also seems little doubt that the volume as it stood was much less of a contribution than it could have been. In fact, the successful telling of Lincoln's history still awaits a historian who can locate the institution's past in a crisp, cogent discussion of its antecedents; who can recite the particulars of its historical development clearly and concisely, without seeing the past mainly as a rehearsal for the problems encountered in its present conditions; and who can recount the relationship between Lincoln University and Africa in a manner that accurately accounts for the waxing and waning of that relationship.

This account of two of Horace Bond's major works of scholarship while he was president of Lincoln University shows that Bond had neither the sustained commitment to scholarship nor the analytical abilities that he had evidenced earlier in his career. In doing research for the NAACP in the *Brown* case, he knew the documents and the sources that should be consulted, and he did the work competently. When the desired political result was achieved, however, Bond lost interest in his material. Bond's history of Lincoln University raises a different set of concerns. Here again, he knew the sources and how to use them in preparing the manuscript. However, he allowed himself to get lost in the study of the years before Lincoln began, and he recounted Lincoln's development in ways that served his present orientations rather than a fair account of the events. He also proved unable to overcome the minutiae of the events he was describing and produce a coherent narrative of Lincoln's past. The one substantial review of *Education for Freedom* demonstrated that this later work was distinctly inferior to the works turned out by the same scholar two decades earlier. While many historians develop as they mature, gaining an increasing mastery of the sources and the circumstances they are studying as well as the wisdom to weigh the results of their research more judiciously, Horace Bond seems not to have achieved this kind of maturation.

In fact, projects related to the historical studies he pursued while writing his dissertation lay unfinished for the rest of Bond's career. One of these was an historiographical critique of Walter Fleming's book on Alabama during Reconstruction. Bond was convinced that Fleming had distorted the historical record, and, to support his argument, Bond went to the trouble of preparing a lengthy outline of Fleming's claims and the sources used to substantiate them. In 1958, after Bond had left Lincoln, John Hope Franklin urged him to get on with that project, now that he was no longer burdened by his presidency.[56] But Bond never finished the work on his Fleming critique. Instead, his scholarly work after he left Lincoln University drifted away from historical concerns.

Chapter 11

After Lincoln

Horace Bond lived for fifteen years after he left the presidency of Lincoln University in 1957. For fourteen of these years, he served on the faculty of Atlanta University, first as the dean of the School of Education and then as the director of the Bureau of Educational and Social Research. He administered the school and then the bureau without obvious difficulties, regularly taught graduate courses in education, and served effectively on various committees.

In the first several years after his dismissal from Lincoln University, Bond was distracted by a bitterness toward "his" school for what he thought was its unfair treatment of him. Worse, he became embroiled in a financial dispute with Lincoln over the terms of the settlement that accompanied his negotiated agreement to resign from the presidency. The dispute was not settled until the mid-1960s, and only then was Bond able to let the wounds of his Lincoln years begin to heal.

In the personal realm, the last fifteen years of Bond's life were perhaps more fulfilling than any other period. His children came into adulthood and took on their own lives. His daughter Jane had finished college, married (Bond often consulted his son-in-law, a lawyer, about his affairs), and had two children. His son Julian had also married, had four children, and meanwhile attained a national reputation through his activities in the Student Nonviolent Coordinating Committee. Horace was extremely proud of his son's success.

During his years at Atlanta University, the elder Bond's scholarly work continued. Immediately after leaving Lincoln, he took up a prestigious lectureship at Harvard University. The publication of his lecture added another book to the Bond bibliography. He published one more book, in 1972, the year he died.[1] Historical research remained a concern, but for most of his publications Bond returned to the field of mental testing. Near the end of his career, Bond had his prominence acknowledged by the institutions that extended several job offers, which he turned down to stay in Atlanta, near his children and grandchildren. The scholarly work Bond produced in these years, however, did not possess the originality and significance exhibited by his work in the 1930s.

Bond had become discontented with the Lincoln presidency long before his resignation in 1957. Because of his unease with the situation at Lincoln, he sought a teaching and research position as an alternative. Late in 1956, he turned down an opportunity to be considered for the vacant presidency of Fisk University; instead, he asked whether there might be a faculty position for him there.[2] It seems clear that he was set to abandon college administration and return to teaching and research full-time.

In 1957, as the situation at Lincoln was coming to a head, Bond began an earnest search for an academic position. When the board met in April and decided to seek his resignation, he wrote several letters to acquaintances in black colleges as well as in the white scholarly and educational world. In May, in the midst of this job search, he received word that he had been chosen to give the Alexander Inglis lecture at the Harvard Graduate School of Education.[3] Bond's selection as Inglis lecturer culminated an effort that he had initiated two years earlier. In 1955, Bond contacted Martin Kilson, a Lincoln graduate then pursuing his doctorate in political science at Harvard, and asked Kilson to check with his advisor to see if he could obtain a position at Harvard. The invitation to deliver the Inglis lecture was the main outcome of this inquiry. While in Cambridge to give the lecture in June 1957, Bond inquired about spending a year at Harvard, during which he could teach part-time (either at Harvard or, nearby, at Tufts University), work on his history of Lincoln University, and write up his Inglis lecture for publication. This proposal did not bear fruit, because, according to Bond, the expense of housing in Cambridge and the costs of enrollment of his two oldest children in a nearby college were prohibitive.[4]

While Bond was still mulling over the possibility of a year in Cambridge, he asked the president of Alabama State College, where he had taught in the 1920s, to consider him for a faculty position there. The response from Alabama was the offer of a professorship in education. Almost at the same time, Bond received an offer to come to Atlanta University as acting dean of the School of Education. The president of Atlanta University, Rufus Clement, was an old friend of the Bond family from their

Kentucky days. Clement's sister, Ruth, was married to Horace's brother Max. Horace Bond delayed acting on either of these offers, hoping that an arrangement could be made in Cambridge; when it was not, he accepted the position at Atlanta University.[5]

Bond had many reasons for choosing Atlanta over Alabama. At Atlanta, he would be dealing only with graduate students and was guaranteed a light teaching load and some time for research. In Alabama, by contrast, he would be working at a largely undergraduate institution and would have a heavy teaching load. Also, in Atlanta his children would be able to enroll in one of the prestigious colleges affiliated with Atlanta University. Finally, life in relatively cosmopolitan Atlanta, with its significant and established black community surrounding the Atlanta University Center, was preferable to life in Montgomery, where the Alabama school was located.

Bond's clear preference, however, had been to obtain a regular position in Cambridge. He apparently thought this was a real possibility, at least for a while.[6] It would have been unprecedented, however. Harvard had no regular, full-time black faculty member; in fact, the institution's first black professor was Martin Kilson, who was offered the position after he finished his Ph.D. A few weeks after learning that there was no chance for him to go to Harvard permanently, Bond rejected an offer from the Pennsylvania State Department of Instruction to become a supervisor of higher education. If this offer had come from a white university, it seems likely that Bond would have accepted. His desires for time for research as well as for recognition of his scholarly accomplishments would have been better met by white institutions, most of which were more securely funded and more willing to grant research time to their faculties than were black colleges. That Bond received no such offer was no surprise, either to him or to his friends. One cannot help but wonder how many white ex–college presidents with credentials and publications significantly inferior to those of Bond received appointments to white colleges and universities in this period. Such were the realities of racism in the American academy in the 1950s.[7]

During Horace Bond's first several years at Atlanta University, he was still disputing his settlement with Lincoln University. Although their quarrel was over financial matters, it seems clear that the emotional shock of his dismissal and the circumstances surrounding it intensified Bond's negative feelings. One of his concerns was the university's lack of official recognition of stock in an African iron-ore company, which Bond had turned over to the university shortly before leaving; a second was the money due him as part of his severance from Lincoln; finally, he worried that Lincoln would renege on its commitment to pay into his Teachers' Insurance and Annuity Association (TIAA) account until he reached the age of sixty-five.

All of these matters were extremely important to Bond, for his financial situation was such that he had to budget conscientiously to meet his expenses. He never owned a house during his years as a college president; the family always lived in campus housing. While this meant that the family's housing costs were minimal, it also meant that no equity was being built up for its future. Given that expenses always seemed to equal salary, the Bonds had little money in reserve. On the issue of the stocks, he was fearful that, if Lincoln did not officially acknowledge that he had donated them to the university, he might be liable for taxes on increases in their value. Though he gave the shares to Lincoln in 1957, they were not acknowledged on any official Lincoln financial statements for several years, and in the interim the stocks had appreciated substantially (they finally showed up in Lincoln's financial audit for the 1961–62 fiscal year).[8]

Bond's salary conflict related to an agreement he had reached with Lincoln's board of trustees at the time of his dismissal in June 1957. They were to pay him for a year after his resignation, and they were also to pay into his retirement account with the TIAA until his retirement. When Bond took the position with Atlanta University in September 1957, Lincoln stopped paying his salary, claiming that his remuneration was a sabbatical arrangement which his acceptance of full-time employment elsewhere negated. Bond was furious, interpreting the suspension of the salary as part of a vendetta being waged against him by the board of trustees. He considered filing a lawsuit to recover the salary funds, but he temporized for a period; he preferred to negotiate, hoping to receive part or all of the money he considered owed to him. At one point during the initial negotiations, he tallied up the amount he sought from Lincoln and what they were willing to pay.[9]

The negotiations with Lincoln were drawn out and, ultimately, unsuccessful. In 1960, Bond consulted a friend who was a lawyer about filing suit to recover the disputed salary and retirement contribution. Bond's friend, Louis Redding, initially demurred, claiming that the official record of the agreement with Lincoln called on Bond to work on his history as a condition of the salary being granted. Bond replied that he had worked on the history and was trying to publish it. Another year elapsed in which negotiations continued between Bond and Lincoln through Redding.[10]

When attempts to solve the matter finally fell through altogether, Redding, who was from Delaware, put Bond in touch with George Brutscher, a Pennsylvania lawyer from a town near Lincoln, who agreed to file the lawsuit. Soon afterward, settlement appeared likely. At that point, Bond interjected the matter of his donated stock, claiming that the terms of the donation, agreed to verbally, though not in writing, required that Lincoln had to use the proceeds for scholarships for African students. This prompted a brief, somewhat exasperated letter from his attorney, who urged him to concentrate on the salary matter and avoid the distractions of other issues.[11]

Lincoln proved unwilling to settle the salary matter on Bond's terms, and Bond and his lawyer agreed to proceed with the suit. By then, it was late 1963, over six years after Bond had left Lincoln. Another six months would pass before the suit was finally settled, almost seven years after his departure. The terms of the settlement called for Bond to receive $7,500, one-fourth of which went for attorney's fees. This left him with a little over $5,000, about half of what he claimed Lincoln owed him. The amount of money Bond gained hardly seems to have been worth the time and energy he expended on the suit, a judgment he had himself reached earlier in the course of the dispute, yet it should be noted that $5,000 was about one-half of his year's salary at Atlanta University.[12]

Bond, of course, welcomed the money, but he also viewed the settling of the lawsuit as a personal victory in a long fight with a by-now almost loathsome enemy. On several occasions in the years before the dispute was resolved, he bitterly chastised the trustees who were active at the time of his dismissal. In response to a query from an Atlanta lawyer as to the trustees' opinion of him, Bond noted that the two faculty trustees "hated my guts." As the suit dragged on, he concentrated his antagonism on the president of the board of trustees, Lewis Stevens. At one point, he noted that Stevens was "a man of vast political ambitions" who did not know how to focus on issues or arguments; instead, he would "believe . . . the last word from the last person he sees." Later, Bond attributed his treatment at the hands of the trustees to political differences: he was a Republican, whereas Stevens, as well as several other board members, were Democrats, and Bond claimed that the Democrats on the board were infuriated when he gave a speech criticizing Adlai Stevenson's ancestors, who were Copperhead Democrats.[13]

In the midst of his dispute with Lincoln, Bond prepared to go public with the issues. He told the editor of a leading black newspaper in Philadelphia that he had not taken the job in the Pennsylvania Department of Education because it would have prevented him from publicly exposing the finaglings of the trustees. These men, who were capable of saying anything about him in their attempt to discredit him, were a threat to the cause of black higher education in the state of Pennsylvania. That was why, Bond claimed, he arranged to have written into the minutes of the board meeting at which he officially resigned a set of resolutions attesting to the virtues of his stewardship at Lincoln. If the resolutions had not gone on record, he believed, the board might have trumped up any number of charges to sully his reputation.[14]

Bond's enmity for Lincoln University was not restricted to the members of its board of trustees. He also harbored ill feelings for those members of the faculty whom he associated with his dismissal, most notably Harold Grim. In 1961, Bond refused to contribute to a Lincoln fund-raising drive as well as to a fund for a gift honoring Grim, and he told the alumnus seeking the funds of Grim's constant criticism of his administration. And he leveled a new charge against Grim: noting that the letter seeking donations to the Grim fund listed Bond's old adversary as a Phi Beta Kappa graduate of Lafayette College, Bond told the fund-raiser that when Lincoln had tried to get a Phi Beta Kappa chapter on its campus, it had come to light that the honorary fraternity had no record that Grim was ever a member.[15]

In 1962, in the middle of negotiations regarding his financial claim against Lincoln, Bond arranged a trip to the campus to obtain some photographs for his history of Lincoln. Bond turned down, however, the opportunity to attend a reception held in his honor and hosted by Lincoln's new president. Bond claimed time pressures as the reason to keep his trip short, but allowing an extra hour or so to attend a social event could hardly have caused him insurmountable scheduling problems. Though he told the president that he intended "no discourtesy" to his former colleagues or to the university, his actions belie his words.[16]

In 1963 Bond received an invitation to the fortieth reunion of his graduating class at Lincoln University. The invitation came from I. J. K. Wells, a longtime friend and steadfast supporter of Bond during his troubled presidency. At the top of the letter was a handwritten note from Wells: "I know how you 'feel' — But show your BIGNESS and come up. It will help you and it will help all." Bond's reply was terse: "I am very sorry, but I cannot be there." He gave no reason, but asked that his old friends be apprised of his regrets at not being able to make the trip.[17]

From all of this one concludes that Bond was deeply wounded by his experiences at Lincoln University, and these wounds were kept alive by his financial claim against Lincoln that dragged on for seven years after his departure from the campus. His bitterness soured most of his dealings with Lincoln and its constituencies; in fact, the feuding seems to have left Bond with a rancor that damaged his relations with his school for the rest of his life. He could not forgive Lincoln for what he thought it had done to him, and, while it does appear that Lincoln treated him shabbily, it seems that he dwelled on his injuries in a way that hampered his ability to turn his attention to other concerns. He also seems to have used his animosity toward Lincoln as a shield against having to consider the ways in which his own actions may have contributed to his problems.

When Bond arrived at Atlanta University in September 1957, it was not certain that he would stay in Atlanta for more than a brief period. His brother Max wrote to him from Tunisia in October, advising him to go back to the writing that he had largely abandoned during his presidency; as for Atlanta, Max advised Horace to look things over carefully, and "if there is one doubt in your mind get the hell out of there before it is too late." It is difficult to pinpoint the source of Max's concern. It may have been awkward, for both Horace Bond and Atlanta's president, Rufus Clement, to have a former president as a faculty member. Max was not convinced, however, that his brother would not prosper at Atlanta under the presidency of his brother-in-law: in fact, Max opined, Atlanta "might be a place where you could spend the rest of your life."[18] That is exactly how things turned out.

Initially, however, Horace Bond's commitment to the deanship at Atlanta as well as the institution's obligation to him were tentative. Hired as a guest professor and acting dean, he sought, scarcely a month after arriving in Atlanta, a semester's leave or other released time to take a position as an educational consultant to the government of Nigeria. In his letter to President Clement in which he described the situation, he indicated that he was not wedded to being a dean but could easily envision having a faculty position. This would allow more flexibility in his employment conditions and provide more of an opportunity for him to take advantage of this and similar offers that might come in the future.[19]

The arrangement in Africa did not work out, however, and in April 1958 Bond took the deanship at Atlanta on a regular basis along with a faculty position as professor of education. Both positions were specified contractually as of five years' duration. He did not have tenure in either role, an indication that his position was still not completely secure. The education dean's job at Atlanta was not onerous, particularly when compared to the Lincoln presidency. Bond had few responsibilities outside of the management of the affairs of the School of Education, a small unit of Atlanta University with a relatively small faculty and student body. At first he took on a few teaching duties, thus indicating that he intended to rejoin the world of academia.[20]

Bond's post as dean of education at Atlanta University lasted for nine years, during which the affairs of the school appear to have run smoothly. This is not to say that there were no controversies or difficulties. From time to time, problems with a colleague over a student's master's thesis would arise, and such troubling issues as the adequacy of secretarial help also surfaced. Yet one gets the impression that the School of Education functioned satisfactorily under Bond's leadership.[21]

In addition, Bond took a prominent role on significant university-wide committees. In 1959 he chaired a committee convened to look into establishing a doctoral program at Atlanta. The committee's report advised that the institution proceed cautiously, for the research priorities of such a degree needed to be well understood by faculty and administrators, sufficient financial support had to be available, additional faculty to support doctoral studies were necessary both at Atlanta University and at the undergraduate colleges in the Atlanta University Center, and a goodly number of high-quality students were required. Bond's committee suggested that the first doctoral degree be offered in biology, where faculty members were qualified for the endeavor. Education might be the next logical area, but only if the doctoral program could be separated from the certification and training functions of the existing School of Education.[22]

In the mid-1960s, Bond chaired a committee, with membership from each of the units of the Atlanta University Center, that developed criteria for the distribution of twenty thousand dollars in research funds to faculty members. At about the same time, he served as Atlanta University's representative to an intercollegiate consortium that was drawing up an application for a southeastern regional educational laboratory. His reports on the meetings of that group show an acute grasp of the political realities involved in setting up such an agency.[23]

In the summer of 1966, Bond discussed with President Clement giving up the deanship of the School of Education. Clement then offered Bond the position of director of a to-be-established Bureau of Educational and Social Research. The president made it clear that Bond's new duties were to be a grantsman for the entire university and to seek financing for his own work as well as for other research projects of Atlanta University faculty. In his letter accepting the position, Bond expressed his desires to maintain his faculty rank and to continue teaching at least one course per semester.[24]

Bond was assuming a new position that meshed with his own priorities as his career was drawing to a close. Earlier in the 1960s, he had successfully pursued a research grant from the United States Office of Education. Shortly after becoming director of the research bureau, he wrote a proposal for federal monies of $100,000 to fund a research agency at the Atlanta University Center. Unfortunately, this proposal was not granted, and Bond was similarly unsuccessful in securing outside funding during his term as director of the research bureau.[25]

Bond's own account of his duties at the research bureau indicated that President Clement set up the agency without providing the necessary funding for its staff or operations. When Clement died the year after Bond assumed his new position, the successive inhabitants of the presidential office did nothing to alleviate the situation. In 1968 Bond referred to his bureau as a "one-man affair" in which his own operations seemed to be at loose ends. He remarked that, because of the circumstances, he "did not have a sense of obligation" to Atlanta University.[26]

In short, Bond's appointment as head of an unsupported research bureau might have been a way of putting an old man out to pasture. He was being removed from the day-to-day operations of the university and its School of Education and was being isolated from faculty concerns. However, Bond seemed content at this gradual disassociation from the university. As he prepared for his retirement, he turned to his scholarly work as a refuge, as he had done earlier in his career.[27]

Although Bond's years at Atlanta University were not marked by significant institutional accomplishments, they do seem to have been a relatively calm and pleasant period in his life. He was freed of the cares and concerns that had dogged his presidencies, and, financially, Bond was as secure as he had ever been. Though he had taken a significant cut in salary (from $10,000 at Lincoln to approximately $7,000 in Atlanta), he was able to recoup some of the loss through summer teaching. Also, his salary was increased regularly during his tenure at Atlanta University, almost doubling to a total of $13,500 for the 1966–67 academic year. In addition, Julia Bond finished her master's degree in librarianship at Atlanta University and was employed in the library there at a salary of over $7,000. In the mid-1960s, Horace Bond was able to purchase a lot near the campus at a quite reasonable price through an urban renewal program; there he constructed a four-unit apartment building, with one unit reserved for him and his wife. The Bonds were finally able to leave institutionally owned housing, in which they had lived since 1939, and avail themselves of the financial advantages of home ownership.[28] Of course, Horace and Julia Bond were far from wealthy, but they were secure and as comfortable financially as they had ever been.

This was also a period in which Horace Bond's children were growing up and beginning to make their own marks on the world. Their father had assiduously husbanded his resources at Lincoln to enable them to study at good private schools. The two eldest children, and particularly the oldest, Jane, had done well academically. Jane consistently scored in the highest range of academic aptitude tests and excelled in her collegiate studies. Her brother, Julian, also scored well on aptitude and ability measures; however, he had more difficulty in school. Like many a bright student, Julian did well in subjects he liked but had difficulty in subjects he did not like, so his academic record was not what it could have been. The youngest Bond, James, had even more problems in his schoolwork. According to his father, James had some kind of psychological block that discouraged him from reading. In order to try and compensate for the situation, Horace tried various devices to get James to read, including contracting with his son to pay him a sum for each book that he read. It was clear to Horace Bond that his youngest child did not have the verbal abilities that the two older children did.[29]

Despite the superior academic record of his daughter, Horace Bond appeared to be more interested in the future of his older son, Julian. This interest was shared by Horace's brother Max, who wrote that Julian was the one who would be Horace's successor. When the family moved to

Atlanta, Julian was enrolled as a student at Morehouse College. In response to a plea from Martin Kilson, Bond's former student, that Julian enroll at Harvard or some other more prestigious institution, Horace remarked that the money would be wasted until Julian got a better sense of the importance of academic study; Morehouse was a good school and also close enough for Horace to monitor his son's progress. Julian's performance in his first year was creditable, though not as good as it should have been. He had difficulty in chemistry, a subject in which his father speculated that he never cracked a book. Bond hoped, however, that his son might suddenly turn over a new leaf and excel in his studies. This is what had happened to Horace himself in his junior year at Lincoln University.[30]

Julian Bond would make his father proud in the next several years, thought not through his accomplishments as a student. Rather, Julian chose the role of civil rights activist. He participated in the drive to integrate lunch counters in Atlanta and served as a leader in the activities of the Student Nonviolent Coordinating Committee. Horace Bond approved of his son's activism and criticized those, such as former president Harry S. Truman, who were opposed to the lunch-counter sit-ins.[31]

Julian went on from his civil rights activities to pursue a career in politics and public speaking. He earned a seat in the Georgia legislature, though he had to gain the right to be seated through the courts when state legislative leaders refused to seat him because of his opposition to the Vietnam War. Perhaps his most notable political moment came when his name was placed in nomination for the vice-presidency of the United States at the 1968 Democratic national convention. (At the time, he was too young to qualify for the office under the United States Constitution.) Horace Bond followed his son's political career avidly. He received frequent letters from his friends noting one or another of Julian's accomplishments and responded with his own proud endorsements of Julian's activities.[32]

Horace was moved by more than the usual parental pride in approving of Julian's career. His son's notoriety along with the accomplishments of the entire civil rights movement provided an opportunity for Horace to rekindle interest in his own work and activities. Both of his 1930s books were reprinted in the late 1960s, spurred by the attention given to black history that was sparked initially by the civil rights movement. Horace attempted to use his son's reputation as an entrée for obtaining a contract for a history of the Bond family, which he was then researching. Also, his own speaking engagements increased rapidly, both in number and in the amount of remuneration, as a result of Julian's spreading fame. He wryly noted to one old friend that he often was chosen as a less costly alternative to his son, who commanded enormous fees and whose speaking schedule was crowded.[33] In the midst of all this flurry of attention surrounding Julian, however, one wonders whether Horace Bond was completely satisfied with his son's accomplishments in politics. What the elder Bond had desired for his son was the kind of academic career and scholarly accomplishments that he had only sampled in his own life.

One area in which both Julian and his sister Jane pleased their father immensely was in their family life. Horace Bond was a doting grandfather who spent much more time with his grandchildren than he ever had with his own children, perhaps as a way of making up for the time he had not given to his own. He told an Atlanta University administrator that it was the fact that he would have to leave his grandchildren behind that caused him to turn down an offer to come to the University of California, Los Angeles, in 1968. No doubt the grandchildren also played a role in his decision to turn down teaching offers from Stanford University and the University of Georgia.[34]

Also while in Atlanta, Bond was able to exercise his skills as a lively and often controversial intellectual combatant. As a college president, he tended to keep his controversies private; this did not mean, however, that they were subdued. As shown in the discussion of his Lincoln presidency in chapter 8, he had a long and often bitter dispute with those whom he considered his enemies on the Lincoln faculty; he also occasionally engaged in sharp exchanges with white scholars and intellectuals with whom he disagreed on one or another issue.[35] All of these exchanges were private, however. Perhaps as a college president, he did not feel that he should take his differences with other scholars into the public arena. Or it may be that the presidency kept him so busy that he could not spare the time to prepare his remarks in the polished way required for publication. Near the end of his Lincoln years, however, a resurgence of an old intellectual enemy—the notion that the low IQ scores of blacks were due to genetic inferiority—pushed him back into the public arena. During the late 1930s genetic interpretations of IQ scores had been largely discredited. In that decade a spate of white criticisms of these interpretations from scholars such as Otto Klineberg forced the genetic determinists into retreat. But in the 1950s, the *Brown* decision sparked renewed charges of the intellectual inferiority of blacks. Southerners, interested in finding whatever ammunition they could to thwart the integration of their schools, resorted to arguments almost identical to those which had been popularized in the 1920s. The resurrection of the old claims about racial differences in IQ scores on army intelligence tests given during World War I provoked Bond's return to this particular fray.

In 1956, southern congressmen intent on derailing school desegregation renewed the argument that, based on the army test data of forty years earlier, blacks were genetically inferior to whites. Bond raised his counter-arguments, basically the same ones that he had used in the 1920s and 1930s. Now, under the auspices of the National Association for the Advancement of Colored People, he reported that the home states of these southern congressmen were characterized by a "voting constituency [that] is in the lower 20 per cent of mental ability of American whites, so far as that mental ability is shown by Army IQ test scores" and that the most vocal of the congressmen, a Georgian, had attended a college that in the 1930s had ranked 201st out of 205 colleges and universities in its average student IQ.[36]

In 1958, one year after Bond arrived in Atlanta, the publication of Audrey M. Shuey's *The Testing of Negro Intelligence* granted some academic respectability to the arguments of the southern politicians. Shuey, a psychologist on the faculty at Randolph-Macon Woman's College in Lynchburg, Virginia, reviewed the results of 288 studies of intelligence test scores of blacks and whites and claimed that these studies forced one to conclude that blacks were innately inferior to whites. In a lengthy review of Shuey's book, Bond countered her analysis with his own long-held environmentalist explanation: "This simply means that everywhere in the United States the American Negro is a subordinated, underprivileged social caste." He recounted the history of the controversy over IQ scores in the 1920s and 1930s, noting that the results of his own studies as well as those of other scholars, black and white, had discredited the explanation that Shuey was now reviving. He speculated that Shuey's book was so popular because it was being used to fight school integration in Florida and was being provided, at no cost, to white citizens' councils in several southern states.[37]

Four years later, Bond was battling with Carlton Putnam, Shuey's doctoral adviser, on a similar issue. Putnam claimed that the scientific accomplishments of George Washington Carver, the famous black scientist, were due to his white blood. (Putnam concluded that Carver was white because Carver had blue eyes.) In a speech that was widely reported in the black press, Bond cited his own recollection, as well as those of several colleagues and acquaintances of Carver, that the Tuskegee scientist did not have blue eyes. He went on to detail the relationship Putnam and Shuey had with right-wing and white-supremacist groups in the South that would grasp at any straw in their campaign against black rights.[38]

Shuey, Putnam, and the groups that used their arguments were really on the fringes of American intellectual life. Still, Bond thought it important to expose the racism in their arguments and the political uses to which they were being put. Moreover, Bond did not confine his published critiques of racial views he thought incorrect to exponents of the far right. Bond was not, however, uniformly unpleasant to white scholars and intellectuals. There are too many examples of polite and productive exchanges between Bond and white historians or other academics that show his generosity and courtesy to his coworkers, whatever their color.[39]

The major intellectual accomplishments of Bond's last fifteen years were not primarily in the field of educational history. Instead, most of his work was in the area of mental and psychological tests, an important focus for him during his doctoral studies and the first years of his career. During his two presidencies, however, he published little in mental testing, though he stayed abreast of current developments. Once relieved of presidential burdens, he was free to return to the testing work. His positions as the dean of the School of Education at Atlanta, and, later, director of a research bureau there meant that his interest in testing would also dovetail nicely with his occupational situation.

Bond's Inglis lectures at Harvard related mainly to the field of mental testing. Though he gave the lectures in June of 1957, they were not published until 1959. After the lectures were delivered but before they were published, the Russians launched *Sputnik*, the first rocket-powered artificial earth satellite, in the fall of 1957, and the momentous event greatly influenced how Bond revised his lectures for publication. In order to interest his readers in his ideas on intellectual talent, Bond skillfully built on both the cold war animosity toward the Soviets, which had been building in the United States since the end of World War II, and the *Sputnik*-induced fear that the Soviet Union was eclipsing the United States in scientific and other intellectual attainments. He began by exposing the falsity of Soviet claims that their scientists came from the working and farming classes; rather, the leading Russian men of science were descended largely from the managerial, intellectual, and other privileged sectors of the middle and upper classes of Soviet society. These scientists were the products of a classically elitist European system of academic education, much like that found in England and Germany.[40]

When he analyzed American intellectual achievements, Bond observed a similar phenomenon. America claimed to be much more democratic than European societies in choosing its intellectual elite, for the choice was made largely on the basis of such objective criteria as standardized test scores rather than on, say, parental background. Furthermore, the movement to raise the intellectual standards in the United States, a reaction to Soviet success with *Sputnik*, could be expected to increase reliance on these scores as identifiers of the talented youth needed to compete with the Soviets. Unfortunately, according to Bond, higher test scores would not necessarily indicate a situation in which opportunity was spread through the social structure.[41]

Bond's analysis of the social background of high scorers on the tests administered to high school students by the National Merit Scholarship Corporation revealed the same skewing that occurred in European countries. Youngsters of higher socioeconomic backgrounds could be depended on to score significantly higher than youth of lower-class backgrounds. Intellectual factors in these varying backgrounds were also extremely important. Bond showed that a librarian's child was 1,120 times more likely to become a merit scholar than a laborer's child. Similarly, the child of professional parents was 30 times more likely to become a merit scholar than the child of farmers.[42]

Bond was convinced that standardized tests were perpetuating in America the same class hierarchy that existed in Russia and the rest of Europe. He vigorously opposed this situation:

> I cannot bring myself to believe that the odds against "high scholastic aptitude" for various occupational classes even remotely resemble the genetic distribution of capacity in the persons concerned. I cannot believe, for example, that there is only one potentially "talented" child among the children of 3,581,000 laborers, while there are 234 among the children of 2,965,000 professional, technical, and kindred workers. Nor can I believe that there is no child—among the 10 million Negroes of the American South—with a "talent potential" worthy of search and subsequent development.

He suggested that a truly American talent hunt would have to go outside of the normal path of identifying ability and look for hidden ability in the black segments of the American population as well as in other environmentally deprived groups, such as rural white southerners.[43]

Bond then described his own work, which showed that such hidden talent did indeed exist. He was studying the family and educational backgrounds of approximately three hundred American blacks who held doctoral degrees. While almost all of the grandparents of these individuals had been slaves, their parents' occupations resembled those of the high-scoring youth on the National Merit Scholarship tests, an indication of the remarkable "social evolution" that had taken place among this relatively small group of blacks. In attempting to isolate the environmental forces that made for such remarkable progress, Bond would work on this study for most of the next decade, and the environmental correlates of academic achievement would be his main intellectual interest for the rest of his career. As he explained to one academic audience, he sought "to discover the secret of how you develop able academic individuals from underprivileged groups."[44]

At times during this period, he attempted to make his research available to popular audiences. In May 1963, he appeared on an Atlanta radio show and told his listeners that many of the black doctorates he was studying had risen to the top from decidedly unfavorable social circumstances. He cited as one example a poor Tennessean who had become a specialist in tropical diseases. The son of a sharecropper, this individual had enjoyed few material or educational advantages in his early life; he did have, however, a mother who encouraged him in his ambition to succeed and a teacher who challenged him to make good on his ambition. Bond remarked that he did not see why this combination of parents who taught a young person good work habits and a teacher who built on those habits and challenged the youngster in school could not be a model for the contemporary poor. Until this model was universally followed, however, in the public schools "the children from the poorest background need more attention—not the same, not less, but *more*—than other children." Bond was here articulating a position consistent with his earlier environmentalism, a position that he had held since the 1920s and that also would undergird such compensatory federal educational programs as Headstart.[45]

Bond pursued his study of the background and career of black doctoral degree holders throughout the 1960s, and in 1967 he entered into a contract with the United States Office of Education to conduct an elaborate study and report the results of the study. Bond's work, *Black American Scholars: A Study of Their Beginnings*, was published in 1972, shortly before his death. There are few meaningful differences between the unpublished report and the published version of Bond's work, leading one to conclude that the study was substantially completed by 1967.[46]

The preface to the published study reiterated Bond's commitment to environmentalism as the best and most democratic explanation of academic ability. He criticized hereditarian explanations of academic ability as "entirely a product of the neo-Darwinism that seized the popular imagination during the second half of the nineteenth century." He ended his preface with a resounding affirmation: "It is with the utmost faith in the equalitarian nature of human ability that I submit this study."[47]

Bond's findings in *Black American Scholars* were based on the return of a survey by 517 black holders of doctoral degrees, an increase of 40 percent over the 300 Bond had mentioned in the 1959 published version of his 1957 Inglis lectures. The questionnaire asked for the date of birth and death, the place of birth, the places lived in, and the educational background of the subject and those of his or her father and mother; the level of elementary, secondary, and higher education achieved by each respondent and his or her parents as well as the kind of institution (private, public, church-sponsored) each attended. In addition, it sought information as to important informal educational experiences, occupations held, unique characteristics, and "kinfolk" with advanced degrees. Bond found in the initial responses to the survey the basis for some rich family histories that could provide convincing explanations for his subjects' achievements. Though these histories could not be quantified or analyzed statistically, they were extremely important. Bond initiated further correspondence with several of the subjects in order to flesh out their families' histories, which he described at length in one of his chapters. He also constructed genealogies of the families responsible for producing the greatest number of black doctorates, incorporating them in one of the many appendixes to the book. Thus even in a work that was ostensibly in the field of mental ability, he made sure that it had a historical dimension. He also had his students in his graduate education classes at Atlanta University write their own family histories in an attempt to educate them about the value of education in their own backgrounds as well as in the hope that they might provide information useful for his survey.[48]

Black American Scholars contained nine chapters which took up 125 pages of text. Ten appendixes consumed another 50 pages, while maps illustrating the geographic origins of black doctorates, their families, and the schools they attended filled another 20 or so pages. The result is an unwieldy volume, a hodgepodge of information and appendixes that cry out for either explication or elimination and maps that are sometimes so poorly produced that they are almost undecipherable. It did contain, however, a wealth of data that could have been the basis for a much more effective volume.[49] Moreover, the early chapters of *Black American Scholars* contained material taken almost verbatim from *The Search for Talent* and from an article Bond had prepared for a reference book, but *Black American Scholars* did not expand on these earlier efforts in any substantial way. Also, though Bond stated his hypotheses early in his book, in later chapters he drifted off on several tangents; when it came time again to restate his hypotheses in the conclusion, Bond did little to prepare the reader for the analyses he provided.[50]

What sustained this volume was Bond's clear commitment to environmentalism as an explanation of the academic achievement of his black doctorates. Yet the book can be read to support a conclusion not completely consonant with environmentalist explanations. For example, the main thesis—that the achievement of blacks is related to family background—is as easily attributable to hereditary factors as to environmentalism. Further, while Bond defined blacks as a group as "underprivileged," he also noted that there were considerable variations in the privileges and advantages they enjoyed. Later, he added that the bulk of his doctorates came from families belonging to the more socially, economically, and educationally advanced sectors of the black population, information that could also be used to support an explanation not in conformity with environmentalism.[51]

During these years, Bond became at times almost obsessed with test scores. He took several standardized tests and reported his scores as well as those he had made on standardized tests earlier in his life. (He seemed well satisfied that his scores were almost always high.) While he offered environmentalist explanations of test data when discussing his own scores as well as those of black doctorates, the high scores he and the other doctorates achieved could also have been used by the environmentalists' detractors, who could say that high scores simply confirmed the relation between measured intelligence and achievement. Further, when the scores were combined with data on family background, one could conclude that black educational attainment came largely from the "better strata" of the black population—the black elite, if you will—an argument that could easily be couched in a way that supported a genetic hypothesis. Bond's unwillingness to discard intelligence tests and desire that the tests be less biased and more fairly administered meant that he would never dismiss them simply as harmful.[52] This meant, in turn, that his arguments could frequently be countered, if not always convincingly, by test advocates who claimed that environmentalism was an overused crutch by which low-ability individuals and groups refused to face the consequences of their own lack of ability.

At some points in his book, Bond himself seemed to question a completely environmentalist interpretation of his data. For example, in discussing how a large group of black doctorates attended a relatively small number of black undergraduate colleges, he concluded: "These institutions are also examples of the development in a racial minority of colleges with a social and class 'elite' enrollment, in which students tend more and more to come from 'white collar,' professional families."[53]

The data that most strongly supported Bond's environmentalist arguments was in his eighth chapter, "Were These the Truly Underprivileged?" Here he described the histories of 16 of his 517 subjects who "might most clearly be classified as 'underprivileged,' or 'culturally' or 'educationally disadvantaged.'" Bond identified these underprivileged by their parents' lack of education, and these 16 Ph.D.'s had parents who had little or no formal education. Bond's brief recounting of their life histories concluded that their unusual achievement was explained by a combination of factors: parental will (that is, an uneducated parent or relative who insisted that the child be educated), contact with an inspiring teacher in elementary or secondary school, and an excellent secondary educational experience. Certainly the importance of teacher and school were consonant with Bond's environmentalism; however, his invocation of "indomitable will, and ambition" on the part of a parent or relative did not seem to support environmentalism. Further, the small size of Bond's group of truly underprivileged as well as his defining the underprivileged by their parents' education rather than by socioeconomic factors made his conclusions subject to counterinterpretation.[54]

In short, *Black American Scholars* appears to have been a noble attempt at making a consistently environmentalist explanation of black intellectual achievement, but it was not always convincing. To be accepted by the community of mental testers, Bond's book would have had to have been substantially less historical and more statistical. It needed more data about the subjects' performance and ability, and it would have had to subject that data to statistical tests of significance. Bond was aware of this weakness in his methods, though he seemed unable or unwilling to do anything about it. In an article published in the early 1960s, he proposed a rule for accurately gauging the true ability of a black child: adding from twenty to twenty-five points to his or her standardized test score. If the child came from an educated home, the "deprivation bonus" should be reduced; if he or she came from a poor home, it should be increased. To this recommendation, however, he appended the notation, "I only wish that this procedure could be established with a greater statistical precision than I can now attempt." [55]

In fact, Bond seldom attempted rigorous statistical analysis of his data. Statistics was not his métier. Historical work—its body of ideas and its methods—was what he knew best. Though he was familiar with test construction, administration, and the literature on testing, the familiarity had been gained early in his career, and he never really attempted to fortify his knowledge to the point that he could legitimately argue with professional testers. His positions—in his articles, in *The Search for Talent*, and in *Black American Scholars*—were geared to members of his race and the friends of his race who were engaged in the political struggle for black advancement, not to the scholarly community concerned with mental testing.

Late in his career, Bond did undertake one project that was related to his earlier historical studies and publications: a history of his family. Though the Bonds had not been profiled as one of the unusual black families in *Black American Scholars*, the academic accomplishments of his relatives were never far from Bond's mind. Since shortly after James Bond's death, Horace Bond had possessed an autobiographical manuscript written by his father, and Horace also was aware of bits of material relating to his paternal grandmother's life. However, he did not seriously contemplate publication of a history of his family until the late 1960s, when Julian Bond gained notoriety as a rising black activist and politician.

In 1968, then, Horace wrote to his brothers and sisters seeking information about their remembrances of their family life. He was intent on writing a history divided into three parts: his father's life, his own career, and his son's accomplishments. Later in that year, he wrote to an editor at Random House who had asked Julian Bond to write his autobiography; Horace explained that Julian had decided not to pursue the project and asked if Random House would be interested in his own history of the Bond family. At the same time, Horace pursued with two other publishers the possibility of publishing his father's autobiography as a separate work.[56]

Horace eventually signed a contract with Farrar, Straus, and Giroux to write a family history that would clearly be a commercial, rather than a scholarly, venture. Before signing the contract, Bond had considered hiring a literary agent, and he contacted one who had been recommended by John Neary, author of a forthcoming biography of Julian Bond. Though there is no record in the Bond Papers that Horace signed an agreement with a literary agent, the commercial nature of his family history seems obvious. At the time the book contract was signed, John Peck of Farrar, Straus, and Giroux wrote Horace to tell him that "I do not see this project as a time-consuming, scholarly work. I see it as a relatively modest book, of whatever length seems right." Peck added that the volume should stress the continuity between the three generations represented by James, Horace, and Julian and that it "would be of tremendous interest to the younger generation."[57]

Approximately one year later, Horace wrote to his editor that Atheneum Publishers had signed a contract with Roger Williams, a white journalist, for him to write a history of the Bond family. This angered Horace. Since Atheneum was one of the publishers to which he had sent the manuscript of his father's autobiography, he thought that Williams might have seen a copy of that document and was using it as a source for his history. Also, Atheneum had reprinted Bond's *Negro Education in Alabama* without having to compensate the author, because the book's original publisher had let its copyright lapse and thus placed it in the public domain. Farrar, Straus, and Giroux eventually canceled the contract with Bond, though seemingly as much because of his failure to write anything as because of the Williams project.[58]

Bond's bitterness toward Roger Williams and Atheneum would never leave him. He did acknowledge, however, "Williams is a good researcher. He has disclosed to me the enormous amount of literature, in the public domain, that does exist." Nonetheless, Bond was convinced that Williams had pirated his father's autobiography and, presumably because of this, hesitated to permit John Neary to quote from the autobiography in Neary's book on Julian Bond. After William's book was published, Horace wrote an angry letter to Atheneum and criticized the book as "wretched" and its author and the publisher as thieves who had stolen the property of the Bond family. Bond further charged that Williams had insulted the family by arguing that the Bonds had a long-lived wish to be "white." Though Bond did not sue Atheneum and Williams, an indication that, at least technically, there had been no violation of the law by the author or publisher, the contract between Atheneum and Williams came so shortly after the publisher considered James Bond's autobiography that one cannot help but wonder about the conduct of both the publishing house and the author.[59]

Though he had lost his contract for publication, Horace Bond attempted to continue with his own project on the Bond family history. He sought Ford Foundation monies to finance a cooperative project on the Bond family by him and a nephew, and a few fragments of a manuscript related to that project are preserved in the Bond papers. However, Bond would die in December of 1972, long before the project could be funded or completed, and, given his lack of progress on the project in the several years before his death, it seems doubtful that he would ever have completed it. His last historical effort, then, came to naught.[60]

The last two decades of Horace Bond's academic career certainly had their highs and lows. Though the distractions of being a college president did not appear to prevent Bond from working on scholarly projects, he was not able to sustain the high quality of scholarship that he had produced earlier in his career. He lost touch with the discipline and intellectual rigorousness that he exhibited during the productive 1930s, when his first two books were published. What distinguishes the young Bond of the 1930s from the older man of the 1950s and thereafter is his inability in the latter period to separate his academic work from his personal and political circumstances. It is not that the early Bond was apolitical or unconcerned about his own plight, that of other black scholars, and of his race as a whole; it is, rather, that as a young man he was able to harness that orientation to a thorough mastery of the facts, methods, and literature that spoke to the historical and contemporary circumstances about which he was writing. In later years he had great difficulty distinguishing the evidence from the arguments he wanted it to support.

In *Black American Scholars* Bond described the unproductive, final stages of the promising career of Martin Delany, a nineteenth-century black physician. The doctor was graduated from the Harvard Medical School, had practiced medicine in Pittsburgh, and had "acquired an international reputation as a scholar." However, he wound up abandoning these areas of accomplishment, because, according to Bond, "the usual fate of the Negro made it necessary for him to enter the cause of racial polemics and advancement."[61] Ironically, Horace Bond's characterization of Delany and his fate could just as fittingly describe what happened to Bond himself in the final decades of his career.

Appendix

Publications by Horace Mann Bond

"Intelligence Tests and Propaganda." *Crisis* 28 (June 1924): 61–64.

"What the Army Intelligence Tests Measured." *Opportunity* 2 (July 1924): 197–202.

"The Langston Plan: A Curriculum for Negro Teacher-Training Schools." *School and Society*, December 27, 1924, 820–21.

"Negro Leadership since Washington." *South Atlantic Quarterly* 24 (April 1925): 115–30.

"Temperament." *Crisis* 29 (June 1925): 83–86.

"Is Vocational Guidance Practical?" *Oklahoma Teacher's Journal* 2 (November 1925): 19–21.

"An Investigation of the Nonintellectual Traits of a Group of Negro Adults." *Journal of Abnormal and Social Psychology* 21 (October 1926): 267–76.

Review of *Whither Democracy . . .* , by N. J. Lennes. *American Journal of Sociology* 33 (July 1927): 149–50.

"Some Exceptional Negro Children." *Crisis* 34 (October 1927): 257–59, 278.

"Human Nature and Its Study in Negro Colleges." *Opportunity* 6 (February 1928): 38–39, 58.

"The Negro Common School in Oklahoma." Parts 1, 2. *Crisis* 35 (April, July 1928): 115–16, 136, 228, 243–45.

"Self-Respect as a Factor in Racial Advancement." *Annals of the American Academy of Political and Social Science* 140 (November 1928): 21–25.

"Will We Ever Be Like That?" *Greater Fisk Herald* 4 (February 1929): 10–13.

"What Lies behind Lynching." *Nation*, March 27, 1929, 370–71.

"Let's Be Honest on Nullification." *Plain Talk*, October 1929, 392–98.

"The Health of the Negro in Relation to Industry." *Bulletin of the National Association of Teachers in Colored Schools* 2 (December 1929): 20–22.

"Two Racial Islands in Alabama." *American Journal of Sociology* 36 (January 1931): 552–67.

"A Negro Looks at His South." *Harper's Magazine*, no. 973, June 1931, 98–108.

"Negro Education: A Debate in the Alabama Constitutional Convention of 1901." *Journal of Negro Education* 1 (April 1932): 49–59.

"Shall Federal Funds Be Spent for Adult Negro Relief or the Education of Negro Children?" *School and Society*, August 12, 1932, 223–24.

"Dr. Woodson Goes Wool Gathering." Review of *The Miseducation of the Negro*, by Carter G. Woodson. *Journal of Negro Education* 2 (April 1933): 210–13.

"The Cash Value of a Negro Child." *School and Society*, May 13, 1933, 627–30.

"Lincoln University: A Laboratory of Leadership." *Lincoln University Herald* 38 (July 1933).

With Charles S. Johnson. "The Investigation of Racial Differences prior to 1910." *Journal of Negro Education* 3 (July 1934): 328–39.

The Education of the Negro in the American Social Order. New York: Prentice Hall, 1934.

"The Curriculum and the Negro Child." *Journal of Negro Education* 4 (April 1935): 159–68.

"Forty Acres and a Mule," *Opportunity* 13 (May 1935): 140–41, 151.

"The Extent and Character of Separate Schools in the United States." *Journal of Negro Education* 4 (July 1935): 321–27.

"The Influence of Personalities on the Public Education of Negroes in Alabama." Parts 1, 2. *Journal of Negro Education* 6 (January, April 1937): 17–29, 172–87.

"Horace Mann in New Orleans: A Note on the Decline of Humanitarianism in American Education." *School and Society*, May 1, 1937, 607–11.

"The Liberal Arts College for Negroes: A Social Force." In *A Century of Municipal Higher Education: A Collection of Addresses Delivered during the Centennial Observance of the University of Louisville, America's Oldest Municipal University*, 341–64. Chicago: Lincoln, 1937.

"The First Thing I Look for in a School Is—Cleanliness." *National Educational Outlook among Negroes* 1 (May 1938): 6–8.

"Redefining the Relationship of the Federal Government to the Education of Racial and Other Minority Groups." *Journal of Negro Education* 7 (July 1938): 454–59.

"Social and Economic Forces in Alabama Reconstruction." *Journal of Negro History* 23 (July 1938): 290–348.

"Education in the South." *Journal of Educational Sociology* 12 (January 1939): 264–74.

"The Position of the Negro in the American Social Order in 1950." *Journal of Negro Education* 8 (July 1939): 583–86.

Negro Education in Alabama: A Study in Cotton and Steel. Washington: Associated Publishers, 1939.

"Seven Aids to Getting a Good Job." *Opportunity* 18 (March 1940): 72–75, 95.

"The Negro Elementary School and the Cultural Pattern." *Journal of Educational Sociology* 13 (April 1940): 479–89.

"Faith in the Death Chamber." *Phylon* 1 (Winter 1940): 112–24.

"The Educational and Other Social Implications of the Impact of the Present Crisis upon Racial Minorities." *Journal of Negro Education* 10 (July 1941): 617–22.

"Negro Education." In *The Encyclopedia of Educational Research*, ed. Walter S. Monroe, 746–72. New York: Macmillan, 1941.

Review of *History and an Interpretation of Wilberforce University*," by Frederick A. McGinnis. *Journal of Higher Education* 3 (February 1942): 114–15.

"The Function of the Academic Program in the Development of Attitudes." *Proceedings: Sixteenth Annual Session, National Association of Deans and Registrars*, Elizabeth City, N.C., March 25–27, 1942, 10–15.

"Should the Negro Care Who Wins the War?" *Annals of the American Academy of Political and Social Sciences* 223 (September 1942): 81–84.

"Planning in a War-Torn World: The Task of Formal Education." *Proceedings: Seventeenth Annual Session, National Association of Deans and Registrars*, Nashville, March 23–25, 1943, 65–68.

"Education as a Social Process: A Case Study of a Higher Institution as an Incident in the Process of Acculturation." *American Journal of Sociology* 48 (May 1943): 73–81.

"The Education of Teachers for Negro Children at Fort Valley State College." *Southern University Bulletin* 29 (May 1943): 59–68.

"The Negro in the Armed Forces of the United States prior to World War I." *Journal of Negro Education* 12 (Summer 1943): 268–87.

"Education for Production as Conducted at the Fort Valley State College: A Report." *Proceedings of the Twentieth and Twenty-first Annual Conferences of the Presidents of Negro Land-Grant Colleges* (1943): 83–87.

"The Role of Negro Education in the Post-War World." *North Carolina Teachers Record* 15 (May 1944): 8.

"Ham and Eggs: A History of the Fort Valley Ham-and-Egg Show." Bulletin 513 of the Georgia Agricultural Extension Service (June 1944), 3–15.

Education for Production: A Textbook on How to Be Healthy, Wealthy, and Wise. Athens: University of Georgia Press for the Fort Valley State College, 1944.

"How Beta Kappa Chi Began." *Beta Kappa Chi Scientific Society Newsletter* 2 (January 1945).

"A New Device for Evaluating the Work of College Students." *School and Society*, February 10, 1945, 94.

"An Ode to the Honorable Secretary of State, James Francis Byrnes, of South Carolina." *New York Herald Tribune*, September 4, 1945, 22.

"What the San Francisco Conference Means to the Negro." *Journal of Negro Education* 14 (Fall 1945): 627–30.

"Education for Political and Social Responsibility: Its Natural History in the American College." *Journal of Negro Education* 16 (Spring 1947): 165–71.

"The Evolution and Present Status of Negro Higher Education in the United States." *Journal of Negro Education* 17 (Summer 1948): 224–35.

"Observations on Education in British West Africa." *Educational Record* 31 (April 1950): 129–40.

"Improving the Morale of Negro Children and Youth." *Journal of Negro Education* 19 (Summer 1950): 408–11.

With Morton Puner. "Jim Crow in Education." *Nation*, November 24, 1951, 446–49.

"The Present Status of Racial Integration in the United States, with Especial Reference to Education." *Journal of Negro Education* 21 (Summer 1952): 241–50.

"The European Heritage: Approaches to African Development, Comment on Paul Henry's Paper." In *Africa Today*, ed. C. Grove Haines, 141–46. Baltimore: Johns Hopkins University Press, 1954.

"Reflections, Comparative, on West African Nationalist Movements." *Presence Africaine* 19 (September 1956): 22–28.

"Forming African Youth: A Philosophy of Education." In *Africa Seen by American Negroes*, 247–62. Paris: Presence Africaine, 1956.

"The Productivity of National Merit Scholars by Occupational Class." *School and Society*, September 28, 1957, 267–68.

Review of *Racial Discrimination and Private Education*, by Arthur S. Miller. *Phylon* 19 (Spring 1958): 128.

"Cat on a Hot Tin Roof." Review of *The Testing of Negro Intelligence*, by Audrey M. Shuey. *Journal of Negro Education* 27 (Fall 1958): 519–25.

Review of *Negroes and Medicine*, by Dietrich C. Reitzes. *Phylon* 19 (Winter 1958): 428–30.

"Talent and Toilets." *Journal of Negro Education* 28 (Winter 1959): 3–14.

The Search for Talent. Cambridge: Harvard University Press for the Harvard Graduate School of Education, 1959.

"The Origin and Development of the Negro Church-Related College." *Journal of Negro Education* 29 (Summer 1960): 217–26.

"Wasted Talent." In *The Nation's Children*, ed. Eli Ginzberg, 116–37. New York: Columbia University Press, 1960.

"The Influence of Cultural Factors on Academic Performance." *Southern University Bulletin* 47 (January 1961): 50–70.

"Some Major Educational Problems in Africa South of the Sahara." *Journal of Negro Education* 30 (Summer 1961): 358–64.

"Howe and Isaacs in the Bush: The Ram in the Thicket." *Negro History Bulletin* (October 1961): 72, 67–70.

"Negro in America." In *Concise Dictionary of American History*, ed. Wayne Andrews, 652–55. New York: Scribner's, 1961.

"Reluctant Almoners." Review of *Adventure in Giving*, by Raymond B. Fosdick. *Saturday Review of Literature*, September 15, 1962, 68–69.

Review of *A History of Sierra Leone*, by Christopher Fyfe. *Phylon* 23 (Winter 1962): 405–6.

"A Century of Negro Higher Education." In *A Century of Higher Education*, ed. William W. Brickman and Stanley Lehrer, 182–96. New York: Society for the Advancement of Education, 1962.

"Teaching: A Calling to Fulfill." *Herald* (Georgia Teachers and Educational Association), March 1963, 5–6.

"The Legacy of W. E. B. Du Bois." *Freedomways* 5 (Winter 1965): 16–17.

"The Negro Scholar and Professional in America." In *The American Negro Reference Book*, ed. John P. Davis, 548–89. Englewood Cliffs, N.J.: Prentice Hall, 1966.

Black American Scholars: A Study of Their Beginnings. Detroit: Balamp Publishing, 1969.

Education for Freedom: A History of Lincoln University. Princeton: Princeton University Press for Lincoln University, 1976.

Notes

Chapter 1: The Prodigy

1 Horace M. Bond to Elnora C. Smith, April 12, 1961, Horace Mann Bond Papers, University of Massachusetts Library, Amherst, Massachusetts, series 2, box 14, folder 42A (hereafter cited as Bond Papers, with a series number, a box number, and a folder number [usually with a capital letter], separated by periods; unless otherwise indicated, the surname Bond, when listed alone, refers to Horace Mann Bond).

2 Bond to Rebecca Reyher, January 23, 1956, Bond Papers, 1.7.35B. Also see Horace Mann Bond, "Notes Written on Myself by Myself: What an Asinine Thing to Do!" Bond Papers, 6.178.55.

3 Max Bond to Horace Bond, May 23, 1968, Bond Papers, 1.5.26D. Letters sent by his mother to Horace Bond can be found in Bond Papers, 1.6.29A.

4 Bond left several fragmentary manuscripts on his family's history. On his grandmother, see "Granny" (1947) and "My Granny Was a Black Mammy," n.d., Bond Papers, 2.6.28.

5 Bond to Richard Bardolph, November 25, 1955, Bond Papers, 2.12.29C; Bond, "Notes Written on Myself."

6 "Life on the Margin: An Autobiography by James Bond," Bond Papers, 1.4.20A.

7 Bond, "Granny."

8 Ibid.

9 Bond to Bardolph, November 25, 1955; Bond to Elnora C. Smith, April 12, 1961, and Bond, "Self-Prattle, Poppycock, Pish-Tush, Etc.," (ca. 1932), Bond Papers, 6.178.55.

10 Elisabeth S. Peck, *Berea's First 125 Years, 1855–1980* (Lexington: University Press of Kentucky, 1982), 3–4, 40, 23–25, 46–48.

11 John Barnard, *From Evangelicalism to Progressivism at Oberlin College, 1866–1917* (Columbus: Ohio State University Press, 1969), 3, 8, 30, 33, 114–15, and

Donald M. Love, *Henry Churchill King of Oberlin* (New Haven: Yale University Press for Oberlin College, 1956), 5.

12 Peck, *Berea's First 125 Years*, 8, 40, and Bond to Smith, April 12, 1961.

13 Bond to Harry Bacon, April 23, 1955, Bond Papers, 2.12.29A, and Bond, "Notes Written on Myself."

14 Bond, "Notes Written on Myself." On Lincoln Institute's beginnings, including James Bond's role, see George C. Wright, "The Founding of Lincoln Institute," *Filson Club Quarterly* 49 (January 1975): 57–70.

15 Bond to Robert J. Moore, June 2, 1960, Bond Papers, 2.13.38D, and Horace M. Bond, "I Was a 'Gifted' Child (or Was I?)," n.d., Bond Papers, 6.178.55.

16 Bond, "Notes Written on Myself," and Max Bond to Horace Bond, May 23, 1968.

17 Bond, "My Aunt Mamie and My IQ" (ca. 1964), Bond Papers, 6.178.55; Bond to Moore, June 2, 1960; and Bond to Reyher, January 23, 1956.

18 Max Bond to Bond, May 23, 1968.

19 James Bond, "The Education of the Bond Family," *Crisis* 34 (April 1927): 41, 60.

20 Barnard, *From Evangelicalism to Progressivism*, 50–51, 76–77, and Bond, "Self-Prattle."

21 Bond, "Self-Prattle."

22 Bond to Reyher, January 23, 1956, and Bond, "Self-Prattle."

23 Bond, "Notes Written on Myself," and Bond, " 'Gifted' Child."

24 Ibid.

25 Bond, " 'Gifted' Child."

26 Bond, "Notes Written on Myself."

27 Bond to Reyher, January 23, 1956.

28 Ibid.

29 Max Bond to Bond, May 23, 1968.

30 "Negro Leader Dies Suddenly," clipping (*Louisville Herald Post*, January 5, 1929), and "Notable Colored Leader's Death Is Heavy State Loss," clipping (*Louisville Herald Post*, January 20, 1929), Bond Papers, 1.5.24.

31 Bond to Bardolph, November 25, 1955, and Bond to Moore, June 2, 1960.

32 Bond to Bacon, April 23, 1955.

33 Bond, "Self-Prattle."

Chapter 2: Lincoln University

1 Horace M. Bond to Martin D. Kilson, February 25, 1968, Bond Papers, 6.175.37.

2 On Lincoln's colonizationist roots, see Horace Mann Bond, *Education for*

Freedom: A History of Lincoln University, Pennsylvania (Princeton: Lincoln University, 1976), 44–68; Bond to Smith, April 12, 1961.

3   Thomas Jesse Jones, *Negro Education: A Study of Private and Higher Schools for Colored People in the United States* (Washington: Government Printing Office, 1917), 690, and Bond, *Education for Freedom*, 394. Bond himself would return to Lincoln University in 1945 as its first black president.

4   Jones, *Negro Education*, 689–91, and Bond, *Education for Freedom*, 108–10, 260–61, 394, 395.

5   Bond, *Education for Freedom*, 366–68, and *Survey of Negro Colleges and Universities* (Washington: Government Printing Office, 1929), 643.

6   *Survey of Negro Colleges and Universities*, 653, 650.

7   Bond, *Education for Freedom*, 260, 275–77; Laurence R. Veysey, *The Emergence of the American University* (Chicago: University of Chicago Press, 1965), 21–56.

8   Bond, *Education for Freedom*, 434–35. For the debate between Washington and Du Bois, see August Meier, *Negro Thought in America, 1880–1915: Racial Ideologies in the Age of Booker T. Washington* (Ann Arbor: University of Michigan Press, 1963).

9   Bond to Smith, April 12, 1961.

10 Ibid.; Bond to Robert M. Labaree, September 2, 1935, Bond Papers, 4.88.70; and Labaree to Bond, April 15, 1940, Bond Papers, 4.103.73A. Labaree was also remembered by Langston Hughes, the black poet and author who attended Lincoln University in the late 1920s; see Langston Hughes, *The Big Sea* (New York: Hill and Wang, 1940), 280, and Arnold Rampersad, *The Life of Langston Hughes*, vol. 1 (New York: Oxford University Press, 1986), 130.

11 Bond, *Education for Freedom*, 402–5.

12 Roger Williams, *The Bonds: An American Family* (New York: Atheneum, 1971), chap. 7, "Short Pants and Scholarship." Also see "Bond, Class Baby, Becomes President," n.d., Bond Papers, 4.100.62D, and Bond, "Notes Written on Myself."

13 Bond to Dr. and Mrs. D. F. Jenkins, April 3, 1960, Bond Papers, 2.13.38C, and Bond to Reyher, January 23, 1956.

14 *The Paw*, 1923 (Lincoln University yearbook), Archives, Lincoln University Library.

15 Ibid., 78–79.

16 Bond, "Notes Written on Myself"; and "Lincoln University, Office of the Registrar, Official Transcript of the Record of Horace Mann Bond," Bond Papers, 3.82.371A.

17 "Official Transcript of . . . Horace Mann Bond."

18 Bond, "Notes Written on Myself," and Bond, " 'Gifted' Child."

19   Bond to E. P. Roberts, January 21, 1945, Bond Papers, 3.82.371A.
20   Bond, " 'Gifted' Child."
21   Ibid.; Bond, "Notes Written on Myself"; and Bond, "I Wouldn't Raise My Boy to Be a Prodigy—by an Ex-Prodigy," Bond Papers, 6.173.19.
22   Bond to Richard Bardolph, November 25, 1955; Bond, "Notes Written on Myself"; and Bond, "I Wouldn't Raise My Boy to Be a Prodigy."
23   Bond, "Notes Written on Myself."
24   Aaron Brown to Bond, January 7, 1958, and Bond to Brown, January 10, 1958, Bond Papers, 2.12.34A; Bond to E. Washington Rhodes, May 8, 1942, Bond Papers, 2.10.15B; and Bond, "Notes Written on Myself."
25   Bond, " 'Gifted' Child," and Bond, "I Wouldn't Raise My Boy to Be a Prodigy."
26   Bond, "I Wouldn't Raise My Boy to Be a Prodigy."
27   Raymond Wolters, *The New Negro on Campus: Black College Rebellions of the 1920s* (Princeton: Princeton University Press, 1975).
28   Ibid., 278–93.
29   These opinions were noted by Langston Hughes in *The Big Sea*, 307.

Chapter 3: Chicago

1   Bond to Robert J. Moore, June 2, 1960, and Bond to Smith, April 12, 1961.
2   Woodie T. White, "The Decline of the Classroom and the Chicago Study of Education, 1909–1929," *American Journal of Education* 90 (February 1982): 167–68.
3   Bond to Frederick Breed, July 22, 1932, Bond Papers, 2.8.2A.
4   James Bond to Bond, March 26, 1924, Bond Papers, 1.1.5C; James Bond to Bond, June 26, 1924, and July 5, 1924, Bond Papers, 1.1.6A; and Bond to Elvin Abeles, December 20, 1953, Bond Papers, 2.11.27D.
5   James Bond to Bond, March 26, 1924.
6   Photostat of transcript of Horace Mann Bond, University of Chicago, October 20, 1944, Bond Papers, 3.82.371B.
7   White, "Chicago Study of Education," 144–74.
8   Ibid., 152. For a lengthy discussion of the conflict between academic and vocational study in graduate education programs at Chicago and elsewhere, see Geraldine Joncich Clifford and James W. Guthrie, *Ed School: A Brief for Professional Education* (Chicago: University of Chicago Press, 1988), chap. 3.
9   White, "Chicago Study of Education," 168.
10   Horace M. Bond, *Negro Education in Alabama: A Study in Cotton and Steel* (1939; reprint, New York: Atheneum, 1969), xi; Bond to Charles H. Judd, December 22, 1936, Charles H. Judd Papers, Regenstein Library, University of Chicago, box 2, folder 5 (hereafter cited as Judd Papers); Bond to Roy

[Davenport], August 22, 1932, Bond Papers, 2.8.2A; and Bond to Edwin R. Embree, November 28, 1932, Bond Papers, 3.71.312D.

11 Bond to W. E. B. Du Bois, April 12, 1926, Bond Papers, 3.37.116B.

12 Biographical information on Freeman may be found in "Frank Nugent Freeman," *University of California in Memoriam*, April 1963, Bancroft Library, University of California, Berkeley, 27–30. "Course Work Taken at the University of Chicago by Horace Mann Bond in Preparation for the Degrees of Master of Arts and Doctor of Philosophy," Bond Papers, 3.82.371B, and Photostat of Transcript for Horace Mann Bond, University of Chicago, October 20, 1944.

13 Horatio H. Newman, Frank N. Freeman, and Karl J. Holzinger, *Twins: A Study of Heredity and Environment* (Chicago: University of Chicago Press, 1937), 362, and John Munroe, "The Inconstancy of the Intelligence Quotient and the Influence of Environment upon Intelligence" (Ph.D. diss., University of Chicago, 1928).

14 Michael Fultz, "A 'Quintessential American': Horace Mann Bond, 1924–1939," *Harvard Educational Review* 55 (November 1985): 427; Robert Labaree to Bond, September 11, 1934, Bond Papers, 2.8.3C; and Bond to Cornelius McDougald and George D. Cannon, July 21, 1956, Bond Papers, 4.102.70A.

15 Horace M. Bond, "Intelligence Tests and Propaganda," *Crisis* 28 (June 1924): 61–64, quotation 63.

16 Horace M. Bond, "What the Army 'Intelligence' Tests Measured," *Opportunity* 2 (July 1924): 197–202, quotation 202.

17 Ibid.

18 Bond, "My Aunt Mamie and My IQ." Bagley's black student at Columbia also published a critique of intelligence testing; see Howard Hale Long, "Race and Mental Tests," *Opportunity* 1 (March 1923): 22–25. For a look at Bond's career-long interest in intelligence tests, see Wayne J. Urban, "The Black Scholar and Intelligence Testing: The Case of Horace Mann Bond," *Journal of the History of the Behavioral Sciences* 25 (October 1989): 323–34.

19 Photostat of Transcript of Horace M. Bond, University of Chicago, October 20, 1944; Horace M. Bond, "An Investigation of the Nonintellectual Traits of a Group of Negro Adults," *Journal of Abnormal and Social Psychology* 21 (October 1926): 267–76.

20 Bond, "My Aunt Mamie and My IQ," and Bond, "Notes Written on Myself."

21 Horace M. Bond, "A Neglected Research Source: The College Psychological Examinations of the 1930s (An Essay on the Method of Historiographic Psychometry)," Harvard University Summer School Convocation, 1966, Bond Papers, 6.172.15.

22 Bond Transcript, University of Chicago, and Bond, "Notes Written on Myself." On Chicago's Department of Sociology and the influence of Robert Park, see Robert L. Faris, *Chicago Sociology: 1920–1932* (San Francisco:

Chandler Publishing Company, 1967), especially 27–30 and 107–8.

23 Bond to James Bond, December 6, 1927, Bond Papers, 1.3.16B; Robert E. Park to Bond, n.d. (ca. 1928), and February 1, 1928, Bond Papers, 2.8.1A; and Park to Bond, January 2, 1929, and January 31, 1929, Bond Papers, 2.8.1B. On Park's notion of the "marginal man," see Faris, *Chicago Sociology*, 108.

24 Horace M. Bond, "Self-Respect as a Factor in Racial Achievement," *Annals of the American Academy of Political and Social Science* 140 (November 1928): 21–25. For a critical discussion of Park's racial views, see Stanford M. Lyman, *The Black American in Sociological Thought* (New York: Capricorn Books, 1973): 27–50.

25 Bond, "Notes Written on Myself," and Bond to Allison Davis, July 21, 1935, Bond Papers, 2.8.4B.

26 Park to Bond, November 21, 1934, Bond Papers, 2.8.3C.

27 Horace M. Bond, review of *Whither Democracy?: Does Equalizing Educational Opportunity Create Hereditary Social Classes?* by N. J. Lennes, *American Journal of Sociology* 33 (July 1927): 149–50. Bond describes the circumstances leading to the publication of this review in a 1957 speech given at the University of Pittsburgh ("The Education of Teachers in a Free Society: A Look Ahead," Bond Papers, 6.171.10).

28 Bond to (Martin) Kilson, March 3, 1969, Bond Papers, 2.15.53A. Bond's teaching Lincoln students proper research methods was described in an interview with Martin Kilson, June 26, 1987.

29 Bond to Thomas Elsa Jones, May 16, 1927, Thomas Elsa Jones Papers, Fisk University Library, box 26, folder 18 (hereafter cited as Jones Papers).

30 Bond to G. T. Buswell, January 2, 1929, Charles E. Judd Papers, box 2, folder 3.

31 Bond to Moore, June 2, 1960.

32 Bond, *Negro Education in Alabama*, and Wayne J. Urban, "Horace Mann Bond's *Negro Education in Alabama*: A Reconsideration," *History of Education Quarterly* 27 (Fall 1987): 363–77. For a full discussion of Bond's dissertation, see chapter 6.

33 Information on Edwards came from a letter to the author from Ralph Tyler, November 10, 1984. Bond, *Negro Education in Alabama*, xi, and Bond, "The Role of the History of Education in Understanding the Struggle for Equalizing Educational Opportunity" (Paper delivered at the National Society of College Teachers of Education, February 28, 1950), Bond Papers, 6.171.6.

34 Newton Edwards and Herman G. Richey, *The School in the American Social Order* (Boston: Houghton Mifflin, 1947), xii.

35 Richard Hofstadter, *The Progressive Historians: Turner, Beard, Parrington* (New York: Alfred A. Knopf, 1968), and August Meier and Elliott Rudwick, *Black History and the Historical Profession, 1915–1980* (Urbana: University of Illinois Press, 1986), 101–2.

36 Bond to Thomas Elsa Jones, March 30, 1927, Jones Papers, box 26, folder 18. On Bond's participation in the Communist meeting, see Ruth R. Pearson to Mr. Bond, January 31, 1926, and the attachment to this letter, titled "Communist Party Involvement," Bond Papers, 2.8.1A. See also "Self-Prattle."

37 Edwin R. Embree and Julia Waxman, *Investment in People: The Story of the Julius Rosenwald Fund* (New York: Harper and Brothers, 1949), and Raymond B. Fosdick, *Adventure in Giving: The Story of the General Education Board* (New York: Harper and Row, 1962), 210–11, 235–36.

Chapter 4: Young Scholar and Academic

1 James Bond to N. B. Young, June 10, 1924, and James Bond to Bond, June 26, 1924, and July 5, 1924, Bond Papers, 1.1.6A; James Bond to Bond, July 24, 1924, and July 31, 1924, Bond Papers, 1.1.6B.

2 James Bond to Bond, May 25, 1925, Bond Papers, 1.2.9B; James Bond to Bond, July 23, 1925, Bond Papers, 1.2.9D; James Bond to Bond, August 11, 1925, Bond Papers, 1.2.9E; and James Bond to Bond, July 30, 1927, Bond Papers, 1.3.15C.

3 James Bond to Bond, December 30, 1924, Bond Papers, 1.1.7D.

4 James Bond to Bond, June 17, 1926, Bond Papers, 1.3.12C.

5 Horace M. Bond, "The Langston Plan: A Curriculum for Negro Teacher Training Schools," *School and Society* 20 (December 27, 1924): 820–21.

6 Horace Mann Bond, "Some Exceptional Negro Children," *Crisis* 34 (October 1927): 257–59, 278, 280; Bond to W. E. B. Du Bois, April 12, 1926, Bond Papers, 3.37.16B; and Horace Mann Bond, "The Negro Common School in Oklahoma," Parts 1, 2, *Crisis* 35 (April, July 1928): 113–16, 136, 138, 228–29, 246.

7 Bond, "Politics in Negro Education," n.d. (ca. 1931), Bond Papers, 6.173.17. On Langston University and I. W. Young, see Zella J. Black Patterson, *Langston University: A History* (Norman: University of Oklahoma Press, 1979), 39–42.

8 Bond's view of Langston University is corroborated in Donald Spivey, "Crisis on a Black Campus: Langston University and Its Struggle for Survival," *Chronicles of Oklahoma* 59 (Winter 1981–82): 430–44.

9 Bond, "Self-Prattle," and "Notes Written on Myself."

10 Bond, "Notes Written on Myself"; Bond to I. J. K. Wells, May 15, 1936, Bond Papers, 2.8.5C; and Horace Mann Bond, "Faith in the Death Chamber," *Phylon* 1 (1940): 112–24.

11 Bond to Thomas Elsa Jones, February 28, 1927, and March 30, 1927, Jones Papers, box 26, folder 18; James Bond to Thomas Elsa Jones, April 16, 1927, Bond Papers, 1.3.14D; Thomas Elsa Jones to Bond, April 11, 1928, Jones Papers, box 26, folder 18; and Bond to I. J. K. Wells, May 15, 1936.

12 Joe M. Richardson, *A History of Fisk University, 1865–1946* (Tuscaloosa: University of Alabama Press, 1980), 104–12.

13 Ibid., 137–40, and Charles S. Johnson to James Bond, December 12, 1928, Bond Papers, 1.4.18B.

14 James Bond to Thomas Elsa Jones, August 25, 1928, Bond Papers, 1.4.18A; James Bond to Bond, October 23, 1928, Bond Papers, 1.4.18C; and "Negro Leader Dies Suddenly," *Louisville Herald Post*, January 15, 1929, clipping in Bond Papers, 1.5.24.

15 About two weeks after his father died, Horace Bond discussed publishing his father's autobiography with Robert Park; see Park to Bond, January 31, 1929, Bond Papers, 2.8.1B. A copy of the manuscript autobiography, "Life on the Margin: An Autobiography," can be found in the Bond Papers, 1.4.20A.

16 James Bond to Julius Rosenwald, July 18, 1924, Bond Papers, 1.1.6B.

17 James Bond to Bond, February 24, 1927, Bond Papers, 1.3.14B, and Leo M. Favrot to James Bond, March 24, 1927, Bond Papers, 1.3.14C.

18 James Bond to Bond, February 26, 1928, and Edwin Embree to James Bond, March 1, 1928, Bond Papers, 1.4.17A.

19 Clark Foreman, *Environmental Factors in Negro Elementary Education* (New York: W.W. Norton, 1932), 22–29, 52; Bond to I.J.K. Wells, May 15, 1936; Franklin O. Nichols to Bond, March 7, 1929, Bond Papers, 2.8.1B.

20 For biographical information on Clark Foreman, see the Julius Rosenwald Fund Papers, Fisk University Library, Nashville, Tennessee, box 121, folder 6 (hereafter cited as Rosenwald Fund Papers); Bond to John McNeal, June 4, 1968, Bond Papers, 4.92.26D.

21 Bond to Foreman, n.d. (1929), Rosenwald Fund Papers, box 175, folder 1.

22 Foreman, *Negro Elementary Education*, 22–29, 52.

23 Horace Mann Bond, "Two Racial Islands in Alabama," *American Journal of Sociology* 36 (January 1931): 552–67.

24 Horace Mann Bond, "A Negro Looks at His South," *Harper's*, no. 973, June 1931, 98–108.

25 Thomas Elsa Jones to Bond, February 14, 1930, and August 25, 1930; Bond to Jones, May 30, 1930; and Jones to Bond, December 4, 1931, all in Jones Papers, box 2, folders 18, 19.

26 Bond to Rebecca Reyher, January 23, 1956.

27 Ibid.; and Julia W. Bond to Mrs. Charles S. Johnson, March 4, 1954, Bond Papers, 1.6.31B.

28 Bond to Reyher, January 23, 1956; Bond to Elvin W. Abeles, December 20, 1953, Bond Papers, 2.11.27D; and Julia Bond to Mrs. Charles S. Johnson, March 4, 1954; Julia Washington Bond, "A Bibliography of Works on Africa in the Negro Collection of the Trevor Arnett Library of Atlanta University" (Master's thesis, Atlanta University, 1964).

29 Bond to Mr. Rucker, February 7, 1933, Bond Papers, 4.87.1.

30 Thomas Elsa Jones to Bond, August 25, 1930, Bond Papers, 4.87.1, and Clark Foreman to Edwin Embree, November 17, 1930, Rosenwald Fund Papers, box 121, folder 7. On Bond's fellowship, see his application (November 14, 1930) in Rosenwald Fund Papers, box 304, folder 10, in which he requested $2,067. For discussion of $1,500 as the amount given, see Bond to Clark Foreman, January 10, 1931, Rosenwald Fund Papers, box 175, folder 1. The Nashville apartment was described to me in an interview with Julia Washington Bond on May 27, 1988.

31 Bond to Mr. Rucker, February 7, 1933; Isaiah T. Creswell to Bond, January 23, 1934, Bond Papers, 4.87.1; on faculty salaries at Fisk in the depression, see Richardson, *History of Fisk University*, 122–25.

32 Horace M. Bond, "Negro Leadership since Washington," *South Atlantic Quarterly* 24 (April 1925): 115–30.

33 Ibid., 128.

34 Ibid., 129–30, quotation 129.

35 See above, n. 6.

36 Bond to W. E. B. Du Bois, June 13, 1931, Bond Papers, 3.37.116B.

37 Bond to the Editor, *Crisis*, May 2, 1933; and W. E. B. Du Bois to Bond, May 18, 1933, Bond Papers, 3.37.116B.

38 Bond, "William Edward Burghardt Du Bois: A Portrait in Race Leadership," n.d. (ca. 1932), Bond Papers, 6.173.18.

39 Ibid.

40 On differences between southern and northern students at Lincoln, see Bond, *Education for Freedom*, 356–57.

41 Allison Davis, who became a close colleague of Bond's at Dillard University in the mid-1930s, wrote in 1927 an article on the black upper classes and masses that seemed to embody many of Bond's ideas on the topic; see Allison Davis, "The Negro Deserts His People," *Plain Talk* 5 (December 1929): 49–54. The significance of this article for Bond and others of his generation was pointed out to me in an interview with J. G. St. Clair Drake on June 26, 1987.

42 Bond to Martin Kilson, May 9, 1962, Bond Papers, 3.31.85D.

43 Richard Robbins, "Charles S. Johnson," in *Black Sociologists: Historical and Contemporary Perspectives*, ed. James E. Blackwell and Morris Janowitz (Chicago: University of Chicago Press, 1974), 56–84.

44 Bond to Mr. [Clark] Foreman, November 14, 1930, Rosenwald Fund Papers, box 175, folder 1; and Bond to Dr. [Thomas Elsa] Jones, November 21, 1932, Jones Papers, box 26, folder 19.

45 On Carter G. Woodson, see Meier and Rudwick, *Black History*, especially chap. 1, "Carter G. Woodson as Entrepreneur: Laying the Foundation of a Historical Specialty," 1–71; Carter G. Woodson, *The Miseducation of the Negro* (Washington: Associated Publishers, 1933).

46 Woodson, *Miseducation of the Negro*.

47   Horace Mann Bond, "Dr. Woodson Goes Wool Gathering," review of *The Miseducation of the Negro*, by Carter G. Woodson, *Journal of Negro Education* 2 (April 1933): 210–13.

48   Bond to I. J. K. Wells, May 15, 1936.

49   Bond to Mr. [Clark] Foreman, November 18, 1929, Rosenwald Fund Papers, box 175, folder 1; Bond to Dr. [I. W.] Young (Langston University president), April 22, 1932, Bond Papers, 2.8.2A; and Bond to Roy [Davenport], n.d. (ca. 1932), and Roy to Bond, n.d. (ca. 1932), Bond Papers, 2.8.2B.

50   W. J. Goedeke to Bond, July 21, 1932, Bond Papers, 6.176.41 (*The Education of the Negro* will be discussed in detail in chap. 6); W. Williams to Bond, March 16, 1933 (regarding a job at the Georgia Normal and Agricultural College in Albany), Bond Papers, 2.8.2C; and Charles W. Florence to Bond, February 24, 1937 (regarding a position at Lincoln University), Bond Papers, 4.103.73A.

51   These two works are the major topic of chap. 6.

52   Bond to John [A. Davis?], n.d., Bond Papers, 3.30.81C.

53   Bond to W. P. Dabney, March 30, 1934, Bond Papers, 2.8.3A.

Chapter 5: Dillard University and the Rosenwald Fund

1   Horace Mann Bond, "Julius Rosenwald: A Mighty Man in Israel," for the Associated Negro Press (ca. 1932), Bond Papers, 6.178.51.

2   Bond to Edwin R. Embree, August 30, 1931, and Embree to Bond, September 9, 1931, Rosenwald Fund Papers, box 175, folder 1; Bond to Embree, November 28, 1932, Bond Papers, 3.71.312D.

3   Edwin Embree's racial optimism is revealed in his book, *Brown America: The Story of a New Race* (New York: The Viking Press, 1931).

4   The composition of the board of the Julius Rosenwald Fund is discussed in John H. Stanfield, "Dollars for the Silent South: Southern White Liberalism and the Julius Rosenwald Fund, 1928–1948," in *Perspectives on the American South: An Annual Review of Society, Politics, and Culture*, ed. Merle Black and John Shelton Reed (New York: Gordon and Breach, 1984), 2:123–25.

5   Embree to Bond, April 16, 1934, Bond Papers, 3.71.312D, and Will Alexander to Bond, May 25, 1934, Bond Papers, 4.88.6A; on Alexander, see Wilma Dykeman and James Stokely, *Seeds of Southern Change: The Life of Will Alexander* (Chicago: University of Chicago Press, 1962).

6   Bond to Embree, August 30, 1931, Rosenwald Fund Papers, box 175, folder 1. The General Education Board and the Rosenwald Fund cooperated in the late 1920s and 1930s by targeting their educational giving to blacks in four university centers in large southern cities: Howard University in Washington, D.C.; Fisk University in Nashville; Atlanta University and other black colleges in Georgia's capital city; and Dillard University in New Orleans.

7   Julia W. Bond to Mrs. Charles S. Johnson, March 4, 1954, Bond Papers, 1.6.31B, and an interview with Julia W. Bond, May 27, 1988.

8   "Conference between W. W. Alexander and Edwin R. Embree on Dillard University, Held in New Orleans, February 20, 1932," Rosenwald Fund Papers, box 191, folder 10, and Bond to Alexander, June 13, 1934, Bond Papers, 4.88.6B.

9   For particulars of the Hutchins experiment at Chicago, see Frederick Rudolph, *Curriculum: A History of the American Undergraduate Course of Study since 1636* (San Francisco: Jossey Bass, 1977), 278.

10 Bond, "The Dillard University Curriculum," n.d. (ca. 1934), Bond Papers, 4.88.6C.

11 Bond to Alexander, June 13, 1934, Bond Papers, 4.88.6B.

12 Interview with J. G. St. Clair Drake, June 26, 1987; Bond to Huey Long, June 15, 1934, Bond Papers, 4.88.6B; Bond to Alexander, January 10, 1934, Bond Papers, 4.88.6A; Bond to Alexander, n.d. (April 8, 1935), Bond Papers, 4.88.6E; and Alexander to Bond, September 28, 1935, Bond Papers, 4.88.7E.

13 Bond to Edgar B. Stern, September 1, 1935, Bond Papers, 4.88.7D, and Bond to Thomas E. Jones, September 2, 1935, Bond Papers, 4.87.1.

14 Drake interview, June 26, 1987, and Bond to Robert M. Labaree, September 2, 1935, Bond Papers, 4.88.7D.

15 "Persons Suggested by E[dwin] R. E[mbree] for Consideration for the Position of President of Dillard University," n.d. (1935?), Rosenwald Fund Papers, box 192, folder 1, and Bond to Robert Park, June 2, 1936, Bond Papers, 2.8.5C.

16 Bond to Park, June 2, 1936, Bond Papers, 2.8.5C; Walter L. Wright to Bond, March 12, 1936, Bond Papers, 4.88.9D; Bond to Wright, March 29, 1936, Bond Papers, 4.89.10B; Bond to Edgar B. Stern, May 7, 1936 (in which Bond's salary for 1936–37 is listed at $3,600), Bond Papers, 4.89.11A; and telegram from Bond to Wright (ca. May 1937), Bond Papers, 4.89.11D.

17 William Stuart Nelson to Bond, June 25, 1936, Bond Papers, 4.89.12B, and Thomas E. Jones to Bond, July 3, 1936, Bond Papers, 4.89.12C.

18 Bond to Charles H. Judd, December 22, 1936, and Judd to Bond, December 29, 1936, Judd Papers, box 2, folder 5; Doak S. Campbell to Bond, July 8, 1937, Bond Papers, 3.72.313B; Bond to Embree, July 9, 1937, Rosenwald Fund Papers, box 323, folder 10; and Embree to Bond, July 12, 1937, Bond Papers, 3.72.313B.

19 Bond to W. P. Dabney, April 2, 1935, Bond Papers, 2.8.4A.

20 "Conference of Explorers and Councilors on Rural Education" (September 21–23, 1934), Rosenwald Fund Papers, box 333, folder 4; and Embree and Waxman, *Investment in People*, 68–74.

21 Horace Bond and Julia Bond, "A Description of Washington Parish," n.d. (ca. January 1935), Bond Papers, 3.72.316; and Horace Bond and Julia Bond,

"The School Itself," 1935, Rosenwald Fund Papers, box 334, folder 1.

22 Edwin R. Embree to Bond, February 2, 1935, Will W. Alexander to Bond, February 14, 1935, and Bond to Frederick L. Allen, March 13, 1935, all in Bond Papers, 3.72.316; Bond, "Forty Acres and a Mule," n.d. (ca. 1935), Bond Papers, 6.173.19.

23 Bond to W. P. Dabney, March 20, 1935, and May 3, 1935, Bond Papers, 2.8.4A.

24 Embree and Waxman, *Investment in People*, 72–73.

25 Edwin R. Embree to Bond, June 24, 1937, and Doak S. Campbell to Bond, July 8, 1937, Bond Papers, 3.72.313B; Bond to Embree, July 9, 1937, Rosenwald Fund Papers, box 323, folder 10; J. Max Bond to Leo M. Favrot, October 7, 1938, General Education Board Papers, Rockefeller Archive Center, Pocantico Hills, New York, box 90, folder 195.

26 Thomas Elsa Jones to Bond, March 15, 1938, Bond Papers, 4.87.2B; and Bond to John J. Coss, September 22, 1937, Bond Papers, 4.92.27E.

27 Embree to Bond, June 24, 1937.

28 "Some of the More Important Aspects of the Fund's Program in Rural Education," n.d., Rosenwald Fund Papers, box 323, folder 7.

29 Bond to Embree, July 14, 1937, Bond Papers, 3.72.313B, and Bond, "Some Exceptional Negro Children," 257–59, 278, 280.

30 Bond to Embree, July 14, 1937, and November 25, 1937, and Embree to Bond, November 29, 1937, Rosenwald Fund Papers, box 323, folder 10.

31 Bond to Dr. Jones, February 1, 1938, Jones Papers, box 26, folder 20, and Bond to J. R. E. Lee, Jr., May 17, 1938, Bond Papers, 4.87.2B.

32 Bond to Doak S. Campbell, May 31, 1938, Bond Papers, 3.72.313D.

33 John W. Davis to Bond, December 27, 1938, and Bond to Davis, January 2, 1938 (1939?), Bond Papers, 2.9.9C.

34 Eddie (T. Edward Davis) to Bond, January 30, 1939, Bond Papers, 2.9.10A; (Cecil) Halliburton to Klops (Bond's college nickname), September 20, 1940, and Bond to Lord Cecil, September 25, 1940, Bond Papers, 2.9.13; Bond to Julius Wanser Hill, January 22, 1940, Bond Papers, 2.9.12A; and Bond to Allison (Davis), July 21, 1935, Bond Papers, 2.8.4B.

35 "Mrs. Jane Bond, Woman Leader, Dies," undated newspaper clipping, Bond Papers, 1.6.29A; Jane Bond to Horace Bond, November 8, 1927, November 8, 1932, July 15, 1935, and March 3, 1936, all in Bond Papers, 1.6.29A.

36 Julia Bond interview, May 27, 1988.

37 Bond to Ollie Stewart, February 13, 1939, Bond Papers, 2.9.10A.

38 Bond to Doak S. Campbell, November 22, 1937, Bond Papers, 3.72.313. For an account of Fort Valley before Bond's presidency, see James D. Anderson, *The Education of Blacks in the South, 1860–1935* (Chapel Hill: University of North Carolina Press, 1988), 115–32. See also J. C. Dixon to Robert W. Patton, August 23, 1937, General Education Board Papers, box 45, folder 407.

39   Bond to Embree, March 25, 1939, Embree to Bond, March 27, 1939, and
     Bond to Embree, April 3, 1939, Rosenwald Fund Papers, box 175, folder 3;
     S. V. Sanford, Chancellor, University System of Georgia, to Bond, May 5,
     1939, Bond Papers, 4.94.32A; Bond to Embree, May 10, 1939, Rosenwald
     Fund Papers, box 175, folder 1; and Bond to Embree, May 13, 1939, Rosen-
     wald Fund Papers, box 326, folder 3. See also F[red] Mc[Cuistion], "Trip
     Report," May 15–17, 1939, General Education Board Papers, box 45, folder
     407; Bond to J. C. Dixon, May 17, 1939, Rosenwald Fund Papers, box 326,
     folder 3.
40   Bond to Embree, August 1, 1939, Bond Papers, 4.94.32D. On Just's career,
     see Kenneth R. Manning, *Black Apollo of Science: The Life of Ernest Everett Just*
     (New York: Oxford University Press, 1983).
41   Bond to Thomas E. Jones, May 25, 1939, and Jones to Bond, June 5, 1939,
     Jones Papers, box 26, folder 21; Jones to Embree, June 5, 1939, Rosenwald
     Fund Papers, box 198, folder 1.
42   Bond to Nolen W. Irby, May 20, 1939, and K. H. Meade to Bond, June 18,
     1939, Bond Papers, 4.94.32A; Eddie (T. Edward Davis) to Bond, June 27,
     1939, Bond Papers, 4.94.32B. In 1953, Bond described the difficulties of a
     black college president in the South: see Bond to Clarence Mitchell, Febru-
     ary 28, 1953, Bond Papers, 2.11.27B.
43   Bond's salary of $4,800 was significantly larger than that of any other Fort Val-
     ley employee. To mitigate this, he budgeted his presidential salary at $2,800
     and added another $1,000 for himself as director of instruction. The final
     $1,000, not listed in the budget, was paid to him by the Julius Rosenwald
     Fund. On these salary arrangements, see Bond to Embree, June 18, 1939,
     Rosenwald Papers, box 326, folder 3, and Bond to S. V. Sanford, June 25,
     1939, Bond Papers, 4.94.32A.

Chapter 6: Scholar of Black Education

1   Books published by Horace Mann Bond, in order of year of publication, are
     The Education of the Negro in the American Social Order (New York: Prentice
     Hall, 1934), *Negro Education in Alabama: A Study in Cotton and Steel* (Washing-
     ton: Associated Publishers, 1939), *Education for Production: A Textbook on How to
     Be Healthy, Wealthy, and Wise* (Athens: University of Georgia Press, 1944), *The
     Search for Talent* (Cambridge: Harvard University Press, 1959), *Black American
     Scholars: A Study of Their Beginnings* (Detroit: Balamp Publishing, 1972), and
     Education for Freedom: A History of Lincoln University (Princeton: Princeton
     University Press, 1976).
2   W. J. Goedeke to Bond, July 21, 1932, and M. V. R. Ungar to Bond, August 9,
     1932, Bond Papers, 6.176.41.

3 "Course Work Taken at the University of Chicago by Horace Mann Bond in Preparation for the Degrees of Master of Arts and Doctor of Philosophy," January 7, 1982, Bond Papers, 3.82.371B.

4 Bond, *Education of the Negro*, 12–13.

5 Ibid., 22–23.

6 Ibid., 76–115.

7 Ibid., 116–50.

8 Ibid., 191–202.

9 Ibid., 228.

10 Ibid., 234, and Horace M. Bond, "The Cash Value of a Negro Child," *School and Society*, May 13, 1933, 627–30.

11 Bond, *Education of the Negro*, 238–59.

12 Ibid., 259.

13 Ibid., 263–304.

14 Ibid., 326–30.

15 Ibid., 331–57, quotation 349.

16 Ibid., 351, 357.

17 Ibid., 358–412; Horace Mann Bond, "Only Way to Keep Public Schools Equal is to Keep Them Mixed," *Afro-American Week*, March 5, 1932, clipping in Bond Papers, 4.178.51.

18 Bond, *Education of the Negro*, 413–17.

19 Ibid., 418–35.

20 Ibid., 436–47.

21 Ibid., 447–63.

22 Ibid., 463. Thirty years after the publication of *Education of the Negro*, Bond discussed the irrelevance of his plan for gradual equalization of school spending by race in Nashville to the way equalization eventually took place — by litigation supported by the NAACP; see Bond's preface to the Octagon Publishers 1965 reprint of *Education of the Negro* (x).

23 Robert M. Labaree to Horace M. Bond, September 11, 1934, Bond Papers, 2.8.3C.

24 E. Franklin Frazier, review of *Education of the Negro*, by Horace Mann Bond, *American Journal of Sociology* 41 (September 1935): 275–76.

25 Charles H. Thompson, review of *Education of the Negro*, by Horace Mann Bond, *Journal of Negro Education* 4 (April 1935): 266–68, and Ambrose Caliver, review of *Education of the Negro*, by Horace Mann Bond, *Survey* 71 (May 1935): 71.

26 Carter G. Woodson, review of *Education of the Negro*, by Horace Mann Bond, *Journal of Negro History* 20 (July 1935): 353–55. Bond's critical review of Woodson's *Miseducation of the Negro* is discussed in chap. 4.

27 Bond to S. E. Carll, n.d. (1934), Bond Papers, 6.176.41. The text of *Education*

of the Negro reads in conformity with the changes requested in the letter; see Bond, *Education of the Negro,* 149.

28 Bond to Gordon J. Laing, April 25, 1938, Bond Papers, 6.177.44. The 1965 Octagon reprint of *Education of the Negro* went through two additional printings.

29 "Course Work Taken at the University of Chicago by Horace Mann Bond"; Bond, Atheneum reprint, *Negro Education.* All references in this chapter are to the 1969 reprint edition.

30 Bond to Charles H. Thompson, July 28, 1936, Bond Papers, 2.8.6A; Lawrence D. Reddick to Bond, December 4, 1936, Bond Papers, 4.89.13D; Bond to Gordon J. Laing, April 4, 1938, and April 25, 1938, Bond Papers, 6.177.44; George A. Works to Bond, June 1, 1937, Bond Papers, 3.86.389B; Carter G. Woodson to Bond, July 12, 1938, and Bond to Woodson, July 16, 1938, Bond Papers, 6.177.44; and Woodson to Bond, April 22, 1939, Bond Papers, 4.179.60. The role that racial discrimination played in Bond's difficulties in getting his dissertation published is a matter for speculation. The well-known problems that black scholars had in finding publishers in this period, as well as the fact that Bond's book continued to be in print into the 1980s lead one to make this kind of speculation.

31 For criticism of stylistic matters, see the reviews of *Negro Education in Alabama* in the *American Sociological Review* 4 (October 1939): 907, and in the *Mississippi Valley Historical Review* 36 (December 1939): 424–25. Also see Lawrence D. Reddick to Dean [Bond], December 4, 1936, Bond Papers, 4.89.13D.

32 In addition to the reviews cited in the previous note, see the reviews in *American Historical Review* 45 (April 1940): 669–70; *Journal of Negro History* 24 (April 1939): 226–29; and *Journal of Southern History* 5 (August 1939): 404–5. Also see Howard K. Beale, "Rewriting Reconstruction History," *American Historical Review* 45 (July 1940): 817.

33 John Hope Franklin, "Reconstruction and the Negro," in *New Frontiers of the American Reconstruction,* ed. Harold M. Hyman (Urbana: University of Illinois Press, 1966), 63; Vincent P. Franklin, "Introductory Essay: Changing Historical Perspectives on Afro-American Life and Education," in *New Perspectives on Black Educational History,* ed. Vincent P. Franklin and James D. Anderson (Boston: G. K. Hall, 1978), 6, 11; and Harvey G. Neufeldt and Clinton B. Allison, "Education and the Rise of the New South: An Historiographical Essay," in *Education and the Rise of the New South,* ed. Ronald K. Goodenow and Arthur O. White (Boston: G. K. Hall, 1981), 252, 256, 262. One author who fails to cite or use Bond's *Negro Education in Alabama* in a work that overlaps Bond's subject matter is William P. Vaughn, *Schools for All: Blacks and Public Education in the South, 1865–1877* (Lexington: University Press of Kentucky, 1974), 1974; Vaughn does, however, cite Bond's 1934 work, *Education of the*

Negro, in his bibliographical essay, 170.

34 Bond to Arthur A. Schomburg, September 5, 1936, Bond Papers, 4.89.13A; W. E. B. Du Bois, *Black Reconstruction* (New York: Harcourt Brace, 1935). For criticism of Du Bois's argument on the dictatorship of the proletariat, see the review by Sterling D. Spero in the *Nation*, July 24, 1935, 108–9. Bond's views on Du Bois are set forth in a letter to Martin Kilson, May 9, 1962, Bond Papers, 3.31.85D.

35 Walter L. Fleming, *Civil War and Reconstruction in Alabama* (New York: Macmillan, 1905). On Fleming's career at Vanderbilt, see Paul K. Conkin, *Gone with the Ivy: A Biography of Vanderbilt University* (Knoxville: University of Tennessee Press, 1985), 244. Bond first criticized Fleming's scholarship in a letter to Edwin R. Embree, November 11, 1936, Rosenwald Fund Papers, box 175, folder 2; see also Bond to John Hope Franklin, July 10, 1958, Bond Papers, 3.30.79B; interview with John Hope Franklin, October 14, 1987, Durham, North Carolina. Professor Franklin has a copy of an outline by Bond sketching out a detailed critique of Fleming's footnotes.

36 Bond, "Social and Economic Forces in Alabama Reconstruction," *Journal of Negro History* 23 (July 1938): 290–348; Bond, "An Interpretation of the Contribution of William Burns Patterson," February 9, 1960, Bond Papers, 6.172.12.

37 Bond, *Negro Education in Alabama*, 45. The significance of Bond's critique of Fleming on the issue of the debt is noted by Howard K. Beale, "Rewriting Reconstruction History," 816.

38 Edwin C. Rozwenc, ed., *Reconstruction in the South* (Boston: D. C. Heath, 1952).

39 William Gilette, *Retreat from Reconstruction, 1869–1879* (Baton Rouge: Louisiana State University Press, 1979); William McFeely, *Yankee Stepfather: General O. O. Howard and the Freedmen* (New Haven: Yale University Press, 1968); and William McFeely, *Grant: A Biography* (New York: W. W. Norton, 1981). Bond defends the humanitarians in *Negro Education in Alabama*, 29. His sensitivity to the economic aspect of the humanitarians' program is in *Negro Education in Alabama*, 117. Bond's book is cited, though not discussed, in the latest synthetic work on Reconstruction; see Eric Foner, *Reconstruction: America's Unfinished Revolution, 1863–1877* (New York: Harper and Row, 1988), 624.

40 Bond, *Negro Education in Alabama*, 26; Jonathan M. Wiener, *Social Origins of the New South: Alabama, 1860–1885* (Baton Rouge: Louisiana State University Press, 1978), 83, 155, 165.

41 Edwards and Richey, *School in the American Social Order*; Merle Curti, *The Social Ideas of American Educators* (New York: Charles Scribner's, 1935). Bond wrote to Curti seeking clarification of a statement Curti made about Washington in *Social Ideas*; see Bond to Curti, November 11, 1936, Bond Papers, 2.8.6A.

42 Edgar W. Knight, *Education in the South* (Chapel Hill: University of North Carolina Press, 1924). On Knight, see Clinton B. Allison, "The Appalling World of Edgar Wallace Knight," *Journal of Thought* 18 (Fall 1983): 7–14.

43 Bond, *Negro Education in Alabama*, 192, argues against Knight, *Education in the United States* (Boston: Ginn, 1929), 474. Bond, *Education of the Negro*, part 2. Louis Harlan, *Separate and Unequal: Public School Campaigns and Racism in the Southern Seaboard States, 1901–1915* (1958; reprint, New York: Atheneum, 1968).

44 Bond, *Negro Education in Alabama*, 273, 278, is critical of, respectively, the General Education Board and the Rosenwald Fund. Contemporary criticism of philanthropy for black education can be found in James D. Anderson, "Philanthropic Control over Private Black Higher Education," in *Philanthropy and Cultural Imperialism: The Foundations at Home and Abroad*, ed. Robert F. Arnove (Boston: G. K. Hall, 1980), 147–77. See also Curti, *Social Ideas*, chaps. 7, 8.

45 Bond, *Negro Education in Alabama*, 240–43, can be compared with the discussion of these issues in Martin Carnoy, *Education as Cultural Imperialism* (New York: David McKay, 1974), chap. 6.

46 Bond, *Negro Education*, 217. Curti treats Curry and Washington in *Social Ideas*, chaps. 7, 8.

47 Bond, *Negro Education*, 217, and *Education of the Negro*, 119.

48 Bond, *Negro Education*, 217.

49 Ibid., 210, 225.

50 Bond, *Education of the Negro*, chap. 6. For a different evaluation of Bond's views of Washington, see Michael Fultz, " 'Quintessential American.' "

51 Louis R. Harlan, *Booker T. Washington*, vol. 1, *The Making of a Black Leader, 1856–1901*, and vol. 2, *The Wizard of Tuskegee, 1901–1915* (New York: Oxford University Press, 1972, 1983).

52 Bond, *Education of the Negro*. On Woodson, see Meier and Rudwick, *Black History*, 1–71. On Bond and Woodson, see Meier and Rudwick, *Black History*, 101–3.

53 Meier and Rudwick, *Black History*, 3–4, and Bond, *Negro Education*, 12, 25, 141.

54 John Hope Franklin, "The Dilemma of the American Negro Scholar," in *Soon One Morning: New Writings by American Negroes, 1940–1962*, ed. Herbert Hill (New York: Alfred A. Knopf, 1969), 60–76, and Meier and Rudwick, *Black History*, 278–82.

55 Horace Mann Bond, "Reflections, Comparative, on West African Nationalist Movements," *Presence Africaine* 19 (September 1956): 22–28; typescript in Bond Papers, 6.171.9.

56 Bond, *Negro Education*, xii.

57 Winthrop Jordan, foreword to J. Hugo Johnston, *Race Relations in the South, 1776–1870* (Amherst: University of Massachusetts Press, 1970), 5–6.

58 Meier and Rudwick, *Black History*, 131–36, 157–58.

59 For a full discussion of Bond's historical work on the *Brown* decision and his history of Lincoln University, see chap. 10.

Chapter 7: Fort Valley President

1 Horace M. Bond to Walter L. Wright, April 13, 1940, Bond Papers, 4.103.73A.

2 Walter D. Cocking, "Report of the Study on Higher Education of Negroes in Georgia," as cited in *The University of Georgia: A Bicentennial History, 1785–1985*, by Thomas G. Dyer (Athens: University of Georgia Press, 1985), 388. On Cocking's activities in Tennessee, see *Atlanta Constitution*, November 14, 1941. Roger Williams suggests that Bond was chosen because of his "light skin," because he was a "name" in Negro education, and because "he was not a racial troublemaker" (Williams, *The Bonds*, 132).

3 Bond to Edwin R. Embree, February 25, 1940, Bond Papers, 4.94.33B.

4 William Anderson, *The Wild Man from Sugar Creek* (Baton Rouge: Louisiana State University Press, 1975).

5 Bond to Fred G. Wale, May 11, 1941, Rosenwald Fund Papers, box 326, folder 6.

6 Ralph McGill column in *Atlanta Constitution*, June 22, 1941, and Bond to A. J. Evans, June 22, 1941, Bond Papers, 4.97.45A.

7 The full-page advertisement by Talmadge appeared in the *Atlanta Constitution*, November 12, 1941; Bond to M. O. Bousfield, November 13, 1941, Bond Papers, 4.94.34C. In later years, Bond proudly recalled the story of the incriminating photo; see Bond to Clarence Mitchell, October 15, 1952, Bond Papers, 3.64.269D, and Bond to Mitchell, December 28, 1956, Bond Papers, 3.64.270E. The story was also told to Talmadge's son, Herman, by Bond's son, Julian; see Herman E. Talmadge, *Talmadge* (Atlanta: Peachtree Publishers, 1987), 214.

8 Dyer, *University of Georgia*, 225–40.

9 Bond to Edwin R. Embree, July 27, 1941, Rosenwald Fund Papers, box 326, folder 6.

10 Bond, untitled memorandum, August 12, 1940, Bond Papers, 2.94.33C; Bond to S. V. Sanford, May 18, 1945, Bond Papers. 4.94.35E; and Bond to A. J. Evans, August 23, 1941, Bond Papers, 4.94.34A.

11 Bond to A. J. Evans, August 23, 1941. Evans was the Fort Valley citizen who was influential in the Talmadge camp (Horace M. Bond to Dorothy Elvidge, November 23, 1940; Edwin R. Embree to General Wood, November 27, 1940; and Embree to Bond, November 27, 1940, all in Rosenwald Fund Papers, box 326, folder 5). General Robert Wood, a Sears and Roebuck executive and Rosenwald Fund trustee, was asked to put in a good word to Talmadge for Fort

Valley State College and Horace Bond. Bond to Fred G. Wale, November 3, 1943, Rosenwald Fund Papers, box 327, folder 1, recounts how a prod from Embree on Fort Valley's behalf meant a quick response from the chancellor of the board of regents.

12 "Regents Drop Holley from State School List," *Atlanta Journal*, April [date unclear], 1943, clipping in Bond Papers, 2.10.16A. Bond's professional rivalry with the Albany College president, Joseph Holley, did not carry over into their personal relations; in fact, Holley asked Bond to help him write his autobiography (see Holley to Bond, June 29, 1943, and Bond to Holley, June 30, 1943, Bond Papers, 2.10.16A).

13 *Missouri ex rel. Gaines v. Canada*, 35 U.S. 337 (1938); Bond to W. R. Banks, May 23, 1945, and Rufus E. Clement to Bond, May 25, 1945, Bond Papers, 4.94.35E; Carter Wesley to Rufus E. Clement, July 9, 1945, copy in Bond Papers, 2.10.19A; Bond, *Black American Scholars*, 177.

14 Bond to Lewis W. Jones, November 14, 1944, Bond Papers, 2.10.17C.

15 Bond to Edwin R. Embree, August 3, 1939, Bond Papers, 4.94.32D, and L. R. Seibert to Bond, September 2, 1939, Bond Papers, 4.94.33A.

16 S. V. Sanford to Bond, May 5, 1939, Bond Papers, 4.94.32A, and Bond to Sanford, June 27, 1939, Bond Papers, 4.94.32B.

17 Bond, "The Objectives, Scope, and Activities of the Fort Valley State College," n.d. (ca. 1941), Bond Papers, 4.95.37A.

18 Untitled notes for a speech to the Fort Valley student body, n.d. (ca. 1940), Bond Papers, 4.95.37A.

19 "Questionnaire: What Ought the Fort Valley State College for Negroes Try to Do in the Next Five or Ten Years?" n.d. (1941), Bond Papers, 4.96.43C.

20 "Questionnaire," and Bond to Herman Talmadge, April 14, 1941, as described in Bond to A. J. Evans, June 22, 1941. A draft of the Talmadge letter is also found in Bond Papers, 4.97.45A.

21 "Fort Valley to Grade Students on Objectives: Evaluation of Life Adjustment to Supplement Usual Grading," n.d. (ca. 1944), Bond Papers, 4.95.37C. For a critique of this type of approach, see Raymond E. Callahan, *Education and the Cult of Efficiency* (Chicago: University of Chicago Press, 1962).

22 Bond, *Education for Production;* Bond to Ellis Arnall, April 21, 1944, Bond Papers, 2.10.17B; and Bond to A. W. Mann, July 8, 1945, Bond Papers, 4.95.36A.

23 Bond to Rufus E. Clement, June 4, 1944, Bond Papers, 4.94.35B, and Bond to Robert M. Labaree, March 28, 1947, Bond Papers, 4.104.76B.

24 Bond, "The Fort Valley State College: A Blueprint for the Future," August 21, 1943, Heritage Collection, Henry A. Hunt Memorial Library, Fort Valley State College (hereafter cited as Heritage Collection).

25 Horace Mann Bond, "Seven Aids to Getting a Good Job," *Opportunity* 18

(March 1940): 72–75, 95, and H. M. Bond, "Ham and Eggs: A History of the Fort Valley Ham and Egg Show," *Georgia Agricultural Extension Service Bulletin*, no. 513 (June 1944): 3–15.

26 Horace Mann Bond, "A New Device for Evaluating the Work of College Students," *School and Society*, February 10, 1945, 94. On William C. Bagley's initial rejection of the article and Bond's refusal to accept that judgment, see Bagley to Bond, December 13, 1944, and Bond to Bagley, December 26, 1944, Bond Papers, 4.94.35D.

27 Bond, *Education for Production*.

28 Ibid., iii.

29 Fred G. Wale to Bond, June 5, 1942, and Bond to Edwin R. Embree, January 7, 1943, Rosenwald Fund Papers, box 327, folder 4. A copy of Bond's manuscript is at the Langston Hughes Memorial Library, Lincoln University. Horace Mann Bond, "The Negro in the Armed Forces of the United States prior to World War I," *Journal of Negro Education* 12 (Summer 1943): 268–87.

30 Horace Mann Bond, "The Educational and Other Social Implications of the Impact of the Present Crisis upon Racial Minorities," *Journal of Negro Education* 10 (July 1941): 617–22; and "What the San Francisco Conference Means to the Negro," *Journal of Negro Education* 14 (Fall 1945): 627–30. The last article was taken from a radio address given on a Macon, Georgia, radio station on March 10, 1945. See also Bond to A. R. Mann, March 8, 1945, "Horace Mann Bond's Proposal relating to Readjustment of Negro Veterans," March 20, 1945; Mann to Bond, March 24, 1945; and Bond to Mann, June 11, 1945, all in General Education Board Papers, box 551, folder 5901.

31 Bond to George M. Reynolds, December 3, 1940, and Reynolds to Bond, December 11, 1940, Rosenwald Fund Papers, box 326, folder 5. Bond to Society of Fellows, Harvard University, January 5, 1944, and Arthur D. Nock to Bond, January 12, 1944, Bond Papers, 2.10.17A.

32 Bond's Saturday teaching at Atlanta University was described in an interview with Julia Washington Bond, March 12, 1986. Also see Julius Wanser Hill to Bond, January 9, 1940, Bond Papers, 2.9.12A. In his letter proposing that Fort Valley become a research laboratory for Fisk, Bond told Charles Johnson that, although he had been trying to do research for five years at Fort Valley, it had been impossible, "because our funds here have been barely sufficient to employ a faculty" and because "we are all so busy doing regular college work that we never get around to doing any fundamental research" (Bond to Johnson, January 12, 1944, Charles S. Johnson Papers, box 2, folder 11).

33 James E. Shepard to Bond, January 10, 1941, and January 16, 1941, Bond Papers, 2.9.14; Bond to Shepard, January 14, 1941, Bond Papers, 4.94.34B; Will W. Alexander to Bond, May 31, 1944, and Bond to Alexander, June 4,

1944, Rosenwald Fund Papers, box 394, folder 10; Bond to Rufus E. Clement, June 4, 1944, Bond Papers, 4.94.35B.

34 Murray H. Leiffer, Garrett Biblical Institute, to Bond, January 12, 1944, Bond Papers, 3.53.212A; "Outline and Suggested Readings for SC 16: The Negro in American Life," n.d. (ca. 1944), Bond Papers, 3.53.212D; Gunnar Myrdal, *An American Dilemma* (New York: Harper and Brothers, 1944).

35 Horace Mann Bond, "The Negro Elementary School and the Cultural Pattern," *Journal of Educational Sociology* 13 (April 1940): 479–89.

36 Horace Mann Bond, "Education as a Social Process: A Case Study of a Higher Education Institution as an Incident in the Process of Acculturation" (Paper delivered at a symposium commemorating the seventy-fifth anniversary of the founding of Fisk University, April 29–May 4, 1941, published as part of the symposium proceedings in the *American Journal of Sociology* [May 1943] and reprinted as part of *Education and the Cultural Process* [New York: Negro Universities Press, 1970], 73–81). For criticism of the term *permanent minority*, see L. D. Reddick to Bond, August 10, 1943, Bond Papers, 3.71.308C.

37 Bond described the editors' reservations about his article and the stories it initially contained in a letter to O. B. Duncan, July 26, 1943, Bond Papers, 2.10.16B.

38 Bond to Edwin R. Embree, January 18, 1944, Rosenwald Fund Papers, box 327, folder 2.

39 Bond to O. B. Duncan, July 26, 1943.

40 Ibid.; William James, *The Will to Believe and Other Essays* (Cambridge: 1898; reprint, Harvard University Press, 1979).

41 Bond, "Philosophy of Education," n.d. (ca. 1943), Bond Papers, 4.96.40A.

42 Bond, "Bring Forth the People out of Egypt: The Mission of Minority Religious Leadership" (Commencement Address Delivered at Gammon Theological Seminary, Atlanta, Georgia, May 19, 1942), Bond Papers, 6.170.1.

43 Bond, "On the Imperative of Faith for a Minority Man" (Spelman College Vespers, Atlanta, Georgia, April 4, 1943), Bond Papers, 6.170.1.

44 Bond, "A Philosophy of Education for Postwar Curricula for Negro Students" (Speech delivered at Paine College, Augusta, Georgia, November 12, 1943), Heritage Collection.

45 Bond, "The Price of Freedom" (Speech delivered at Church of the Master, New York, New York, n.d. [April 27, 1947]), Bond Papers, 6.170.3.

46 Mrs. Edward M. Yard to Bond, April 7, 1945, and Bond to Yard, April 9, 1945, Bond Papers, 2.10.18A; Bond to Francis J. Biddle, attorney general, October 31, 1944, Rosenwald Fund Papers, box 327, folder 2; and Bond to Thomas E. Dewey, March 5, 1945, Bond Papers, 2.10.18A.

47 Bond to Walter L. Wright, April 13, 1940, Bond Papers, 4.103.73A.

48 Bond to J. W. Holley, September 14, 1942, Bond Papers, 2.10.15C. For a

criticism of black college presidents in this era, see Charles H. Thompson, "Control and Administration of the Negro College," *Journal of Educational Sociology* 19 (April 1946): 494.

49 Bond to William A. Griffey, April 1, 1940, Bond Papers, 2.9.12B; Horace M. Bond to J. C. Dixon, August 12, 1940, and unheaded note, August 12, 1940, both in Bond Papers, 4.94.33C; and Bond to Edwin R. Embree, August 18, 1940, Bond Papers, 4.94.33D.

50 Bond to Embree, January 24, 1940, Rosenwald Fund Papers, box 326, folder 5, and Bond to Walter L. Wright, July 6, 1945, Bond Papers, 4.103.74A.

51 See above, n. 33, for correspondence regarding graduate deanships; James E. Shepard to Bond, June 20, 1944, and Bond to Shepard, June 27, 1944, Bond Papers, 2.10.17C.

52 "Report of the President of Fort Valley State College, 1944–1945," n.d. (June 30, 1945), 1–2, Bond Papers, 4.95.37C.

53 Ibid., 3–5.

54 Ibid., 6–7, 11–13.

55 Ibid., 10.

56 Charles W. Flowers to Bond, September 6, 1933, Bond Papers, 4.103.73A; Robert M. Labaree to Bond, April 15, 1940, Bond Papers, 4.103.73A; Walter G. Alexander to Bond, February 17, 1941, Bond Papers, 4.100.62A; Bond to Joseph W. Baker, May 15, 1942, Bond Papers, 2.10.15B; Alexander to Bond, December 31, 1944; Bond to Alexander, January 5, 1945; and Alexander to Bond, May 31, 1945, all in Bond Papers, 4.103.73B.

57 Embree and Waxman, *Investment in People*, 30–31, and Fosdick, *Adventure in Giving*, vii.

58 Robert M. Labaree to Bond, April 15, 1940.

59 Fred G. Wale to Bond, June 9, 1944, Rosenwald Fund Papers, box 327, folder 6.

60 Fred G. Wale to Edwin R. Embree, "Summary of Our Discussion on Program in Rural Education," December 29, 1944, Rosenwald Fund Papers, box 323, folder 8; Fred G. Wale to Bond, January 15, 1945, Rosenwald Fund Papers, box 327, folder 3; and Wale to Embree, "Rural Education," February 27, 1945, Rosenwald Fund Papers, box 323, folder 8.

61 Edwin R. Embree to George W. Goodman, April 24, 1942, Rosenwald Fund Papers, box 294, folder 1; Bond to Embree, June 4, 1945, Rosenwald Fund Papers, box 327, folder 3; and Embree to Bond, July 12, 1945, Bond Papers, 3.72.314B.

62 Bond to Embree, January 25, 1946, Rosenwald Fund Papers, box 294, folder 4. On the Rhodes scholarship, see Bond to Embree, January 5, 1947, and Embree to Bond, January 7, 1947, Bond Papers, 3.72.314B.

63 Bond to Embree, August 1, 1945, Bond Papers, 3.72.314B, and Bond to Claude Barnett, August 3, 1945, Bond Papers, 3.33.94B.

64 E. W. Rhodes to Bond, July 13, 1945, containing an undated clipping of Rhodes's column from the *Philadelphia Tribune*, and Bond to Rhodes, August 1, 1945, Bond Papers, 4.103.74B.

65 Horace Bond to Julia Bond, July 17, 1942, Bond Papers, 2.10.15B.

Chapter 8: Lincoln Again

1 Wolters, *New Negro*, 278–93.

2 For the names of four other candidates, see J. W. Holley to Bond, June 19, 1945, Bond Papers, 4.103.73C.

3 Walter G. Alexander to Bond, May 31, 1945, Bond Papers, 4.103.73B.

4 Walter G. Alexander to Charles S. Johnson, March 25, 1945, and Johnson to Alexander, April 9, 1945, Charles S. Johnson Papers, Fisk University Library, Nashville, Tennessee, box 2, folder 11. A copy of Johnson's letter to Alexander with a handwritten notation reading "This letter was of great help" is in the Bond Papers, 4.103.73B.

5 W. E. B. Du Bois, "The Winds of Time: New Day at Lincoln," *Chicago Defender*, May 18, 1946, copy in Bond Papers, 3.37.116A. The particulars of Lincoln's aid from the state of Pennsylvania and the scholarships it granted because of that aid are spelled out in "Report of an Evaluation of Lincoln University for the Committee on Institutions of Higher Education, Middle States Association of Colleges and Secondary Schools, in March of 1953," Bond Papers, 4.112.119C.14.

6 Horace [Bond] to I. J. K. Wells, July 1, 1945, and H. M. Bond to W. L. Wright, July 2, 1945, Bond Papers, 4.103.73E; DuBois, "Winds of Time."

7 [Bond] to Edwin R. Embree, August 1, 1945, Bond Papers, 3.72.314B.

8 "A Special Report on *Lincoln University*, with Particular Reference to the Theological Seminary, to the Commission on Institutions of Higher Education, Middle States Association of Colleges and Secondary Schools," March 30, 1955, Bond Papers, 4.112.119C.

9 Bond to Alma Forrest Polk, February 12, 1947, Bond Papers, 2.10.21A, and [Bond] to Robert M. Labaree, March 28, 1947, Bond Papers, 4.104.76B.

10 W. A. C. Hughes, Jr., to Bond, July 14, 1945, Bond Papers, 4.103.74B.

11 Bond to Hughes, July 28, 1945, Bond Papers, 4.103.74B.

12 For example, see Bond to Robert W. Johnson, M.D., July 9, 1949, Bond Papers, 4.101.63F, or John E. Gatling to Bond, October 28, 1952, Bond Papers, 4.104.78B; interview with John A. Davis, New Rochelle, New York, November 22, 1987.

13 J. Plus Barbour to Frank Wilson, dean of students, May 15, 1947, Bond Papers, 4.104.76B; and Horace M. Bond to I. J. K. Wells, August 8, 1947, Bond Papers, 4.102.67B.

14 Bond to I. J. K. Wells, June 11, 1946, Bond Papers, 4.102.67A.

15 Ibid., and Bond to Cornelius McDougald, Jr., May 13, 1947, Bond Papers, 4.101.63D.

16 I. J. K. Wells to Bond, September 13, 1949, and Bond to Wells, September 17, 1949, Bond Papers, 4.111.112A.

17 Davis interview, November 22, 1987.

18 [Bond] to Labaree, March 28, 1947.

19 Ibid., and E. Washington Rhodes to T. McKeen Chadsey, attorney general of Pennsylvania, September 9, 1947, Bond Papers, 4.113.126B.

20 Davis interview, November 22, 1987.

21 For the dedication of the yearbook of the Lincoln University class of 1923 to Harold Grim, see *The Paw*, 1923, p. 5. On Grim's official duties early in Bond's presidency, see *Lincoln University Bulletin, Catalogue Number 1945–46*, 7.

22 H. F. Grim to Dear Alumnus, November 22, 1947, Wilfred N. Mais, Jr., to Bond, December 4, 1947, and Bond to Mais, December 11, 1947, all in Bond Papers, 4.106.86B.

23 Board Minutes, Board of Trustees of Lincoln University, November 11, 1948, 3, Langston Hughes Memorial Library, Lincoln University, contains both a discussion of the new statutes and President Bond's caution that faculty go through proper channels to approach the board. A copy of these minutes is also found in Bond Papers, 4.177.149C.

24 Bond to Cecil [Halliburton], February 26, 1949, Bond Papers, 2.11.23A; Wells to Bond, September 13, 1949, and Bond to Wells, September 17, 1949.

25 H. F. Grim to Bond, December 7, 1949, and Bond to Grim, December 8, 1949, Bond Papers, 4.106.86C.

26 Edwin R. Embree to Bond, February 10, 1949, Bond Papers, 3.72.314B, and Bond to Cecil [Halliburton], February 26, 1949, Bond Papers, 2.11.23A.

27 Bond's interest in African students surfaced early in his presidency (see Bond to Carl Murphy [President, the Afro-American Newspapers], January 11, 1946 [1947], Bond Papers, 4.97.46B). In April 1950, Horace Bond's brother Max wrote that he was taking a job in Liberia and urged his brother to establish a center for African studies at Lincoln (see Max Bond to Horace M. Bond, April 5, 1950, Bond Papers, 1.5.26C). Later that year, the formation of such a body was announced (see "Lincoln University Announces an Institute of African Studies," General Education Board Papers, box 665, folder 6908). Chapter 9 contains a full account of Bond's African activities.

28 Bond to Joel Dirlam, March 27, 1951, and Bond to John A. Davis, June 3, 1951, Bond Papers, 4.105.84B.

29 [Lincoln faculty members] to Lewis M. Stevens, May 31, 1951, Bond Papers, 4.106.87B; Philip S. Miller to George D. Cannon, June 1, 1951, Bond Papers, 4.101.64B; and Bond to Frederick T. Gruenberg, June 26, 1951, Bond Papers, 4.105.84B.

30 Bond to Lewis M. Stevens, July 13, 1951, Bond Papers, 4.118.156A.

31 Lewis M. Stevens to Bond, August 10, 1951, and Bond to C. R. Whittlesey, September 4, 1951, Bond Papers, 4.118.157D.

32 Bond to Lewis M. Stevens, September 11, 1953, Bond to the Faculty Committee on Personnel, September 12, 1953, and Bond to John [Davis], November 12, 1953, all in Bond Papers, 4.105.84D.

33 Bond to Joseph N. Hill, January 26, 1952, Bond Papers, 4.107.94B, and Lincoln University Faculty to Lewis M. Stevens, June 1, 1952, Bond Papers, 4.105.84C.

34 Bond, "Statement on Faculty Members as Trustees," n.d. (1951), and Bond to Maceo W. Hubbard, October 12, 1951, Bond Papers, 4.118.158. On the appointment of a faculty member to raise funds from the alumni, see Bond, "A Seven-Year Report to the Alumni by the First Negro President of Lincoln University," n.d. (1952), Bond Papers, 4.101.64D.

35 Bond to Donald C. Yelton, June 11, 1954, June 21, 1954, and July 25, 1956, and Yelton to Bond, August 2, 1956, and August 10, 1956, all in Bond Papers, 4.111.113A; William R. Cole to Bond, August 29, 1956, Bond Papers, 4.111.113B; Bond to Cole, September 11, 1956, Bond Papers, 4.111.113A; and A. O. Grubb to Bond, September 13, 1956, and Bond to Grubb, October 11, 1956, all in Bond Papers, 4.111.113B.

36 "Resolution," May 29, 1952, of William H. Molbon, president, and other members of the Detroit Alumni Chapter, Bond Papers, 4.101.64B, and Bond to James Fitzgerald, August 8, 1952, Bond Papers, 4.101.64C.

37 [Bond] to Walter L. Wright, September 4, 1945, Bond Papers, 4.103.75B, and Bond to David Swift, July 22, 1949, Bond Papers, 2.11.23C; Davis interview, November 22, 1987.

38 For Bond's account of his difficulties with orthodox Presbyterians, see his letter to David Swift, July 22, 1949, Bond Papers, 2.11.23C.

39 John E. Gatling to Bond, October 28, 1952, and Bond to Johnnie, November 21, 1952, Bond Papers, 4.104.78B. Chapter 2 describes the poll of Lincoln's students.

40 Bond to Faculty Member, November 4, 1952, Bond Papers, 4.101.64C; Bond to William H. Molbon, November 19, 1952, and December 22, 1952, Bond Papers, 4.101.64D; and Bond to Whirlwind [R. Walter Johnson], March 9, 1955, Bond Papers, 4.101.65E.

41 Cornelius McDougald to Bond, April 15, 1955, and Bond to McDougald, May 5, 1955, Bond Papers, 4.102.69A; Bond to McDougald, May 27, 1955,

Bond to Frank T. Wilson, June 10, 1955, and Bond to McDougald, July 13, 1955, all in Bond Papers, 4.1012.69B; Introduction [Draft of Response to Alumni Study by Bond], ca. 1956, Bond Papers, 4.102.70A; and "Progress Report and Summary Data Collected for Study of Conditions and Trends at Lincoln University," by Donald W. Wyatt, Alumni Historian, Bond Papers, 4.102.69D.

42 H. F. Grim to Bond, November 14, 1950, and Bond to Grim, November 14, 1950, Bond Papers, 4.106.86D; Grim to Bond, January 2, 1951, and Bond to Grim, January 3, 1951, Bond Papers, 4.106.87A; Bond to Lewis M. Stevens, February 10, 1951, Bond Papers, 4.106.87A; and Bond to Stevens, April 4, 1952, Bond Papers, 4.106.87C.

43 Grim to Horace M. Bond, April 19, 1952, Bond to Grim, April 21, 1952, Grim to Bond, April 26, 1952, and Grim to Lewis M. Stevens, April 27, 1952, all in Bond Papers, 4.106.87C; Bond to Maceo Hubbard, David G. Morris, and Harold T. Scott, May 14, 1952, Bond Papers, 4.101.64B.

44 Grim to Bond, May 20, 1952, Bond Papers, 4.106.87D; Bond to Lewis M. Stevens, July 1, 1952, Bond Papers, 4.117.150A; and Bond to the Executive Committee, August 14, 1952, Bond Papers, 4.117.150A. The letter to the executive committee is full of strikeovers and penned-in corrections, leading one to believe that it was not sent. Harold R. Scott to Bond, May 20, 1952, Bond Papers, 4.101.64B, and Bond to Maceo [Hubbard], October 30, 1952, Bond Papers, 4.101.64C.

45 Grim to Bond, October 31, 1953, and Grim to Whom It May Concern, November 16, 1953, Bond Papers, 4.106.88A; Grim to Bond, January 30, 1954, Bond Papers, 4.106.88B; and Grim to Paul Kuehner, February 28, 1956, and Bond to Grim, March 1, 1956, Bond Papers, 4.106.89A.

46 Grim to Bond, March 29, 1956, and Bond to Grim, March 30, 1956, Bond Papers, 4.106.89A; Grim to Bond, December 11, 1956, Bond Papers, 4.106.89B; and Grim to Bond, January 25, 1957, Bond Papers, 4.106.89C.

47 Lewis M. Stevens to Bond, April 6, 1953, Bond Papers, 4.112.122A, and "Minutes of the Lincoln University Board of Trustees," April 18, 1953, Bond Papers, 4.117.150C.

48 "Inaugural Address of Horace Mann Bond as the Fifth President of Lincoln University," June 4, 1946, Lincolnania, box 2a, Archives, Langston Hughes Memorial Library, Lincoln University, 4 (a copy is also in Bond Papers, 4.170.2).

49 Edwin R. Embree to Bond, June 11, 1946, Bond Papers, 3.72.314B; and Embree to Bond, December 17, 1946, Rosenwald Fund Papers, box 294, folder 4.

50 Bond to Embree, December 21, 1946, and Embree to Bond, December 23, 1946, Rosenwald Fund Papers, box 294, folder 4.

51 Thurgood Marshall to Harris [*sic*] M. Bond, June 13, 1949, and Bond to Marshall, June 15, 1949, Bond Papers, 3.63.262.

52   Bond to Robert D. Calkins, January 8, 1951, Bond to Calkins, April 3, 1951, and Calkins to Bond, April 9, 1951, General Education Board Papers, box 665, folder 6908.

53   Bond to Faculty Member, April 23, 1953, Bond Papers, 4.112.122A; "Mrs. Reyher——Bond: Questions and Answers, November 8, 1955," Bond Papers, 4.113.123B; and Bond to Herbert E. Millen and Lewis M. Stevens, February 2, 1956, Bond Papers, 4.120.169D.

54   Bond to Lewis M. Stevens, April 3, 1957, Bond Papers, 4.114.131B; Bond to Julius Rosenwald II, April 23, 1957, Bond Papers, 4.106.89D; Bond to Stevens, May 1, 1957, Bond Papers, 4.107.94F; "Dr. Bond Resigns at Lincoln University: Will Lecture at Harvard University," News Release, June 4, 1957, Bond Papers, 4.114.132D; and Lewis M. Stevens to Armstead O. Grubb, June 7, 1957, Bond Papers, 4.107.90.

55   Bond to Lewis M. Stevens, May 29, 1957, Bond Papers, 4.114.132A, 1–3.

56   Ibid., 3–8.

57   Ibid., 8–10.

58   Ibid., 10.

59   Ibid., 11–13.

60   Ibid., 13–15.

61   Ibid., 15–16.

62   "Report of an Evaluation . . . in March of 1953," Bond Papers, 4.112.119C, 2, 4, 7, 8.

63   Ibid., 5, 11, 16, 14–15.

64   Ibid., 16.

65   Ibid., 3, and "A Special Report on Lincoln University," March 30, 1955.

66   Bond spelled out the particulars of the Ford grant in a letter to "Dear Trustee," December 20, 1955, Bond Papers, 4.106.88D; Davis interview, November 22, 1987.

67   "Lincoln U. to Control $1 Billion Barnes Art Collection," *Philadelphia Inquirer*, September 27, 1988.

68   Interview with H. Alfred Farrell, March 25, 1987, and interview with De Forrest Rudd, March 25, 1987; letter from David E. Swift to author, September 8, 1987.

69   Interview with J. G. St. Clair Drake, June 26, 1987; interview with Julia Washington Bond, May 27, 1988.

70   For example, see Bond's intemperateness in an exchange of letters with Elliott Rudwick (Bond to Rudwick, January 30, 1951, and Rudwick to Bond, January 31, 1951, Bond Papers, 2.11.25B).

71   Interview with De Forrest Rudd and interview with H. Alfred Farrell, March 25, 1987; interview with Martin Kilson, June 26, 1987.

72   Interview with John A. Davis, November 22, 1987, and interview with Frank T. Wilson, March 25, 1987, Lincoln University, Pennsylvania.

73 On Bond's search for a teaching job in the late 1940s, see Edwin R. Embree to Bond, February 10, 1949, Bond Papers, 3.72.314B; see also Bond to William C. Gray, April 4, 1954, Bond Papers, 2.12.28A, and Bond to Robert C. Weaver, March 29, 1956, Bond Papers, 2.12.30C.

Chapter 9: Africa

1 Bond, "My Aunt Mamie and My IQ"; Bond to Richard Bardolph, November 25, 1955, Bond Papers, 2.12.29C; and Bond to Robert J. Moore, June 2, 1960, Bond Papers, 2.13.38D.

2 On Bond at Lincoln University and the University of Chicago, see chaps. 2 and 3, and Wayne J. Urban, "The Graduate Education of a Black Scholar: Horace Mann Bond and the University of Chicago," *History of Higher Education Annual* 7 (1987): 29–43.

3 "Inaugural Address of Horace Mann Bond as the Fifth President of Lincoln University," June 4, 1946.

4 K. Ozoumba Mbadiwe to Bond, June 8, 1949, Bond Papers, 3.22.25B; Bond to Ruth Sloane (Department of State), September 10, 1949, Bond Papers, 3.22.25D; and Bond to Carl Murphy, May 17, 1949, Bond Papers, 3.22.25B. On an honorary doctorate for Kwame Nkrumah, see I. J. J. A. Dickson to Bond, November 14, 1950, and Bond to Dickson, November 21, 1950, Bond Papers, 3.18.2E.

5 Bond to Carl Murphy, May 17, 1949.

6 Bond to W. Montague Cobb, December 1, 1949, Bond Papers, 3.18.2B.

7 Bond to Ruth M. Sloane (Department of State), December 3, 1949, and Sloane to Bond, December 13, 1949, Bond Papers, 4.100.59B. "Lincoln Head Off to Africa to Aid People," *Philadelphia Daily News*, November 29, 1952, clipping in Bond Papers, 3.22.29F.

8 Bond to Mrs. John Adams (Barnard College), August 18, 1950, Bond Papers, 3.18.2C. Bond cooperated with St. Clair Drake and other American academics to avoid deportation for Lincoln student Mugo Gatheru (interview with J. G. St. Clair Drake, June 27, 1987, and Bond to Drake, November 17, 1952, Bond Papers, 4.100.60A). Bond identified himself as a member of the Institute for African-American Relations in a letter to Robert Blum (September 21, 1954, Bond Papers, 3.56.232C). He was invited to become a member of the Board of the All-African Student Union of the Americas; see Benedict C. Njoku to Bond, August 31, 1955, Bond Papers, 3.28.66C. See also "To Help Establish a Nigerian (West African) University (A Proposal for a Cooperative Undertaking by Associated Universities and Colleges of Pennsylvania)," n.d. (October 13, 1956), Bond Papers, 3.19.6C. On Bond's efforts for Atlanta University, see his letter to Nnamdi Azikiwe, September 16, 1957, Bond Papers, 3.34.99C.

9   Nnamdi Azikiwe to Bond, October 15, 1957, Bond Papers, 3.34.99C, and Kwame Nkrumah to the President of Lincoln University, February 4, 1957, Bond Papers, 3.23.33A. Bond described an invitation he received to attend the inauguration of Liberian president Tubman in a letter to L. E. Detwiler, October 10, 1955, Bond Papers, 3.57.233F.

10 Horace Mann Bond, "Observations on Education in British West Africa," *Educational Record* 31 (April 1950): 129–40.

11 Bond, "God Be Glorified in Africa: A Statement Prepared for Circulation to the Executive Committee of the Board of Foreign Missions of the Presbyterian Church in the United States of America on Behalf of the Extension of Mission Work in Africa Generally, and in Liberia, Specifically," December 15, 1949, Bond Papers, 6.173.22; Bond, "Africa for the Middle-Class Mind: An Address Delivered at the Howard University Charter Day Exercises," March 2, 1951, Bond Papers, 6.171.6; and Bond, "Africa: An Area of Study in Writing Negro History," n.d. (presented October 16, 1959), Bond Papers, 6.172.11.

12 Bond, "Impressions of the All-African Peoples Conference, Accra, December 5–12, 1958," n.d. (ca. December 1958), Bond Papers, 3.23.37C.

13 Horace Mann Bond, "Howe and Isaacs in the Bush: The Ram in the Thicket," *Negro History Bulletin* 25 (October 1961): 72, 67–70.

14 Harold R. Isaacs to Bond, December 17, 1959, Bond Papers, 3.174.27.

15 H. F. Grim to Bond, May 20, 1952, and Grim to Lewis M. Stevens, June 4, 1952, Bond Papers, 4.106.87D; Grim to Laurence Foster, November 23, 1956, and Grim to Bond, December 12, 1956, Bond Papers, 4.106.89B; Grim to Bond, February 1, 1957, Bond Papers, 4.106.89C; and interview with John A. Davis, November 22, 1987. Bond's dismissal is discussed fully in chap. 8.

16 L. E. Detwiler to Bond, May 23, 1952, Bond to Kwame Nkrumah, May 29, 1952, and Bond to Detwiler, May 29, 1952, Bond Papers, 3.22.29A.

17 On Tydings and Richberg, see Bond to Kwame Nkrumah, September 2, 1952, Bond Papers, 3.22.29C; on Avery, see L. E. Detwiler to A. Casley-Hayford (Minister of Agriculture and Natural Resources, Gold Coast), September 13, 1953, Bond Papers, 3.22.29G; and on Senator Duff, see document headed "Objective," July 25, 1957, Bond Papers, 3.23.35B.

18 Bond to Kwame Nkrumah, August 19, 1952, Bond Papers, 3.68.292A; Bond to Lewis M. Stevens, n.d. (not sent; September 1952?), Bond Papers, 3.22.29E; and Bond to A. A. Alexander, September 9, 1953, Bond Papers, 3.18.4C.

19 For the Liberia proposal, see Bond to Johnston Avery, February 26, 1953, Bond Papers, 3.56.229D. On financial arrangements with Lincoln's board of trustees, see Bond to Lewis M. Stevens, January 30, 1953, Bond Papers, 3.56.229C.

20 Bond to L. E. Detwiler, September 16, 1952, Bond Papers, 3.22.29D; Detwiler to Bond, January 26, 1953, Bond Papers, 3.56.229C; and Bond to Detwiler, May 24, 1957, Bond Papers, 3.57.236B (all deal with Bond's stock). On Bond's

selling stock to friends, see Claude Barnett to Bond, March 4, 1958, and Bond to Barnett, March 31, 1958, Bond Papers, 3.33.94B. On the dispute with Lincoln University over stock, see Austin H. Scott (Business Manager, Lincoln University) to Bond, September 22, 1957, and Lewis M. Stevens to Bond, September 27, 1957, Bond Papers, 4.114.134B. Also see Bond to Lewis Pinckney Hill, n.d. (September 30, 1957), Bond Papers, 4.114.134C.

21 Bond to Johnston Avery, July 8, 1954, Bond Papers, 3.56.232B, shows Bond responding negatively to a black competitor for economic influence. Lewis M. Stevens to Bond, January 28, 1957, and Bond to Stevens, February 11, 1957, Bond Papers, 3.19.7C.

22 "Programme for the Visit of Dr. H. R. [*sic*] Bond, President, Lincoln University," 1954, Bond Papers, 3.23.32.

23 Bond to Kwame Nkrumah, June 16, 1952, Bond Papers, 3.22.29B, and "The Big Dreamer: Louis Edgar Detwiler," *Time*, August 1, 1960, 62, clipping in Bond Papers, 3.58.241D. On Bond's competing venture in Africa, the Ghanus Corporation, see untitled document headed "June 12, 1957," Bond Papers, 3.23.35A, and "Objective," July 25, 1957, Bond Papers, 3.23.35B.

24 Minutes of the Board of Trustees of Lincoln University, April 23, 1949, Bond Papers, 4.117.149C; interview with John A. Davis, November 22, 1987; and Horace M. Bond to Bank of Nova Scotia, June 7, 1958, Bond Papers, 3.58.237C.

25 Interview with Martin Kilson, June 26, 1987.

26 Bond to Johnston Avery (Technical Cooperation Administration), February 26, 1953, Bond Papers, 3.18.3F.

27 "Proposed Topics for Discussion at the Cleveland Conference, 1955," Bond Papers, 3.36.107E, and Bond to the Editor, *Portland [Oregon] Journal*, July 13, 1954, Bond Papers, 3.18.5B.

28 Bond to John Utley (African Desk, Department of State), April 21, 1953, Bond Papers, 3.18.4A; Bond to Sidney M. N. Berry (United States Information Service), May 26, 1954, Bond Papers, 4.102.72D; Bond to Robert Blum (Foreign Operations Administration), September 21, 1954, Bond Papers, 3.56.232C; Bond to Valoris Washington, August 3, 1953, Bond Papers, 3.18.4C; and Bond to Val Washington, December 28, 1956, and Washington to Bond, January 5, 1957, Bond Papers, 3.19.7B.

29 Robert W. Williams to Bond, September 22, 1953, and Bond to Williams, September 29, 1953, Bond Papers, 3.25.49A.

30 "Institute of African-American Relations, Inc.," n.d. (ca. 1953), Bond Papers, 3.25.49A; "AAI: Draft Statement of Purposes (with Mr. Pifer's Changes)," April 14, 1958, Bond Papers, 3.25.52B; and Bond to Lewis M. Stevens, February 11, 1957, Bond Papers, 3.23.33B.

31 Theresa Allain to Bond, February 23, 1959, Bond Papers, 3.30.80B; "Gentle

Imperialism for Africa," *New York Age*, July 11, 1959, clipping in Bond Papers, 3.25.53E; William M. Steen, "Memo to the Board Members of Color," April 25, 1962, Bond Papers, 3.27.59C; and Bond to Harold K. Hochschild, March 25, 1963, Bond Papers, 3.27.60D.

32 [Bond], "Report on the First Congress of Negro Writers and Artists, Held in Paris, France, The Sorbonne, September 19–22, 1956," Bond Papers, 3.36.111B, and Bond to John A. Davis, October 13, 1959 (regarding John Hope Franklin's resignation from AMSAC), Bond Papers, 3.30.81C. Franklin confirmed racial exclusivity as his reason for resigning from AMSAC in his interview with me on October 14, 1987. For the objections of a white scholar regarding racial exclusivity in AMSAC, see Milton R. Konvitz to James Harris, December 16, 1960, and (Bond) to Konvitz, n.d. (not sent? December 1960), Bond Papers, 3.31.82D.

33 (Bond), "Report on the First Congress"; John A. Davis to Messrs. Bond, Ivy, and Fontaine, May 5, 1957, Bond Papers, 3.36.111D; and Davis to Bond, August 5, 1957, Bond Papers, 3.30.78A, which included the first page of the proposed constitution of AMSAC.

34 John A. Davis to Bond, August 5, 1957, and (Bond), "Report on the First Congress."

35 CORAC was originally known as the American Information Committee on Race and Caste. In a letter to Bond, John Davis noted that CORAC preferred that its relationship with AMSAC not be acknowledged in the AMSAC constitution, as had been proposed; Davis added, however, that CORAC "was warmly enthusiastic about continuing and expanding its support of the Society" (Davis to Bond, October 31, 1957, Bond Papers, 3.30.78B). On Bond's selection as a director of CORAC, see Frederick R. Van Vechten to Bond, November 29, 1957, Bond Papers, 3.30.78B. The "CORAC Progress Report for Board of Directors Meeting, June 14, 1958, 8 A.M.," Bond Papers, 3.37.112C, devotes half a page to CORAC activities and two and a half pages to AMSAC. At least to CORAC directors, the organizations appeared to be intimately related.

36 (Bond), "Report on the First Congress"; Alvin W. Rose to Bond, April 15, 1959, and Bond to Rose, April 27, 1959, Bond Papers, 3.30.80B; and Bond to John A. Davis, "Report, Tour in Africa, September 17–October 13, 1963," Bond Papers, 3.24.47B.

37 Frank E. Pinder to Bond, April 18, 1963, and Bond to the Editor of the *Ghanaian Times*, April 25, 1963, Bond Papers, 3.83.373B. Pinder was with the United States Information Service, as identified in Bond to Director, United States Information Service, January 9, 1963 (should be 1964), and the reply, Frank S. Pinder to Bond, January 23, 1964, Bond Papers, 3.120.12A.

38 On W. E. B. Du Bois, see Elliot Rudwick, *W. E. B. Du Bois: A Study in Minority*

Group Leadership (Philadelphia: University of Pennsylvania Press, 1960), and Manning Marable, *W. E. B. Du Bois: Black Radical Democrat* (Boston: Twayne, 1988). On Paul Robeson, see Martin B. Duberman, *Paul Robeson* (New York: Knopf, 1988). On the CAA, see Hollis R. Lynch, *Black American Radicals and the Liberation of Africa: The Council on African Affairs, 1937–1955* (Ithaca: Cornell University Africana Studies and Research Center, 1978).

39   On Bond and Du Bois, see chap. 3.

40   Bond to John A. Davis, June 21, 1962, Bond Papers, 4.123.181B, and Bond to Davis, September 21, 1961, Bond Papers, 3.31.84B.

41   Maye Grant to Bond, January 6, 1962, and John A. Davis to Grant, January 12, 1962, Bond Papers, 3.24.44.

42   Martin Kilson to John A. Davis, n.d. (April 10, 1962?), Davis to Kilson, April 25, 1962, Kilson to Bond, May 4, 1962 (May 6?), Kilson to Davis, postmarked May 6, 1962, Bond to Kilson, May 9, 1962, and Davis to Kilson, May 18, 1962, all in Bond Papers, 3.31.85D; interview with Martin Kilson, June 27, 1987.

43   *Newsweek*, March 6, 1967, 31, published a chart that specified AAI and AMSAC as recipients of CIA funds and identified some of the agencies used as intermediaries for these funds. On attempts to save AMSAC after the CIA disclosures, see American Society of African Culture, Executive Council, Agenda, October 7, 1967, Bond Papers, 3.32.90G; also see John A. Davis to Averell Harriman, April 1, 1968, and "Annual Report of the American Society of African Culture," June 29, 1968, Bond Papers, 3.33.91A. On the death of AMSAC, see Davis to Bond, April 9, 1969, Bond Papers, 3.33.91C.

44   "Summary Statement of IAAR Income and Expenses, March 16, 1954, to June 30, 1957," Bond Papers, 3.25.51A, and "African-American Institute Budget, 1961–62, Summary of Income," Bond Papers, 3.26.56A. On Mercer Cook and the Congress for Cultural Freedom, see "Overseas Release . . . 9," August 5, 1960, which contains the item headed "Dr. Mercer Cook Named to Post with Congress for Cultural Freedom." On the Congress for Cultural Freedom and the CIA, see Christopher Lasch, *The Agony of the American Left* (New York: Vintage Books, 1969), chap. 3.

45   John A. Davis to Bond, August 29, 1958, and Bond to Kwame Nkrumah, September 4, 1958, Bond Papers, 3.30.80A; "Opening Remarks, Horace M. Bond, American Society of African Culture, Henry Hudson Hotel, 8:00 P.M., June 13, 1958," Bond Papers, 3.30.79B.

46   Bond, "African-American Relations, 1752–1961," n.d. (March 12, 1961), Bond Papers, 6.172.12.

47   Bond to Nnamdi Azikiwe, August 16, 1957, Bond Papers, 3.34.99C.

48   Bond to Kwame Nkrumah, n.d. (July 1966), Bond Papers, 3.68.294; interview with J. G. St. Clair Drake, June 26, 1987.

Chapter 10: Still a Scholar?

1 Bond, *Education for Freedom.*
2 The questions were appended to a letter from John A. Davis to Bond, August 14, 1953, Bond Papers, 3.64.269E; they are also cited in Richard Kluger, *Simple Justice* (New York: Knopf, 1975), 778. The full citation for the *Brown* case is *Brown* v. *Board of Education of Topeka, Kansas*, 347 U.S. 483 (1954).
3 Kluger, *Simple Justice*, 784.
4 Bond, *Negro Education.*
5 Bond to Robert L. Carter, July 8, 1953, and Mabel Smythe to Marion Wright, July 9, 1953, both in Bond Papers, 3.64.269D. On Wright's background, see Meier and Rudwick, *Black History*, 104–5.
6 John A. Davis to Bond, August 14, 1953, Bond Papers, 3.64.269E, and Conference Program, September 25–28, 1953, Bond Papers, 3.64.270A.
7 Kluger, *Simple Justice*, 784, and William Preston Vaughn, *Schools for All: The Blacks and Public Education in the South, 1865–1877* (Lexington: University Press of Kentucky, 1974).
8 *Missouri ex rel. Gaines* v. *Canada*, 35 U.S. 337 (1938); Kluger, *Simple Justice*, 678–79; and Horace Mann Bond, "The Present Status of Racial Integration in the United States, with Especial Reference to Education," *Journal of Negro Education* 21 (Summer 1952), 241–50.
9 Bond to John A. Davis, August 29, 1953, Bond Papers, 3.64.269E.
10 "Chart Demonstrating the Twelve States Seeking Admission or Readmission during Reconstruction Understood That Congress Interpreted the Fourteenth Amendment as Prohibiting the Legal Requirement of Segregation in Education," n.d. (1953), Bond Papers, 3.64.270B. The chart included a discussion of Nebraska, in addition to the eleven Confederate states, since Nebraska was admitted to the Union for the first time during Reconstruction.
11 Bond to Mabel Smythe, October 5, 1953, Bond Papers, 3.64.270A.
12 Ibid.
13 Brief for Appellant [NAACP] in Nos. 1, 2, and 4 and for Respondents in No. 10 on Reargument, 19, reproduced in Philip B. Kurland and Gerhard Casper, eds., *Landmark Briefs and Arguments of the Supreme Court of the United States: Constitutional Law*, vol. 49 (Arlington: University Publications of America, 1975).
14 Ibid., 142–57.
15 Brief for the State of Kansas on Reargument, 33, reproduced in Kurland and Casper, *Landmark Briefs.*
16 Ibid.
17 Brief for the Appellant.
18 Supplemental Brief for the United States on Reargument, 117, 116, reproduced

in Kurland and Casper, *Landmark Briefs.*

19 Appendix to the Supplemental Brief for the United States on Reargument, 160–393, reproduced in Kurland and Casper, *Landmark Briefs.*

20 *Brown v. Board of Education*, 347 U.S. 483. Chief Justice Warren's opinion is reprinted in Kluger, *Simple Justice*, 983–91, quotation 984.

21 Alfred H. Kelly, "An Inside View of *Brown v. Board of Education,*" *Congressional Record* 108 (September 11, 1962), 19025–28. Kelly's paper was originally delivered to a meeting of the American Historical Association on December 28, 1961. Senator Strom Thurmond of South Carolina had the paper inserted in the *Congressional Record* in an attempt to block the appointment of Thurgood Marshall as a federal judge.

22 Rita Norton, "The Horace Mann Bond Papers: A Biography of Change," *Journal of Negro Education* 53 (Winter 1984): 29.

23 Kelly, "An Inside View"; C. Vann Woodward, *Thinking Back: The Perils of Writing History* (Baton Rouge: Louisiana State University Press, 1986), wherein Woodward traces his *Strange Career of Jim Crow* to his work on the *Brown* case; and John Hope Franklin, *Reconstruction* (Chicago: University of Chicago Press, 1961).

24 Kelly, "An Inside View," 19025; and Horace Mann Bond, "Reflections, Comparative, on West African Nationalist Movements," *Presence Africaine* 19 (September 1956): 22–28.

25 Robert L. Carter to Bond, June 21, 1954, Bond Papers, 3.64.270C; and Bond to Thurgood Marshall, July 14, 1954, Bond Papers, 4.123.180.

26 Bond to Stanton Belfour, May 21, 1954, Bond Papers, 4.123.180; interview with J. G. St. Clair Drake, June 26, 1987; and interview with John Hope Franklin, October 12, 1987.

27 Bond to Charles R. Whittlesey, October 19, 1955, Bond Papers, 4.123.181; and Bond to John M. Fogg, Jr., May 13, 1956, Bond Papers, 4.123.181.

28 Bond, *Education for Freedom*, 3–8.

29 Ibid., 6, 21–37.

30 Ibid., 59.

31 Ibid., 134–39.

32 Ibid., 143–68.

33 Ibid., chaps. 16, 19–24.

34 Ibid., chap. 21, esp. 409; also see 434–35, 360–61.

35 Ibid., chaps. 22, 23.

36 Ibid., chaps. 16 (esp. 300–1), 19, and 20, and pp. 413–18.

37 Ibid., chaps. 17, 18, and pp. 371–81.

38 Ibid., 352–55.

39 Ibid., 356–57.

40 Ibid., 383.

41 Ibid., 370–81.

42 Ibid., 380, 384; Wolters, *New Negro*.

43 Bond, *Education for Freedom*, 388–89.

44 Ibid., 384. The faculty member who opposed an integrated staff in the 1920s and whom Bond perceived as opposing his presidency was Philip Miller.

45 Du Bois, "Winds of Time"; and Pauli Murray to Bond, August 4, 1954, Bond Papers, 4.123.180.

46 "Report of an Evaluation of Lincoln University for the Committee on Institutions of Higher Education, Middle States Association of Colleges and Secondary Schools in March of 1953," and "A Special Report on *Lincoln University*, with Particular Reference to the Theological Seminary, to the Commission on Institutions of Higher Education, Middle States Association of Colleges and Secondary Schools," March 30, 1955, Bond Papers, 4.112.119C. Bond, in *Education for Freedom*, 434, simply mentions in one sentence that the seminary was closed in 1959; he gives no accounting of the forces involved in its closing. This mention must have been added to the manuscript, either by Bond or by the Lincoln committee involved in the book's publication, after his presidency ended in 1957.

47 Bond, *Education for Freedom*, 400, 483.

48 For a discussion of presentism as a problem in historical research, see David Hackett Fischer, *Historians' Fallacies: Toward a Logic of Historical Thought* (New York: Harper and Row, 1970), 135–40.

49 Richard E. Neustadt and Ernest R. May, *Thinking in Time: The Uses of History for Decision Makers* (New York: Free Press, 1986).

50 John Ciardi (Twayne Publishers) to Bond, December 1, 1954; George Stevens (J. B. Lippincott) to Bond, May 2, 1955; Bond to Elizabeth Paschal (Fund for the Advancement of Education), July 22, 1955; and Pauli Murray to Bond, August 31, 1955, which contained a copy of Marie F. Rodell to Pauli Murray, November 22, 1954 (Rodell, Murray's literary agent, declined to represent Bond and his Lincoln history), all in Bond Papers, 4.123.180. Edward Uhlan (Exposition Press) to Bond, June 14, 1962, Bond to John A. Davis, June 21, 1962 (which enclosed "A Request for a Grant to Publish *God Glorified by Africa: The History and Sociology of Lincoln University*"), Bond to Arthur G. McDowell (Pennsylvania Historical and Museum Commission), January 16, 1964, Bond to Hugh M. Gloster, December 17, 1968 (regarding the Negro University Press), Richard L. Wentworth (Louisiana State University Press) to Bond, January 7, 1969, Gordon Hubel (University of Pennsylvania Press) to Bond, February 3, 1969, and Maurice English (Temple University Press) to Bond, July 17, 1969, all in Bond Papers, 4.123.181.

51 Gordon Hubel to Bond, April 14, 1969, Bond Papers, 4.123.181.

52 Bond to Hildrus A. Poindexter (Lincoln University Alumni Association Rep-

resentative on the Lincoln University Board of Trustees), September 15, 1968, and February 4, 1969, Grace Frankowsky to Bond, May 28, 1971, and Grace Frankowsky to Dr. and Mrs. Bond, April 3, 1972, Bond Papers, 4.123.181.

53 Emory Wimbish, Jr., to Dr. and Mrs. Horace M. Bond, March 27, 1972, Bond Papers, 4.123.181, and Bond, *Education for Freedom*, xx.

54 Review of *Education for Freedom*, by Horace Mann Bond, *Choice* 14 (June 1977): 579.

55 June O. Patton, review of *Education for Freedom*, by Horace Mann Bond, *Journal of Negro History* 62 (July 1977): 307–9.

56 See above, chap. 6, n. 35.

Chapter 11: After Lincoln

1 Bond, *Search for Talent*, and Bond, *Black American Scholars*.

2 Philip M. Widenhouse to Bond, November 27, 1956, and Bond to Widenhouse, November 30, 1956, Bond Papers, 2.12.31B.

3 Bond to Charles H. Wesley, April 4, 1957, Bond Papers, 4.114.131A; Bond to Ralph Tyler, April 19, 1957, Bond Papers, 4.114.131B; and Bond to Lewis M. Stevens, May 29, 1957, Bond Papers, 4.114.132A.

4 Bond to Martin Kilson, Jr., April 4, 1957, Bond Papers, 4.114.131A; interview with Martin Kilson, June 26, 1987; and Bond to George J. Brutscher, October 20, 1963, Bond Papers, 4.114.135D.

5 Bond to H. C. Trenholm, June 15, 1957, Trenholm to Bond, June 17, 1957, and Bond to Trenholm, June 19, 1957, Bond Papers, 4.114.133A; Bond to Rufus E. Clement, June 28, 1957, Bond Papers, 4.114.133B; and Bond to Clement, n.d., Bond Papers, 4.114.133C.

6 L. D. Reddick to Horace (Bond), June 10, 1957, and Bond to Reddick, June 15, 1957, Bond Papers, 4.114.133A.

7 Bond to Andrew Bradley, August 12, 1957, Bond Papers, 4.114.133D. For the difficulties black scholars have had in white universities, see John Hope Franklin, "Dilemma of the American Negro Scholar," and Michael R. Winston, "Through the Back Door: Academic Racism and the Negro Scholar in Historical Perspective," *Daedalus* 100 (Summer 1971): 678–719.

8 Bond to Frank J. Hutchings, Sr., April 21, 1961, Bond Papers, 4.105.80E, and Bond to George J. Brutscher, April 10, 1963, Bond Papers, 4.114.135D.

9 Bond to John Bell Keeble, n.d. (ca. 1957), and "Bond v. Lincoln University," n.d. (ca. 1957), Bond Papers, 4.114.134C.

10 Louis L. Redding to Bond, November 25, 1960, and Bond to Redding, November 28, 1960, Bond Papers, 4.114.134D; Bond to Redding, June 30, 1961, Bond Papers, 4.114.135D; and Redding to Bond, April 11, 1962, and Bond to Redding, April 12, 1962, Bond Papers, 4.123.181.

11 George J. Brutscher to Bond, March 14, 1963, Bond Papers, 4.114.135B; Bond to Brutscher, April 10, 1963, and Brutscher to Bond, May 15, 1963, Bond Papers, 4.114.135D.

12 Brutscher to Bond, October 17, 1963, Bond to Brutscher, October 20, 1963, Brutscher to Bond, March 25, 1964, Bond to Brutscher, March 30, 1964, Brutscher to Bond, March 31, 1964, and Redding to Bond, April 2, 1964, all in Bond Papers, 4.114.135D.

13 Bond to Keeble, n.d. (ca. 1957), Bond Papers, 4.114.134C, and Bond to Thomas P. Harney, May 25, 1959, Bond Papers, 4.114.134D.

14 Bond to E. Washington Rhodes, August 5, 1958, Bond Papers, 4.114.134D, and Bond to Keeble, n.d. (ca. 1957).

15 Bond to Hutchings, April 21, 1961.

16 Bond to Marvin Wachman, April 12, 1962, Bond Papers, 4.123.181.

17 I. J. K. Wells to Dear Classmate, May 12, 1963, and Bond to Wells, May 21, 1963, Bond Papers, 4.101.66D.

18 Max and Ruth (Bond) to Horace and Family, October 13, 1957, Bond Papers, 1.5.26D.

19 Bond to Louis L. Redding, June 30, 1961, Bond Papers, 4.114.135D, and Bond to Rufus E. Clement, October 30, 1957, Bond Papers, 4.134.222A.

20 Rufus E. Clement to Bond, April 22, 1958, Bond Papers, 4.134.222A; Bond to Louis L. Redding, June 30, 1961; and Bond to Brutscher, October 20, 1963.

21 Edward Weaver to Bond, June 27, 1959 (two letters), Bond Papers, 4.135.223A.

22 "The Report of the Committee on Ph.D. Studies," n.d. (ca. 1959), Bond Papers, 4.136.229D.

23 Rufus E. Clement to Bond, July 22, 1964, Bond Papers, 4.139.247A; "Announcement of Grants-in-Aid for Research, The Atlanta University Center Research Committee," November 9, 1964, Bond Papers, 4.139.247D; and Bond to Clement, August 21, 1965, Bond Papers, 4.135.226B.

24 Clement to Bond, July 23, 1966, and Bond to Clement, July 25, 1966, Bond Papers, 4.136.227B.

25 Horace Mann Bond, "A Study of Factors Involved in the Identification and Encouragement of Unusual Academic Talent among Underprivileged Populations," January 1967, Project No. 5–0859, Office of Education, U.S. Department of Health, Education, and Welfare; "Application to the Regional Research Office of the Office of Education for a Grant of $100,000 to Support a Research Consortium involving Atlanta University and Morris Brown College for a Two-Year Period," n.d. (April 1, 1967), Bond Papers, 4.139.248B.

26 Bond to Wendell P. Jones, August 31, 1968, Bond Papers, 2.15.51C.

27 Bond to T. Edward Davis, January 30, 1969, Bond Papers, 2.15.53A.

28 Rufus E. Clement to Bond, January 15, 1958, Bond Papers, 4.134.222A, and Bond to Wendell P. Jones, August 31, 1968.

29 Bond to Howard Zinn, April 5, 1960, Bond Papers, 2.13.38C. On Julian Bond at the George School, see Bond to I. J. K. Wells, May 25, 1953, Bond Papers, 4.102.68A, and James A. Tempest to Bond, June 21, 1956, Bond Papers, 1.1.4A. The contract between Horace Bond and his son James, dated September 2, 1957, whereby James would be paid for each book he read and reported on, is found in Bond Papers, 1.5.26C.

30 Max (Bond) to Horace, May 23, 1968, Bond Papers, 1.5.26D; Martin L. Kilson, Jr., to Bond, June 4, 1958, and Bond to Kilson, June 6, 1958, Bond Papers, 2.12.34B.

31 Bond to Harry S. Truman, April 15, 1960, Bond Papers, 2.13.38C.

32 On Julian Bond's career up to 1970, see John Neary, *Julian Bond: Black Rebel* (New York: William Morrow, 1971); Hildrus A. Poindexter to Bond, September 9, 1968, Bond Papers, 4.123.181C; and Bond to Mr. Harold Cooper and Mrs. E. Cooper Kerr, October 1, 1968, Bond Papers, 2.15.52A.

33 Bond, *Negro Education*; Bond, *Education of the Negro*; Bond to Robert L. Bernstein, October 14, 1968, and Bond to John Hawkins, March 15, 1969, Bond Papers, 1.7.36A; Bond to T. Edward Davis, January 30, 1969.

34 Bond to T. Edward Davis, January 30, 1969; Bond to Thomas A. Jarrett, September 14, 1968, Bond Papers, 4.136.228A; and George H. Knoles to Bond, May 7, 1969, and Bond to Joe Williams, May 14, 1969, Bond Papers, 2.15.53B.

35 Bond to Elliott Rudwick, January 30, 1951, Rudwick to Bond, January 31, 1951, and Bond to Rudwick, February 26, 1951, Bond Papers, 2.11.25B; Bond to Samuel Eliot Morison, February 26, 1951, and Morison to Bond, March 15, 1951, Bond Papers, 2.11.25A; Bond to David Potter, October 12, 1951, and Potter to Bond, January 4, 1952, Bond Papers, 2.11.25C.

36 "Southerners Branded 'Moron' by NAACP," unidentified newspaper clipping (ca. 1956), Bond Papers, 3.64.270D.

37 Horace Mann Bond, "Cat on a Hot Tin Roof," review of *The Testing of Negro Intelligence*, by Audrey M. Shuey, *Journal of Negro Education* 27 (Fall 1958): 519–23.

38 Bond, "George Washington Carver's Blue Eyes, the Nutmeg Yankee, and the Mental Capacity of Black Folks" (Address delivered to the American Teachers Association, July 26, 1962), and "Bond Challenges Putman [*sic*] Claim That Dr. Carver Was Blue-Eyed," clipping from *The Call* (Kansas City, Missouri), August 3, 1962, Bond Papers, 6.172.13.

39 For one example of cordial relations between Bond and a white scholar, see Bond to August Meier, February 16, 1956, Bond Papers, 4.123.181, and Meier to Bond, April 16, 1959, Bond Papers, 2.13.36C.

40 Bond, *Search for Talent*, 13–20.

41 Ibid., 21–23.

42 Ibid., 24.

43 Ibid., 26.

44 Ibid.; 27–31; and Bond, "How to Breed a Scholar," February 14, 1963, Bond Papers, 6.172.13.

45 "Script for Radio Broadcast: Education for the Long Haul, or Education: The Slow Process of Families, Schools, and Generations," May 5, 1963, Bond Papers, 6.179.58.

46 Bond, "Academic Talent among Underprivileged Populations," and Bond, *Black American Scholars*. Bond decided to submit his manuscript to its eventual publisher, Balamp Publishing, after seeing a pamphlet the firm had published on black scientists; see Bond to James M. Jay, September 17, 1971, as well as several other letters to Jay in Bond Papers, 6.177.48.

47 Bond, *Black American Scholars*, iii.

48 Ibid., 11, 100–110, 170–79, 203. Boxes 141 through 150 of the Horace Mann Bond Papers contain the family histories that Atlanta University students compiled as students in Bond's classes.

49 Bond, *Black American Scholars*, iv–v, 190–92.

50 Chapter 1 of *Black American Scholars* repeats verbatim much of *The Search for Talent*, 5–20; chapter 2 repeats much of Bond, "The Negro Scholar and Professional in America," in *The American Negro Reference Book*, ed. John P. Davis (Englewood Cliffs, N.J.: Prentice Hall, 1966), 548–89, an article at best tangentially related to the focus of *Black American Scholars*.

51 Bond, *Black American Scholars*, 120, 4–5, 116–17.

52 Bond, "My Aunt Mamie and My IQ."

53 Bond, *Black American Scholars*, 115.

54 Ibid., 100–110.

55 Horace Mann Bond, "The Influence of Cultural Factors on Academic Performance," *Southern University Bulletin* 47 (January 1961): 68–69.

56 Max (Bond) to Horace, May 23, 1968; Bond to Robert Bernstein, October 14, 1968, and John Peck to Bond, February 21, 1969, Bond Papers, 1.7.36A.

57 Bond to John Hawkins, March 15, 1969, and John Peck to Bond, July 16, 1969, and August 7, 1969, Bond Papers, 1.7.36A.

58 Bond to Peck, September 21, 1970, and March 3, 1971, Bond Papers, 1.7.36B; and Bond to Hawkins, March 15, 1969.

59 Bond to Peck, March 3, 1971; John Neary to Horace Mann Bond, November 12, 1970, Bond Papers 1.7.36B; and Bond to Atheneum Press, December 6, 1971, Bond Papers, 1.7.36D.

60 Bond to Dear Kinfolk, September 8, 1971, Bond Papers, 1.7.36C; and "The Secret of Success of All Notable Families," n.d. (1971), Bond Papers, 1.7.36D.

61 Bond, *Black American Scholars*, 15.

Index